The Quiet Furies

ELTON B. McNEIL, the author of this book, is a clinical psychologist and Professor of Psychology at the University of Michigan. He is a graduate of Harvard and the University of Michigan and is a past-president of the Michigan Psychological Association. He is the author of a number of psychological books, monographs, and articles published during the last 20 years.

WITHDRAWN

The Quiet Furies

MAN AND DISORDER

Elton B. McNeil

Prentice-Hall, Inc., Englewood Cliffs, New Jersey

Illustrations by Edith Dines

© 1967 by Prentice-Hall, Inc., Englewood Cliffs, New Jersey. All rights reserved. No part of this book may be reproduced in any form or by any means without permission in writing from the publishers. Printed in the United States of America. Library of Congress Catalog Card Number: 67-25950

Current printing (last digit): 10 9 8 7 6 5 4 3 2 1

Prentice-Hall International, Inc., London. *Prentice-Hall of Australia, Pty. Ltd.,* Sydney. *Prentice-Hall of Canada, Ltd.,* Toronto. *Prentice-Hall of India Private Ltd.,* New Delhi. *Prentice-Hall of Japan, Inc.,* Tokyo.

Contents

vii

Introduction

THE VOYEUR FINDS IT NECESSARY to look rather than to do, and the reader of casebooks may similarly be tempted to peek at the secrets of others solely for the purpose of reassuring himself about his own superior stability. If this is to be the fate of this effort, then I will have failed to achieve my original goals. This book was intended to make more familiar and less mysterious the kinds of disorder to which all human lives are subject to a greater or lesser degree. In these cases are you, me, everyone. They do not show sickness of a biological sort; they demonstrate how the normal problems of living can escalate beyond recognition. This is an account of the hidden selves of a number of people whose problems and inappropriate behavior led them to seek or need assistance in being productive participants in our society. Psychotherapy is one means of restoring order where chaos has come to prevail but it is only one of many means and it is still an imperfect tool. People have reorganized themselves without professional help since time began and there is little reason to believe that self-help will not always be the most vital factor in adjustment. Psychotherapists are needed as much to organize the resources of those closest to the victim of disorder as they are to restore psychological order to the sufferer himself.

The events in the disordered lives reported here are true and as accurate as I can make them given the vagaries of memory and the inevitable distortions of time and distance. Yet, no one of these cases is exactly true if truth is defined very rigorously. I have carefully disguised the recognizable self of each. I did not see them professionally for the purpose of gathering case material; they represent only a fragment of those I have come to know in the last fifteen years; they are people to whom I became most attached as persons; and they have inalienable rights to privacy. My hope is that their difficulties will be made reasonable and credible enough to prove instructive and insightful to others without harm or injury to the principals. There is, of course, no possibility that any human being in close

personal contact with another can reproduce the full essence of that experience. Case presentations are synopses and shorthand accounts of a
mountainous mass of detail, impression, reaction, and conversation, and
such abbreviated glimpses of the life of another must of necessity seriously
distort reality.

These cases of disordered lives are best employed as suggestive skeletal
outlines of possible patterns of response to the inevitable stresses of life.
The cases reported were selected to illustrate a number of basic lessons in
adjustment and maladjustment among human beings not much different
from those with whom we all come in contact in daily life. The more
bizarre and distorted aberrations of psychic existence have been passed
over because they so often are believable primarily because anything and
everything is conceivable in an "insane" universe. To most of us, the
"insane" are beyond the bounds of usual logic and live on a planet so
distant from our own that its alien ways are accepted as oddities that need
no explanation.

These cases were chosen to reinforce the observation that emotional
and psychological disorders are a usual aspect of existence and do not
always have a strange and eerie quality about them. They will serve best
to help us understand the nature of psychological man if they enable us to
observe similar patterns in persons of our own acquaintance and if they
teach us to view one another with eyes that see beyond the surface and
perceive the underlying reasons for all human behavior.

The preparation of case material for public consumption ought to
reflect a theoretical point of view that serves as a skeleton to be fleshed out
by the cases themselves. Unfortunately, perhaps, not every psychotherapist
is born and dies with an unfailingly theoretical point of view. Mine is
eclectic but its nearest approximation is the point of view espoused by
O'Kelly and Muckler.* The paraphrasing of their views will be helpful
here since it is a scientific explanation but should at the same time make
sense to the unspecialized reader.

Man free from stress always constitutes a special case from which little
is learned. We must turn to the human under pressure—the human for
whom problem-solving is not working—to see clearly the internal psychic
state of man. When stress becomes sufficiently intense, we find our
energies increasingly devoted to the issue of "compensating" or "adjusting." If these efforts resolve our difficulties in living, we return to the
equilibrium of normal existences. If our troubles deepen, our problems
worsen, and stress increases, the kind and quality of our response to life
and other persons deteriorates accordingly, and we devote our energies
to a psychological agenda that has little relation to the amenities of daily
life. This is what is meant by disorder in life. The expected patterns of

* L. O'Kelly and F. Muckler, *Introduction to Psychopathology* (Englewood Cliffs,
N.J.: Prentice-Hall, Inc., 1955).

normal response fail to appear while bizarre and unpredicted reactions take their place.

Fundamental to this observation about order and disorder is the task of avoiding or reducing the experience of anxiety. The neurotic employs a multitude of devices to relieve himself of the onslaught of anxiety and its attendant pains. When these anxiety-reducers fail or are bypassed for more primitive forms of defense, we have the disorder we label psychosis. The disorder we are discussing is, of course, defined in great part by the tenor of the times and interpreted according to current theories of sickness and health. We can still observe that the extremity of the psychotic's attempt to adjust produces a disintegration of expected patterns of response such that we become wary of them and no longer feel comfortable in interaction with them. When the attempt to solve problems under stress produces unusual and barely understood forms of interpersonal congress, most of us react negatively and decide that only sickness can account for the distortions of emotional and intellectual response.

What we call "neurosis" is a less clearly distressing form of disordered living. The neurotic has problems that are equally incapable of resolution by rational means and, more dangerous, resemble normals in so many respects that he is most often indistinguishable from those less troubled.

Each of us is neurotic in one sense or another. Each of us carries through life a set of unsolved problems, prejudices, and biases in response to our fellow human beings. Since neurosis so often disguises itself as normality and so often is indistinguishable from it, a major problem of adjustment is focused on the correct or incorrect diagnosis each of us makes of the other. The disorder of a single life usually has repercussions in the lives of others, and that is the issue. Normality, then, becomes a very relative term and its limits are more elastic than most of us suspect. We are all, simultaneously, normal and abnormal. These cases simply illustrate the range of possible disorder in our lives.

Finally, my personal and professional concern about protecting the anonymity of this mixture of patients and persons I have known has run so deep that in each of the nearly one dozen successive rereadings of the completed cases I have made changes in content designed deliberately to disguise the identity of the participants. In each instance, I weighed carefully the nature of the incident, characteristic, or behavioral sequence that might make the person recognizable and have substituted another clinically consistent event in its place. Perhaps I have been too cautious and, perhaps, the hard core of reality has been sacrificed. The cases are true in every respect but the pieces of the various puzzles are often interchangeable clinically.

The Quiet Furies

The Invisible Sickness
–GEORGE L.

GEORGE L. WAS NOT what you would call a handsome man. His features were far from classic, his manner quiet and self-effacing. Being an English professor suited him exactly and he even looked like the stereotyped typical professor. It was as if he were genetically destined to be a professor and could not escape his fate.

Bespectacled, quiet, intense, and devoted to shaping young minds—these described George in part but left out too much to be accurate. George did of course have some professorial characteristics that fit the stereotype. For example, he could never learn to tie his necktie properly. He would begin by wrapping the tie around his neck and adjusting both ends to the same length. As a result he always ended up with the narrow back portion of the tie about three inches longer than the front. This asymmetrical catastrophe was then studiously tie-clipped into place as evidence for all to see that he had again flunked his daily test of sartorial elegance.

His students and colleagues felt there was a Christ-like quality in George's devotion to his work, and, in fact, an ex-student once wrote that George missed his calling by not becoming a religious leader. George wasn't religious in a classic sense but he was intensely reverant about human life and subscribed devoutly to the idea that the state of mankind could be improved substantially if everybody worked full time at it. He seldom mentioned this aloud since it sounded pretty corny in sophisticated company.

Whenever anyone commented on his slightly Christ-like demeanor, George would launch into a somewhat defensive, somewhat aggressive, cynical laying waste of all that most people considered holy. It was an unconvincing display—George *was* Christ-like. But, it made him nervous

since his self-image was that of a person waspishly anti-establishment.
George's problem was that he knew the words but couldn't carry the
tune of protest. He was, congenitally, a nice guy and this birth defect was
beyond remedy at the age of 45. You liked him at once for his honesty
and openness, and you soon respected him for his dedication to the vital
issues of life. Yet, you knew he was a "patsy," and that others would take
advantage of him.

Among George L.'s problems was a crushing personal and social conscience. He cared intensely about the image he presented to other people
and worked day and night to be, within reason, the kind of person
others expected him to be. He was always on time, met his classes when
sick or well, read term papers religiously, demeaned his talents publicly
by pointing out his personal and professional shortcomings, admired the
"operators" among his colleagues, and was regularly distressed by the
discrepancy that existed between his aspirations and his achievements. He
was a little corny and sentimentally serious by current standards when he
expressed his values and ideas about life but he was always inspiring to his
students and they not only admired him but became devoted to him. A
tight-knit cult of students swore they "would never forget him."

Sometimes George had anxiety-laden dreams in which he found himself in a situation in which he had "let somebody down terribly" by not
doing what he was supposed to do at the time he was supposed to do it.
In these dreams he always felt mortified and he would awaken in misery
and go into work early that day. He just "felt better" if he could get at
his work a little earlier. Incidentally, the chairman of the English department was a brilliant diagnostician who recognized at once George's
fatal flaw. The chairman looked like a friendly Buddha but his chubby
sincerity masked a practical administrative mind that never missed an
opportunity to be nice to a masochist by mistreating him. George always
carried an impossible course load but he never complained. It often
seemed to me that he sold the tickets, showed the movie, pushed the pop-
corn, and swept out the theater of education while the chairman had the
important task of counting the profits. It became obvious, before long,
that George unconsciously enjoyed being walked on almost as much as
the chairman was pleasured by accomodating him with an overload of
professional responsibility.

George's two children were also a problem to him, not because they
were rebellious. In fact, their mature view of life was admirable. They
were quiet, sensitive, and self-contained human beings who were made
uncomfortable by the bluff, hearty, hail-fellow-well-met types to which
they were exposed. Working as diligently as he did and accepting professional responsibility to the extent that he did, George worried regularly about the possibility that he was neglecting his children by not being
as close to them emotionally as he thought he ought to be. He was

constantly oppressed by the feeling that he had failed as a parent by not being able to weigh the parts of life with sufficient care and clarity to decide what was important in the long run. In reality, his children were very attached to him. But this did not reassure him about his way of life. He frequently had serious conversations with colleagues regarding their "honest" view of his children. It was questionable if he ever got a totally honest answer but he seemed to need this regular reassurance.

George was compelled to do things for other people. If he came over to your house for an evening's conversation he always brought expensive liquor or something exotic to eat. He worried about how people accepted him and always made it a package deal—George L. and a gift. George also never complained about personal discomfort or inconvenience. He lived just beyond the city limits and some years ago he and six other families formed a kind of small community cooperative in which they not only worked as a group to construct their individual homes but through which they owned community property (a power lawnmower, a community water system, private street lights). As fate inevitably arranges, two of the six members of the community viewed their communal role as something akin to being uncrowned royalty living in gallant splendor among colorful and loyal serfs. This meant that sharing the common labor of the group was distinctly beneath their dignity and required that the bulk of their community contribution be devoted to logical arguments about community policy followed by rationalizations regarding their inability to contribute a proper share of the labor. Over a period of years George was victimized by these two families in a variety of ways. He took it, grumbled privately, and extended himself to be even more cooperative and hard working as an example to the others. It didn't work, of course. The two parasitic families shirked their responsibilities in direct proportion to his assumption of increased duties.

It was as though George had been born to suffer. His emotional investment in the chronic injustices of life seldom was applied to himself. All his resentment was directed toward the plight of deprived children neglected by an unresponsive society insufficiently concerned with human wreckage. The glaring discrepancy between the lip-service people pay to social problems and what they are willing to provide to solve them irritated him without end. The apparent hypocrisy of humanity galled George constantly. People just didn't give a damn about others and civilization was getting exactly what it deserved. In some ways George was alienated from his own society by the callousness and disinterest he saw in all those about him.

It was his unexpected plans for divorce that shocked the academic community. George was apparently such a devoted family man that he called home each day just to check on how things were going and to

remind his wife of a variety of things of which she was already aware—
that the children would be home early from school today, or that the
steaks should be defrosted for supper. He was, perhaps, too "apparently"
devoted to his family. His wife, for example, suffered a powerful but
silent resentment about these daily calls since she always sensed that
George treated her as if she had a limited intelligence. She always made a
wry joke about it if a neighbor was there at the time the call came: "It
must be George checking to see if I know the difference between hot and
cold water." She tolerated this quirk in George and learned a variety of
ways to assure that his constant supervision of her would roll off her
back and not interfere with her labors as a wife and mother. It was a
minor annoyance and George was otherwise a steady if unspectacular
mate.

George's marital problem, I later discovered, lay outside the close
family circle he maintained, and George's problem with the female of the
species had more to do with his childhood perceptions than it did with
the current state of his happiness or unhappiness as a married man. George
was not the kind of person who "played around" every chance he got. He
appeared quite businesslike and circumspect around the office. He was
avuncular to his own office staff but he underwent a startling transforma-
tion whenever he found himself in close contact with the chairman's secretary. This woman held a strange fascination for him and he confided
intimate details of his personal life to her and manufactured excuses to
see her whenever he could. There was a moth-and-flame attraction that
was bound to be a fatal combination.

The two of them became a departmental item before long. Everyone
knew that they shared a few too many quiet luncheons together and
many suspected that their Saturday labors were a mixture of work and
play. There was no real proof of the true depth of their relationship but
the sharp-eyed secretarial staff at once launched its usual program of
assassination-by-gossip and enjoyed the scandal immensely. The inevitable,
because it was inevitable, happened. First, one secretary accidentally discovered them in an intimate embrace in the file room. Next, George's
wife invaded the privacy of one of their motel excursions and blackened
his eye with a vigorously swung purse. George moved out of the family
home, and the boss's secretary quit her job and began divorce proceedings
against her engineering-student husband. The grounds for her divorce
were obscure but socially polite—incompatibility.

The scandal became even more choice and juicy when George L.
and the boss's secretary openly travelled to New York together to attend
a professional convention. The sight of George L. holding hands with
the secretary in the lobby of the convention hotel and exchanging deep
and secret glances with her was particularly shocking to his friends, not
only because it seemed so totally out of character for him but because

there was at least a difference of 20 years in their ages. In the last two months, it was true, George had been acting in a somewhat strange manner but this latest public display of unconventionality topped it all off. George had frantically immersed himself in an unaccustomed round of social events; he was drinking too much, acting sophisticated and gay, night-clubbing, and telling dirty jokes.

It was as if George had become a different person. He neglected his professional work almost completely and undertook a host of new and short-lived hobbies and interests. George began to dress youthfully. He abandoned his previous circle of scholarly acquaintances and took up with the cool jazz, protest, and coffee-house clan. It was a pathetic sight to see him try to wrestle age to a standstill, and, when our paths crossed, he always looked as if his anchor were dragging a little. He was losing weight and exercising regularly but these efforts were clearly painful to him and his physique was not nearly approaching Adonis-like proportions. He looked very much what he was—a middle-aged man trying desperately to repair the ravages of time and addiction to comfort. I was most concerned about the physical vigor of many of the activities he now pursued with unbounded enthusiasm. He became an ardent squash player, for example. Tennis might have been all right at his age but hard-fought competition on the squash court seemed too much for a man of his years. He began to look like a prime candidate for a cardiac arrest and the pace seemed literally to be killing him.

Interestingly, during this time (nearly six months) George never managed to take the necessary steps to divorce his wife. He was quite upset about the possible effect his newly found emotional attachment might have on his children, but he could not bring himself to talk to them or to explain what had happened. Whenever George wanted to speak to his wife, he would have his secretary call her to make sure he did not accidently come in contact with the kids and find himself stuttering and stammering about what was happening to all of them.

The upshot of the whole affair was that George L. never divorced his wife. His flaming romance with the boss's secretary extinguished itself almost as quickly as it had blazed to life in the first place and his disinterest in her, as I later discovered, took place shortly after she quit her job as the boss's secretary. George was sheepishly reconciled with his wife and accepted an offer from a small Eastern university where he now seems to have returned completely to his previous way of life. For six months George L. was painfully transformed into a pathetically different human being, one who learned the hard way that at his age the pattern of a lifetime is extremely difficult to change.

Nearly a year has passed since these uncomfortable events took place, and when I last talked to George, he was almost exactly the same person I once knew so well. Almost, I say, because he seems now to bear an even heavier burden of guilt than before and has redoubled his efforts to seek atonement for his extramarital escapade by way of increased diligence and dedication to his students. George was being reborn through his students every day of his life.

George was a friend rather than a patient and he came to me first to ask me to meet with his children and try to explain to them what was happening to the family. I agreed to speak to any child of his who wished to see me but I rejected his request to play the part of *pater familias* at this early stage of his marital difficulties. As he described in detail his view of his problems, I began to suspect that the last thing in the world that would be a satisfactory solution for him would be an escape from reality via a quick second marriage. In fact, the more he described the nature of his affair with the boss's secretary, the more I began to think that his paramour was a symbol of an unresolved problem that had remained alive in him from his early childhood. This secretary he was so "mad about" resembled quite closely his account of the personal characteristics that were most accurately descriptive of his mother.

The boss's secretary was, unconsciously, the equivalent of "the big man's woman"—his father's wife. The fact that this secretary did not physically resemble his mother was inconsequential as far as his unconscious was concerned. The attraction for George had less to do with the personal qualities of the particular female, it seemed to me, and more to do with the fact that she be a person privy to the secrets of the boss-man and a person who might have influence with the departmental father figure. Every anxiety George could recall about suffering the wrath or displeasure of his father had now been transferred, without his conscious knowledge, to the person of his boss. George told me that this feeling had happened to him a number of times in the past and that he had always been great friends with females who occupied this role. This was, however, the first time that he had resonated with so responsive a chord as to be swept away in a tide of overwhelming emotion and gross misjudgment. When this particular secretary responded warmly and sympathetically to him, he was unable to resist temptation and incapable of keeping the relatonship on a businesslike level.

As George said, it just felt as though he had casually drifted into the romance without knowing how far he had gone. It seemed to him his emotions were genuine at the time and that this woman in this position was the answer to a number of deep cravings that had always nibbled timorously at the edge of his conscious mind. When he eventually became reconciled with his wife he felt a mixture of penetrating shame and puzzlement about the trap he had fallen into and his inability to find a way out. When I was talking to him one day about the similarity of the feelings he had toward his mother and the emotions he was experiencing with regard to his love affair, he broke down and began to cry violently. This event was the beginning of the end.

George himself made the connection between the mother he wanted so desperately to love only him and the anger and resentment he felt toward a father who always seemed to interfere in his love affair with his mother. His father (the boss) always had everything his own way and commanded the attention and affection of his mother despite the urgency of George's own felt needs. George ran a distant second to his father and was compelled to continue running this losing race currently even though all the original contestants had stopped running long ago. George's failure to win the object of his love in early life had goaded him into an impossible unconscious contest again and again, and, as I watched him run frantically, I was also able to detect the desperation he felt so deeply. He was forever running but he knew he was losing. His emotional entanglement with this particular boss's woman was a nightmarish distortion of feelings that most of us long ago managed to cope with in more mature ways.

Typically, the male who loves his mother comes to realize the hopelessness of his quest for her exclusive ownership and seeks, in her stead, a reasonable substitute for the unattainable. For George, this event never took place. Symbolically, and in fantasy, George still felt he could win even though the odds were clearly against him. He was fighting an ancient battle but its purpose was as clear as it had been when he was only three years old.

George had a variety of problems, each of them highly visible to his friends as well as his critics. Yet, George's diagnosis was a strange one. George was normal. George was normal and he was a typical citizen at the same moment that he was atypical in our society. Had George never been involved in scandalous behavior he would have been invisible socially and his name would have been remembered only by those closest to him. George was, like most of us, ordinary. He had grown to maturity carrying with him a great many disordered remnants of his past life and these unsolved problems both shaped his adult personality and plunged him into a social trap from which he could not escape. George faced a challenge that all of us face, but he solved it badly and impulsively. He was as much the victim as the cause of his enmeshment with life and, like most of us, did the best he could with what resources were available to him.

The average person seldom becomes as acutely aware of the imperfections in his personality structure as George. It was as if the whole structure of his life had collapsed on him and he was unable, alone, to disengage himself from the rubble of his existence. George had all the virtues and few of the faults that the majority of us have, but, when he came face-to-face with impossible circumstances, he was without the necessary resources to manage them. Each of us undergoes a certain amount of natural upheaval in life and we weather it badly or well depending, in great part, on the resources at our command. With George it was a case of too little and too late. He lacked what he needed at the moment in his life when it was most vital that he not be short of supplies.

Yet, George was normal. As normal as most of us are and as subject to the vagaries of fate. Look around you and think about your closest friends. If they are young people, they have ahead of them a life filled with trials and tribulations beyond their capacity to envision. It is possible that more than one of your close friends will be divorced, remarry badly, be depressed and upset, not know which way to turn for advice and guidance and, yet, be normal.

Normality is a very strange thing. One can be normal and experience a great many painful blows in life. Normality is not determined by what fate deals a person. It is judged, rather, in terms of the manner with which one responds to and rebounds from these events. Life was never advertised as less than a harsh struggle and it is how we manage this combat that determines what will become of us. George was normal and he suffered all the pains and afflictions most normals do. Perhaps he had somewhat more than his share, but life is like that—so much of it is accident and uncontrollable circumstance that it sometimes surprises me that so many of us manage to survive relatively intact.

George was normal. As you read the personal histories of those less than normal you must be wary of judging too quickly or judging too harshly. Your normal life may be as incident-laden as was George's. "Normal" encompasses a great and broad range of humanity that continually fights adversity and it includes those among us who visibly or invisibly protest against the way things are and seem briefly to be maladjusted to life. To live is to have problems and in solving these problems we grow emotionally, but we grow at the cost of the formation of measurable scar tissue in our psychic structure. One day you may come across George or his counterpart and be tempted to discuss his way of life as inappropriate as a model for your existence. I would ask only that you be tolerant and understanding of the frailty of mankind.

George destroyed his reputation as a teacher when his personal life ceased to be a model of an idealized public morality. In this action he achieved once again a tension-laden expression of his basic masochism—his need to be punished and put-upon by people in order to feel worthwhile as a human being. In the early conflict with his father over being dispossessed in the affections of his mother, George learned to be passive and to gain acceptance by self-sacrifice. The Oedipal contest he lost in childhood was reborn, in disguise, in his affair with the boss's secretary. Like the refighting of all lost battles, this conflict was destined again to make him the loser since the course of ancient history is seldom altered by new interpretations of the way things should have been rather than the way things really were.

George was, as most of us are, a person of many parts and aspects, only some of which were available for conscious inspection when he peered inside himself. As he viewed his professional and personal life, he was pleased but restless. Something was missing but that something only became apparent in the holocaust of a self-created crisis of emotional involvement. George learned what every used-car salesman knows almost instinctively—the purchaser of a four-door, basic black, manual shift, six cylinder car has a deep rooted longing for the impractically snappy, multi-colored, overpowered sports model. For George L. it was very much like finding himself in what he took to be the wrong—and slowest —line in a bank or supermarket. Maybe he had made the wrong choice and was missing out on life.

So George impulsively changed lines only to find that the second choice was little better than the first. What he lacked in his relationship with his wife, he found in the arms of his paramour, but his new solution to an ancient problem proved to be less than adequate at this susceptible time in his life. George learned a lesson about life but it was a costly course of instruction. His relationship with his wife can never be quite what it was before, and his confidence about knowing himself will never again be what he once thought it was. "Once burned, twice shy" will undoubtedly be his motto in the future but the fundamental needs and longings that impelled him once to ill-considered action remain alive, if dormant, within him. These needs may never surface again to complicate George's life in so extreme a fashion, but they remain an important part of his total psychological makeup. George will continue to be a complex human being—like most of us—and he will continue to lead some part of his life with some measure of anger and despair below the surface.

George is as normal as you, and I, and most others we know. Disorders are not the province of the few. They are, rather, the state of being of all of us at some time in our lives.

Transient Situational Disorder:
Gross Stress Reaction

To Whom It May Concern
—Doug E.

PROLOGUE *Transient situational disorders* encompassing a gross
stress reaction can occur as a consequence of natural
catastrophes (accidents, floods, fires, tornadoes, earthquakes),
reactions to a variety of chronic stresses issuing from daily life
(divorce, unemployment, failure), or can be the outcome of
traumatic reactions to war and combat. The memory of most of
us has never been free of the strain of war and the prospect of a
future without mortal conflict is improbable indeed. The
transient situational personality disorders of war are thus,
regrettably, a source of continued concern in our civilization.
The case considered here is one dating from World War II but
its relevance to modern times is inescapable since the emotional
difficulties portrayed are the timeless consequences of
exposure to severe stress with which one cannot cope and
from which there is no escape. All human vessels split if the
pressure within them is great enough and World War II, the
Korean conflict, and the war in Viet Nam have been grisly
laboratories in which we have conducted a series of savage
natural experiments with the effect of stress on the psychic
structure of human beings.

One of the prime differences between transient situational
disorders and neurotic and psychotic disorders is the visibility

and reasonableness of the stress which disorganizes the
personality. The man in combat can understand the sudden
disintegration of his comrade-in-arms since he is himself
pressured by similar stress and strain and knows intimately what
it is to teeter on the brink of total psychological collapse.
Neurosis and psychosis are incomprehensible to most of us
because the stress that triggers them is internal, invisible, and "not
reasonable or sensible" to the onlooker.

In previous wars, transient situational disorders were
attributed to a variety of causes: shell shock (tiny hemorrhages
of the brain produced by the concussion of an explosion),
combat exhaustion (with its suggestion of a physical basis for
psychological collapse), and war neurosis (a theoretical
contradiction according to most theories of how neurosis is
developed in childhood). The disorders of combat have
symptoms resembling those typical of a neurosis or psychosis but
the course of transient situational disorders is often responsive
to mild, short-term therapy. In the Korean "police-action,"
for example, front-line psychiatrists observed that a rapid
return to combat of moderately injured soldiers prevented
the development of serious situational disorders
traceable to gross stress.

The clinical picture of the transient situational disorder is
one of irritability and hypersensitivity in a victim who is
aware he is losing self-control but is helpless to turn back the tide
that is engulfing him. The slightest stimulus can bring on
a massive overresponse in which the victim appears
terror-stricken and displays a violent startle response.
He is, in short, nervous and jumpy. He is bone-weary, whipped,
dejected, and desperately needs the rest provided by sleep
but finds again and again that despite his exhaustion he can't
get comfortable or loosen his despairing grip on wakefulness.
In part, he is so tense that he never stops listening to what is
going on around him and, in part, he dreads the terrifyingly
realistic dreams that will awaken him screaming
and shaking in terror.

The steady erosion of self produced by the threat of death,
the necessity of killing others, unbelievable exhaustion,
separation from the security of family and loved ones,
and continued exposure to new and dangerous situations for

which one seems totally unprepared and helpless all occur
in a setting in which freedom to act independently is denied
the individual. Rapidly mounting anxiety increases violently with
each "near miss," with the sudden death of one's comrades,
and a steady loss of faith in one's leaders. Psychological resources
needed to meet danger and cope with it successfully begin
to disappear as home and family become dim,
vague memories and death becomes a foregone conclusion—
merely a matter of time and bad luck.

As a last desperate hope, the victim of these continuous
stresses may pray fearfully and unashamedly for the million
dollar wound—the nonmutilating, nonfatal passport out of an
intolerable situation. A mixture of fear, guilt, and shame becomes
the constant companion of the combat soldier. If it is only a
superficial wound there is little escape from the awareness that
it is in the lap of fate whether or not you get yours this time
or the next time around.

When these severe stresses are superimposed on a basically
immature and inadequate psychological makeup and are,
perhaps, coupled with a growing sense of guilt over one's failure
to be a "good soldier," we have all the needed elements for
personal catastrophe. The victim starts to sweat and to tremble
as though the world is about to fall in on him. There is no escape
and there is no help from any quarter. The least noise
startles him, he smokes cigarettes endlessly, he has twitches
and tics, darts glances over his shoulder, and becomes the walking,
talking stereotype of the "nervous wreck." At this juncture, he
may become confused, stuporous, and helpless to defend
himself or to function effectively.

Had fate dealt with him less severely he might have lived
out his days in a relatively stable and adjustive fashion.
Forced to look death squarely in the eye day after day,
he loses the staring contest and becomes a casualty of civilized
man's violent form of interaction with his fellow beings.

"Doug is bugged, Doug is bugged, Doug is bugged," kept repeating itself over and over in his head. Who wouldn't be bugged? He hadn't slept
soundly for what seemed like a month now and he knew he was jittery.
He had been counting the number of missions he had already flown but
was bothered by the outside possibility that he had freakishly miscalcu-

lated and was flying one more mission than he had to. He wondered if the clown keeping count knew what he was doing. Maybe he couldn't count. And, of all the stinking luck, today he was flying with a green crew that looked so young, dumb, and scared that it would be a miracle if they didn't kill themselves before they got off the ground. He didn't bother to learn their names because if they got back alive he would never fly with them again anyway. "Christ!" he thought, "they must be scraping the bottom of the barrel if this is what they are sending into combat. My sister is tougher than these guys. Why in hell do I have to fly with these jerks? Talk about a rotten break."

And this morning! Like every other morning that son-of-a-bitch of a duty sergeant busted into the barracks at 4 a.m., slammed the damn screen door, snapped on those miserable lights, and read the roster of flight crews "destined for glory on this foggy day in jolly old England." Same old joke every morning. A comedian. Doug wondered if the duty sergeant would sound so damn cheery if *he* had to make the run into Berlin today. Doug knew it was Berlin because the bartender at the pub had told him. All those bartenders must be Nazi spies, he thought. They always know where the hell we're going but "our" Colonel wouldn't tell you his serial number if his life depended on it. And how come some of those other clowns didn't fly once in a while? Why did he have to go on every god damn mission? No rest camp, no rotation, no nothin' but fly, fly, fly. He'd never make it. Today smelled bad. He knew he was going to get it today.

Christ, it was cold! How the English could ever amount to a pile of squat in this climate was beyond him. The cold cut right through him but he was sweating anyway. It seemed like he was sweating all the time in the last couple of weeks and he had picked up a nervous habit of wiping his hands on his flight suit all the time. He knew he had to stop that before the other guys noticed and began to kid him about it. Then he remembered—George and the eggs.

Those greasy, slimey, powdered eggs and dishwater coffee when you were falling over from sleepiness and sick to your stomach anyway. The worst part of breakfast was being served by George L. George used to be a member of the crew but he turned chicken and saw the Chaplain for a punk-out from combat. It was great psychology their Colonel had invented. He had decided that anybody who turns yellow had to be a mess servant for the "heroes" in the outfit. As he ate he tried not to look into George's eyes. Doug thought about his own fears and recalled that when he first came into combat he carried a G.I. issue tommy gun and had wild fantasies of shooting his way out of Germany single-handed after he crashed. He was a hell of a lot smarter now. He didn't even carry a jack-knife with a long blade. No point in provoking people.

Doug had been, at first, the epitome of cockiness. He was never very religious and when his crew suddenly "got religion" and started to attend services on Sunday he told them, "You pray for me and I'll oil your guns." He always oiled their guns on Sunday because he was scared too but couldn't admit it. To demonstrate his supposed fearlessness, he had once hung a sign on the tail turret of the B-17 announcing that he was "Open for Business—24 hours a day." After a particularly scarey mission, he had quietly torn the sign to shreds and began to worry about inviting heavenly punishment for his irreverent attitude.

Doug was scared. As scared as he had ever been in his 19 years, but he couldn't admit it and couldn't do anything about it. And, today, he was flying with a new crew who were so scared they thought he was cool. So, he had to appear to be combat-wise, sophisticated, casual, cool, confident, and reassuring. He felt none of these things, and he wished secretly he were back on the Shady Lady with Captain Willard and his own crew. At least with them he had half a chance. The guys knew each other and had been through a lot together—you didn't have to worry about them. Today was going to be a big sweat but there was no way out. Maybe he could see the Chaplain and tell him how scared he was.

Doug E. gave up when they were hit by ME 109's on the outskirts of Berlin. It seemed like the skies were full of them and fighter planes flying "area cover" were nowhere to be seen. When the waist gunner shot up their own right wing, it was just too much. Doug went clear out of it and began to mumble to himself and shout meaningless orders to the crew. As he began to scream incoherently, the co-pilot jumped out of his seat and dragged Doug unceremoniously aft into the radio compartment. He wrapped Doug in an electric blanket, gave him a shot of morphine, strapped him down securely, and told the other crew members to keep an eye on him. The radio operator was killed ten minutes later and his bleeding body fell on Doug.

They got back, somehow, to their base at Bury St. Edmunds but they had to fly the tree tops all the way. Doug was taken to the station hospital (one medic plus a once-in-a-while flight surgeon) and in a couple of days was transferred to a base hospital. By then he was agitated and didn't recognize the members of his crew who came to visit him and he was wide awake every night with horrifying recollections of his last mission.

Doug's breakdown was long overdue, and he had been flying behavioral distress signals for some time before it took place. He remembered, for example, a nightmare that occurred every time he suspected an unusually dangerous mission was scheduled for the next morning. In the dream, Doug would go through all the motions of preparing for a mission, but, inevitably, everything seemed to go wrong. As Doug said,

> Just as we would lift off from the end of the runway I would begin a frantic search through my flight bag to make certain everything I needed was there. It never was, of course. I was always horrified to discover I had forgotten my oxygen

mask, I couldn't find the top half of my electrically heated suit, the spare bolts for the caliber 50 machine guns were missing, and I couldn't recall if I remembered to load the extra cannisters of ammunition. I would then make fumbling, frantic efforts to plug in my intercom to tell the Captain we had to turn back but I could never get the intercom to work. I would usually wake up screaming something like "turn back, turn back, turn back."

Doug's dream was a transparent one. The moment he drifted into sleep and relaxed conscious control over the content of his thoughts, his all-consuming anxieties would instantly emerge and try to inform him in a symbolic and disguised fashion that he was missing too much psychological equipment to go into combat. He had lost or misplaced the resources that he needed to come back alive and he didn't have what it takes to make it all the way.

One other dream Doug had was simpler yet even more horrible. In this night fantasy he was always taking-off from an airport in a large metropolitan area and as the climb-out began it would suddenly become apparent that even under full power the plane was never going to gain enough altitude to clear a solid row of buildings that suddenly appeared directly in his path. Frozen with horror he would watch helplessly as he hurtled toward the buildings at an extremely rapid and undoubtedly fatal rate. He would awaken screaming, panicked, and sweating just before the crash, and lie awake the rest of the night, afraid to go back to sleep.

Doug had not simply folded without a fight. He had, simultaneously, tried foresight and forgetfulness as ways out of his frightening dilemma. Forgetfulness was the easier of the two. When the weather was bad (as it chronically seemed to be in England) and Doug could wangle a three-day pass, he would roar off to London on the prowl for "broads and booze." Since London in 1943 had an oversupply of American soldiers, Doug more often than not had to take what he could get among the prostitutes who were still available late at night. Since Doug most often had reached a state of staggering drunkenness, anything resembling the human form was acceptable to him. The next day, hung over and disgusted with himself, he would painfully thread his way back to more normal society and vow to spend his future leave time in a more constructive and less dissolute manner.

When his squadron was on alert for a mission the next day, Doug would proceed at once to the noncommissioned officers' club and spend the evening drinking himself into insensibility. As the evening wore on and the hour grew late, he would head for the barracks carrying with him some piece of furniture from the club. His favorite "toting piece" was an empty practice bomb that had been converted into a standing lamp. It became a kind of good-luck piece for him and he began to become superstitious about it. If he got drunk and carried it back to the hut, he believed he would then survive the mission, whatever the odds, in order to complete the magic ritual by carrying the bomb-lamp back to the club. He recalled that the bomb was painted Air Force Blue and had fighter bomber cutouts on the shade. More than once, Doug was still drunk when he boarded the B-47 Flying Fortress for the mission but he was usually in condition to fight by the time they reached enemy territory. Stark, abject terror is a great soberer of men.

Doug was very adept mechanically and he employed this unusual aptitude in his program of foresight. He figured out that if he welded extra ammunition cannisters to the standard number found on most planes he would acquire 30 per cent more rounds of ammunition and a similar margin of combat safety. It was a minor matter, but whenever Doug got anxious he also felt an overwhelming desire to urinate. So Doug installed no less than seven "relief tubes" on the plane. No member of his crew had to travel far to a rest room but he never solved the problem of involuntary loss of bowel control during moments of high stress.

In line with his program of self-protection, Doug was an unrelenting scavenger of airplanes incapacitated in combat. Scrounging parts and pieces of intact equipment, Doug rigged an intercom system that allowed everyone on the crew to talk to all others at the same time. In addition, he double-armored his own upper turret gun position so that nothing short of cannon-fire could injure him.

Foresight and planning proved insufficient to assure Doug of invulnerability. He was still scared and a couple of close calls confirmed his conviction that his days were numbered. Once he was sitting on an empty amunition box when an anti-aircraft burst destroyed the box and left him untouched but well-slivered from the splinters of the box. At another time red hot flak (anti-aircraft fragments) sliced the electronic gunsight between his eyes and stopped no more than an inch from his skull. Doug knew that no human being could create a safe environment for himself when fate, accident, and luck had so much to do with survival.

Doug also discovered that his forgetfulness was temporary and the remembering even more painful afterwards. He was helpless to save himself and could not drown this awareness. At the moment of this dual discovery he was ready to crack and it was indeed only a matter of time. The time of his collapse was 1943 and times were very bad. Nearly 23 per cent of all front-line evacuations during this period were for what was then called "battle-fatigue." In fact, more G.I.'s were being evacuated from combat for emotional distress than were being inducted into the service back in the States, and becoming "nervous in the service" was far from an isolated or rare event. Doug was about to become a common statistic even though he thought his problem was unique to him.

As we learned through bitter experience in the Korean and Viet Nam conflicts, the evacuation of Doug from combat was probably the worst psychiatric move possible. With immediately available helicopter-powered psychiatric aide close to the front lines, the rate of psychiatric disability in Viet Nam was reduced to one-half of the rate in Korea. In part, this is an unfair comparison since the soldier's awareness that his tour of duty is fixed at 12 months allows him to focus on an honorable escape from tension in a measurable span of time. Doug, in contrast, had not been rotated for R and R (rest and rehabilitation) in four solid months of combat. In fact, at the moment he completed 23 missions he was informed that 30 missions, rather than 25, must be flown to complete one's duty-tour. The last two missions yet to be flown frightened him enough; the thought of an additional seven was truly hopeless. His luck could never last that long. He was operating on sheer nerve now and knew he would never make it to the end because they had moved the finish line too far down the track.

The most difficult aspect of treating Doug was dealing with the towering sense of guilt he experienced about deserting his combat crew in their hour of need. He could never forgive himself for what he took to be child-like weakness in the face of danger, and he knew that his father would never forgive him for not having the guts to carry on when the chips were down. His father was a career officer in the infantry who set high standards of personal heroism for all his sons and could accept nothing less than outstanding courage and absolute fortitude from his male offspring. Doug had never really felt at ease with these paternal demands. Being Virginia-born and an army brat seemed to require that he be better than most others when it came to manliness. Again and again, Doug mentioned that his defection from combat would "kill" his father but I was never quite sure if this was what he feared or what he secretly wished.

In Doug's early days he had tried valiantly to be what his father wished him to be. He got into fist fights with other kids (although he reported he was scared to death whenever he fought), and, as he became skilled with his fists he was both a moderate bully and a very reluctant David frequently forced to attempt to slay some local Goliath. He tried out for most high school sports but, as he said, "he ran too slow and jumped too low" to amount to anything. He could remember that his father attended every football game and cheered wildly. He could always recognize his father's voice in the crowd and sometimes wished one of the tackles would get injured so the coach would have to put him in the game. It was agony to dissect each game later that day because his father was systematically critical of the coach (whom Doug admired) and kept insisting that Doug pass on to the coach some of these pearls of wisdom. He knew that all week his dad would bug him, asking, "Did you tell the coach about spreading that end out farther?" Doug would be forced to reply that he had mentioned it during one of the team's skull sessions.

Doug never mentioned it to the coach, of course. He was only on the second team and hadn't played a total of five minutes during the whole season. He did have some wild, secret fantasies, not uncommon to the bench warmers of the world, of being put in the game, making some brilliant, spectacular play, and having the head coach finally notice him and ask the line coach why they weren't using Doug more in the regular line up. The fantasy never came true and Doug remained second string throughout the time of his eligibility. What really hurt was that his father began to be "too busy" to go to the games in his senior year. With equal frequency Doug began to skip practice. When he quietly left the team, no one seemed to notice, but the discussion of football strategy abruptly stopped occupying the family on Saturday nights.

Both Doug and his parents were well practiced in ignoring failure and second-rate performance and they treated broken expectations as if the hopes had never existed in the first place. Doug had failed in his own and his father's eyes in all the important tests of life, but his feelings about failure and success had never been discussed openly with anyone. Doug never knew how others felt when they failed or how other people felt when they witnessed someone in the process of failing. Doug's experience had always been limited to suffering his personal version of guilt, worthlessness, and anxiety, and he found it difficult to believe that others could accept a lack of perfection with any comfort or even a faint semblance of grace. Doug was a poor loser because he was gambling more than he could afford and that meant he would be a desperate gambler who would rely more on fate than good judgment. Since he felt things just *had* to work out, he had faith that indeed they would. It took him some while to comprehend the wide gap between reality and his fantasy version of it as it referred to failure and personal worth.

Doug's recovery was gradual and unspectacular. A clearer picture began to emerge when, as we talked of the demands his father had made on him, we analyzed their uncompromising nature and examined the pattern of behavior he had developed to achieve acceptance, and compared this pattern with his reaction to the stresses of combat. The need to convert a demanding but emotionally distant father into a warm, loving, accepting, and admiring "dad" had determined the direction that much of his life had taken. When Doug volunteered for duty in the Air Force he had constructed an elaborate explanation of the correctness of his behavior while hiding his real motivation—to please his father. He recalled that when he told his father he had enlisted, his father was pleased but critical of his choice of a "sissy outfit like the fly-boys." Even this ultimate gesture—quitting college in the middle of the term—had somehow turned out badly. Doug consoled himself with the thought that he would be away from his father and on his own for a change.

As we traced the course of Doug's breakdown in combat, it appeared to me that there had been a multitude of warning signals, each more strident in its call for help than the last, but that Doug had failed to recognize or heed any of them. His primary mistake was to keep his problems bottled up for fear others would never understand and would only belittle his fears. He was afraid that they, like his father, would make even greater demands on his waning supply of heroism. He lived with his fears, but they proved to be evil roommates.

Doug's symptoms disappeared, bit by bit decreasing in intensity with every new insight about his life and the kind of person he had become. Interestingly, I was always able to chart his improvement about a week in advance of the time he became aware that he was getting better. At the end of therapy he reported that he often felt he was improving but was afraid it was only temporary relief that would ultimately be followed by a deeper immersion in even more painful symptoms. Doug had a pessimistic outlook on life that precluded the possibility that he would succeed at anything important and he viewed therapy with the same jaundiced eye.

Doug is a successful manager, now, in a branch office of a national trucking concern. His life is free of the extreme stresses of combat and he reports a complete absence of symptoms. When he is at cocktail parties and the conversation drifts into stories of how the paunchy, middle-aged gentlemen assembled won World War II single-handed, Doug tends to stress the glory of his combat days and to gloss over his undignified exit from its perils. Doug's exaggeration of his contribution to the war effort coupled with his selective recall only of the good aspects of soldiering, are reasonable adjustments to past trauma and are adjustments typical of most male members of every society.

Doug's case is not an unusual one, really. With or without therapeutic intervention, victims of transient situational disorders come to some re-definition of their lives and, for better or for worse, manage an adjust-ment on new terms to a life free of stress but haunted by the memory of collapse when it happened before. They lead normal lives but they live with ghosts of the past.

In Doug E.'s case the trauma of combat was dealt with shortly after the disintegration that served admirably to remove him from the situation that was the source of gross stress. Not all sagas of personal encounter with short-lived situational disorders have a happy ending and the ending to this case is far from being all sweetness and light. Carrying him safely past his immediate crisis was a necessary but not sufficient step in teaching him to manage future stress in his life.

Doug E. never again reacted with such violence to the pressures of life but then he was never again confident of his capacity to manage the chal-lenge of things new or unexpected. Successful as he was, he more than once withdrew gracefully from the invitation to a different brand of combat—open conflict in the business world. Doug's "failure" under stress was costly to the conduct of the rest of his life. It made him tentative when he should have been bold, reluctant when he should have been adventurous. Transient or not, the situational disorder Doug E. experienced scarred him psychologically and left him the victim of an invisible wound. This wound of breakdown under severe stress made the difference between what he was and what he could have been in life. Many of us have fallen short of our capabilities but few have had so visible and unmistakable a basis for our shortcomings.

We know a great deal more now about what happened to Doug E. We know that the human organism can only sustain itself psychologically if it has a relatively intact physiological situation. Experimental subjects who deliberately deprive themselves of sleep undergo very similar experiences of anxiety and psychological disorganization. The terror that confronted Doug E. with regard to survival is the kind of stress that can destroy the psychological well-being of any of us. Man cannot survive long in a state of constant physiological alert and alarm. In this case, of course, Doug E.'s early life had ill-equipped him for survival in a world laden to the breaking point with stress.

If Doug E. confronts severe stress again in his life, the probability is great that he will again suffer total psychological collapse. He has learned to be wary of becoming immersed in situations beyond his control and he has learned to live with his personal limitations. Perhaps this is enough.

Neatness Counts!

–Georgia M.

PROLOGUE *Life is* a continual tug-of-war between love and hate,
right and wrong, order and disorder, cleanliness and dirt.
Yet, most of us manage to maintain a precarious balance between
these extremes, and only a few of us become caricatures of
normality in which a single aspect of life almost becomes
one's sole reason for being.

In a psychoneurotic disorder marked by an
obsessive-compulsive reaction, for example, we find human life
frozen into a rigid pattern of inescapable thoughts and absolutely
necessary actions if anxiety is to be avoided and sanity preserved.
The unwilling victim knows his or her pattern of life is irrational,
silly, stupid, futile, irritating to others, and hopeless,
but absolutely indispensable to continued psychic comfort.

Each of us has suffered obsessive thoughts and been the prey
of compulsive actions but these have usually been confined
to haunting melodies we could not shake from consciousness
or persistent concern with situations that lack any simple,
elegant solution—worrying. We have all felt better after a ritual
crossing of fingers or knocking on wood, but few of us
have been terrorized by the thought that we might, for example,
rise in some public gathering, surrounded by friends,
and shout some obscenity that would shock and repel
all those who know us. The specter of a socially unacceptable

impulse bursting the cage that confines it and running amuck
in society is not a part of the constant worry patterns
of most of us.

Suppose you were to find yourself obsessed all day with
thoughts of murdering those you thought you loved best?
At first these vagrant mental images might easily be dismissed
from mind and lost in a flurry of work or play. Then,
these murderous thoughts would begin to appear when
unsummoned, persist throughout one's waking hours,
inhabit one's dreams, and dictate the performance of certain
of your actions and behavior. At that moment, you would be
experiencing a full-blown obsessive-compulsive neurosis.
It is not unlikely that you would be plagued with thoughts
that you are going insane and that you must be a disgustingly
abnormal and horrifying person to think such evil,
wicked, sinful thoughts.

As you fight to quell these unsettling thoughts, you are
likely to engage in a series of actions designed to neutralize
or eliminate these breakthroughs of impulse and to defend
yourself against the full awareness of the truth of the unconscious
and unacceptable urge that fills your life. Survival comes first,
and the pattern of behavior you devise to meet the threat
you feel is about to engulf you may be painful to those
who are closest to you, but you have no choice in the matter.
You do what you feel you must to escape the anxiety
ravenously gnawing at you.

The obsessive-compulsive person is driven to organize
the world in a fashion designed to reassure, to assuage anxiety,
and to make tolerable just living from one moment to the next.
The obsessive person is often a socially submissive individual
bound hand and foot by convention, conscientiousness
in the extreme. A rigid person who seems regularly
to be inadequate in meeting the challenges of life. He may
already have organized his daily existence along methodical,
predictable lines only to discover that this degree of
systematization is insufficient to ward off the threat life poses.
Suddenly, despite his attempts to build a stout fort
to protect himself from attack, he discovers that the enemy
is swarming over his defenses and he must rebuild the walls
to an even greater height.

The last-ditch dictum becomes "a place for everything

and everything in its place." The logic is that if the outside world
is chaotic, messy, disorganized, and untrustworthy, at least
one's personal life can be ritualized, timed, ordered, organized
and made free of surprises via ritual, regularity, and rigidity.
Life constrained in this fashion is absolutely predictable, avoids
excessive exposure to temptation, and eliminates contact with
those particular temptations that might prove to be irresistible.
Little wonder that sudden or violent disruptions of this robot-like
programming of events in one's life are viewed as threatening
and dangerous. Spontaneous invitations to "cut loose"
and "leave the dishes in the sink" are greeted only with horror
and misgivings by the truly obsessed person.
For them, order spells safety.

At the base of obsession-compulsion is a sense of
worthlessness and culpability as a human being. Guilt,
self-condemnation, and fear of punishment become the
unconscious springs of motivation yet the seemingly senseless
actions of the affected individual make a psychological sense to
the astute observer. What is safe gets substituted for what is
unsafe, the thinkable replaces the unthinkable, clean thoughts
are substituted for their reprehensible other selves and anxiety
is temporarily held at bay. The fear that one is not perfect
(as everyone knows one ought to be) gets translated into actions
that are calculated to correct this deficiency in a socially
admirable fashion. When one feels unclean, exaggerated
cleanliness is the only answer. Obsessive love can compensate
for deep-reaching hate and, if it is effective, no one,
including the self, need be the wiser.

Obsessive-compulsive patterns of behavior are
self-defeating, primarily because of the difficulties they create
in relationships with others. If one has never suffered anxiety
attacks relievable only by compulsive behavior, the actions
of the victim may seem bizarre, uncalled for, and worthy
of criticism. The hostility and resentment of others that such
encounters occasion drives the victim deeper into the distress
of costly measures that are bound to fail in the long run. The
compulsive act designed to satisfy the obsessive thought fails
because it serves to remind its victim of the fundamental anxiety
that is being eluded in the first place. Checking the gas jets
to make sure they are turned off merely stimulates, again,
the unconscious impulse to turn each of them full on.

GEORGIA M. ACTED OUT her fundamental problem as she sat nervously in my office. On this particular day, my office happened to be neater than usual, but Georgia M. apparently did not share my view of neatness. She was able in a speedy, all-encompassing glance to catalogue every detail of what had been neglected and what was unclean. She lowered herself into the proffered seat with some tentativeness—gingerly, as if it were crawling with filth.

As she talked she touched the objects on my desk in turn, shifting their positions slightly. She idly but disapprovingly ran her finger along a book case shelf, discovered some dust, and made a great show of dusting off her hands. She hand-brushed her clothes continuously as she talked and was one of the busiest and most efficient lint-removers I had ever seen.

I had several reactions as I watched her fuss away furiously at the condition of my office. It occurred to me that I would one day be able to observe improvement simply by watching the ratio of comfort-discomfort she would show on future visits. Like many people, I have never felt very comfortable in homes where everything is spick-and-span, exactly ordered, spotless, and fragile-looking. According to every American housewife, the usual condition of her house is "a mess." A mess, then, is the normal condition, but for some people what is normal is painful and intolerable. Such was the case with Georgia M.

Most "messy" houses I have entered have been staggeringly well kept, and it always seemed apparent that this frequent self-accusation on the part of housewives is a ritualized, conventional disavowal of responsibility —enter at your own risk. It is also a solemn and fashionable declaration that they would never have presented such a sloppy scene to offend your eyes had you given decent and proper advance notice of your coming. The regularity with which American women voluntarily declare their homes a disaster area does, however, tell us about the cultural ideal held out as a model for American womanhood. Cleanliness is next to godliness and neatness counts in our society. So much so, that European cultures have deridingly depicted us as an excessively scrubbed, well-plumbed, deodorized, sterile, and only slightly human version of a civilization.

Cleanliness is probably better than dirtiness. Tidiness is no doubt better than untidiness. But, according to Georgia M.'s husband, if neatness was an olympic sport Georgia would easily have been captain of the team. As he said,

> You remember that old joke about getting up in the middle of the night to go to the john and coming back to the bedroom to find your wife has made the bed? It's no joke. Sometimes I think she never sleeps. I got up one night at 4 a.m. and there she was doing the laundry downstairs. Look at your ash tray! I haven't seen one that dirty in years! I'll tell you what it makes

me feel like. If I forget to leave my dirty shoes outside the
back door she gives me a look like I had just crapped in the
middle of an operating room. I stay out of the house a lot and
I'm about half-stoned when I do have to be home. She even
made us get rid of the dog because she said he was always
filthy. When we used to have people over for supper she
would jitterbug around everybody till they couldn't digest
their food. I hated to call them up and ask them over because
I could always hear them hem and haw and make up excuses
not to come over. Even the kids are walking down the street
nervous about getting dirt on them. I'm going out of my mind
but you can't talk to her. She just blows up and spends twice
as much time cleaning things. We have guys in to wash the
walls so often I think the house is going to fall down from being scrubbed all the time. About a week ago I had it up to here
and told her I couldn't take it any more. I think the only reason she came to see you was because I told her I was going to
take off and live in a pig pen just for laughs.

Georgia's obsessive concern with cleanliness forced her to take as many
as three showers a day, one in the morning, one before supper, and one
before going to bed, and, on hot days, the number of showers would rise
in direct proportion to the temperature. Her husband could not understand how she got dirty overnight, but Georgia always dismissed his ob-
jections by observing that "it isn't any skin off his nose if I take good care
of myself" and that "he would be the first to holler if I turned sloppy."
The trouble in this family ran deeper than just neatness, of course.
Georgia was aware, in part, of the effect she was having on her family
and friends, but she also knew that when she tried to alter her behavior
she got so nervous that she felt she was losing her mind. She was frightened by the possibility that "I'm headed for the funny-farm." As she said,

I can't get to sleep unless I am sure everything in the house
is in its proper place so that when I get up in the morning the
house is organized. I work like mad to set everything straight
before I go to bed, but, when I get up in the morning, I can
think of a thousand things that I ought to do. I know some of
the things are ridiculous, but I feel better if I get them done,
and I can't stand to know something needs doing and I haven't
done it. I never told anybody but once I found just one dirty
shirt and washed, dried, and ironed it that day. I felt stupid
running a whole wash for one shirt but I couldn't bear to leave
it undone. It would have bothered me all day just thinking
about that one dirty shirt in the laundry basket.
What really bothers me is this whole business of sex. My
husband acts like he wants it all the time and he always brings
it up at times when it's impossible because I have so much to

do. By nighttime I am tired and we live on different sleep
schedules. I always have a million things to do and he's ready
to go to bed. I like to make preparations, too. I think we both
ought to take a shower and the bed should have clean sheets on
it. But, he gets mad and says "the hell with it" and sulks. He's
just like a big overgrown kid. In the last month he hasn't said
anything about sex and I am beginning to think he is fooling
around with some other woman. I got so suspicious that I thought
about following him once or twice, but, with the kids and the
house to take care of, I couldn't get free. Now he says he's going to leave me and that's the only reason I came to see you.

Adding it all up, I wasn't very encouraged by the prospect of making
progress with this family. Georgia certainly had a problem. The children
were suffering, and the marriage was about to come apart at the seams. I
wished they had come to me before the marital issue had gotten quite as
knock-down-and-drag-out as it seemed to be at the moment but it is often
that way.

I asked both Georgia and her husband to see me regularly, but separately. My clinical goals with the husband were: 1) to explore in full the
nature and extent of the symptoms Georgia was displaying, 2) to assess
what resources the husband had that might be useful in establishing some
new patterns of interpersonal relations with his wife, and 3) to examine
the structure of complicity in the game they were playing. I reasoned
that it took two to dance this complicated tango of life and that, somehow, he must contribute to the maintenance of so severe a set of symptoms. Did he marry her with this obsessive prospect lurking in his unconscious? Did he reward or encourage the first appearance of extraordinary
neatness in her? Was she acting out a part of himself that would never
otherwise reach the surface of his consciousness? There were a million
such unanswered questions. Why did he insist, only now, that she enter
therapy? Why had he tolerated this condition so long? Why his evident
glee in relating in fine detail the excruciating agony caused by her behavior? Why did his relationship with his children seem distant and cold (he
never mentioned their names; he always designated them by relative age—
the oldest kid, the middle kid, and the youngest kid)? Why did he always
compare his wife to his own mother?

The first stages of therapy with Georgia and her husband Bill were re-
markably alike, a fact which impressed itself on me because, at times, I
would confuse who said what. At first there was resistance. It was not
that they lied; it was rather that I never got more than part of the truth
at any one time from either of them. It was as frustrating as being handed
pieces to a picture puzzle one at a time. You needed a good memory to
keep any kind of perspective because the same event would be described
several times before, suddenly, I realized they were both talking about

the same thing. It is an unsettling experience to become aware all at once that the argument being described is the same one you had discussed previously but failed to recognize when retold by the other combatant. More than once I was tempted to bring them together to discuss their two views of the same argument in the vain hope that with me acting as a judge the reality of the battle might finally emerge and be recognized by all. It was, as I said, a vain hope born of frustration since I knew full well that reality was clearly in the eye of the angry beholder. For some weeks it was like wading through a swamp of glue with both of them until we could have an hour free of resistance—an hour in which I would not silently say "en garde" as the conversation began.

Bill opened up first. He was describing something Georgia had recently done when he jumped from his chair and shouted, "Hey, that's just what my mother always used to do!" Then, as suddenly as he had jumped, he broke down and started to cry. I could only suspect what was taking place (this was his fourteenth hour with me), so I began to probe to find some solid ground for a firmer therapeutic footing. What poured out that hour changed our relationship dramatically. It was as if we had finally gotten the engine of insight started.

Bill had been raised in a small town in Illinois in which he had lived out the classic stereotype of the small-town boy. Barefoot and a little too fat for popularity, he hunted, fished, and spent his time at the local courthouse and lumber yard where the other kids gathered.

Bill's problem was, as I suspected, his mother. His father was a farmer and worked long hours in the fields and barn. He never said much and Bill learned to work silently beside him when he got old enough. When he did comment, Bill observed, it was usually pungent and crisply to the point. Bill recalled his father once saying, "the angels ain't as careful about Heaven as your mother is about that house. She should never have married a farmer 'cause farmers are in love with dirt. That's what makes things grow, and if it don't grow we don't have nothin'."

Bill could recall no other paternal comment directed at his mother's fastidiousness but item after item bounced into consciousness once he began to look closely at his early life. The parlor that was locked except on Sundays or special occasions and draped with dust shields during the week, the ritual of "washing outside" before going to supper, the classification of clothing as "work" or "Sunday-go-to-meetin'," and the ritual of having one's hands inspected for cleanliness before meals all came alive again in memory after the long unconscious sleep of repression. As the forgotten events washed across his consciousness he reacted much as one viewing color television for the first time. He was as much amazed at the clarity of his recollections as he was impressed by the events he thought long dead and forgotten.

Bill M., it appeared, had married a magnified version of his mother, and his oppressive guilt and sense of conscience, coupled with basic resentment of his mother's demands on him, had paved the way for trouble. He had decided unconsciously to be again the victim of an obsessively clean, demanding female. It was painful at the same time that it brought security and comfort. Georgia would never change until Bill solved some of his own problems. She sensed, somehow, that he applauded what he most strenuously objected to. She could not become someone else until he was capable of change.

Georgia M. was raised in a quite different setting. Different, in that it was a small town in Northern Michigan. Her parents were, in many ways, the opposite of Bill's. The prickling, violent, mutual resentment between her parents had always been open and frequently loud. Her early life had been disorderly in the extreme with nothing ever making sense twice in a row. There was nothing she could depend on as an anchoring point for her personal development. School offered her a way out because there, and only there, two and two always made four.

Georgia was somewhat ashamed of her parents and objected strenuously but fruitlessly to a number of their habits. Her father worked hard all day and wanted to relax when he got home. Since supper was always served in the kitchen, her father Charlie always came to the table in dirty work pants and no shirt. He had the "terrible" habit of buttering a whole piece of bread and then folding it over when he ate it. At other times he would use his bread like a mop to soak up the remaining gravy on his plate. Her father and mother said "ain't" where "isn't" was grammatically proper, and they were "coarse" and "vulgar" in conversation.

Georgia left home when she was 16 and attended high school in a larger neighboring town. On her own for the first time, she organized her life to suit herself and constructed a succession of myths to describe her origins and the character of her parents. After graduation from high school she moved 300 miles further south to a large metropolitan area in which she could totally reject her humble beginnings. She cultivated exotic and "arty" interests and seemed to spend the bulk of her time looking down her nose at the common people and all others who had "bad taste." She learned to speak a little restaurant French and consciously rejected the meat and potatoes school of eating to live rather than living to eat.

None of this was enough, however. Georgia equated freedom from parents with freedom from her past self, but she soon discovered that no matter how fast she ran she could never lose her former self. Freedom made her nervous because she could no longer make her parents scapegoats and blame them for all the anxious feelings she had. Georgia had been neat beyond reasonable expectations from the time she was a very young girl. She was fastidious in the care of her clothes, her room, and her personal possessions and had an immature tantrum whenever her things were rearranged as her mother cleaned. A number of hours of discussion with Georgia eventually revealed that this neatness served a number of purposes for her. It produced order where previously there had been disorder, of course, but this didn't explain her unusual need for a perfectly safe world. Not everyone is so frightened by the condition of the world. Her concern with dirt was intimately connected to the idea of disorder in her mind. Disorder and dirt meant two things to her. First, these twin evils meant that someone was being lazy, irresponsible, and expressing hostility to others. Whenever her mother's house was messy, it always made Georgia feel that her mother didn't care about her father and was immune to his anger about living in a "pig-pen." Georgia knew her mother deliberately neglected the housework to express irritation with her father, and Georgia feared that one day he would really walk out on them as he often threatened. These fears of marital discord resulting in separation were one basis for her excessive concern with spick-and-span housecleaning. Dusting furniture became, for her, a magic way of warding off husbandly (fatherly) discontent and possible divorce. The difficulty was that her husband was not her father and this unconscious confusion of the two was wreaking havoc with her marriage. Georgia was doing exactly what she unconsciously thought her mother ought to have done in life. Georgia's problem was that her actions were inappropriate because they had more to do with things in her anxious childhood than they did with her present adult life.

In addition, Georgia had long been obsessed with inescapable thoughts of sin, hellfires, and damnation. When she was very young, she was dismayed to discover that she was prone to thinking about sex. She recalled that once she was totally engrossed in a fantasy of what it must be like when her parents had intercourse when her mother happened to discover her and tongue-lashed her angrily for being slothful and lazy. This sudden confrontation with a mother she had been imagining in awkward and exotic sexual positions while doing "that dirty thing" so startled her that for a moment she felt her mother could read her mind and know what she had been thinking. Georgia was sure no other decent child ever wondered about or imagined such evil things and she was convinced something was wrong with her mind.

This combination of guilt over sinful thoughts and the need to quell her rising anxiety about losing one or both of her parents proved to be her psychological undoing. Undoing was exactly the proper word in her case. By her avoidance of sexual contact with her husband, her obsessive concern with neatness, and her anxious involvement in making the world a safe and orderly place in which to exist, Georgia was attempting to undo that part of her previous life she was most upset about and had least learned to live with and adjust to. As an adult she was still a captive of childish problems she had never been able to manage with any substantial success. The trouble was that the more Georgia relived the past and tried to undo its anxious hours, the more she was reminded of her ancient anxieties, and the more these provoked her into a new frenzy of redoubled effort to wipe out the past by sheer brute force. It was a losing game that was expensive to play.

As Georgia relived emotionally some of her early experiences and began to re-evaluate them in light of her adult responsibilities and status, she was willing to make an attempt to control the expression of her symptoms and to tolerate the anxiety this always produced. The beginning was a quite limited one. She decided to do her laundry every other day—rather than daily—and to discuss with me the feelings this act of gross neglect provoked in her. She was startled to discover this was a manageable experience and that the heavens didn't crash in on her as a consequence of her dereliction of duty. From these small beginnings we progressed to even more daring steps when she felt she could manage them, such as hiring a cleaning lady and showering only once a day.

This attempt to live life in a different fashion produced an unusual anxiety in Bill. He began to worry and get depressed despite the fact she was altering those habit patterns to which he most objected. From then on, it became a therapeutic game of tennis. She served, he returned, and once in a while they both called foul or argued that there was no point in continuing the game. The rapidly bouncing ball of increasing marital disharmony was difficult to deal with, but in somewhat less than a year it was apparent that the tide of discontent was being swept back a bit at a time.

Georgia and her husband remain in therapy with me at the present time but I see them only once a week and I see them together rather than separately. They have learned how to argue openly with one another without being afraid that harsh words will destroy their marriage and they have learned something of the value of honest expression of one's feelings in times of acute psychological distress. A reasonably solid foundation is developing for their marriage and while it may never become a model for others, it will survive and, perhaps, prosper.

There is one drawback to this case. Georgia has become almost as calculatedly messy as she was neat. I have started to discuss this with her and to examine its reasons. It will take time, of course, but at least she has stopped criticizing the usual condition of my office. The most startling change is the one that has been brought about indirectly in the children. Both Georgia and her husband report that the kids seem much happier and better behaved than before. The youngest girl has taken to approaching either or both parents at odd times, hugging them, and telling them how much she loves them. Children are resilient and can bounce high once the pressure is removed from them. Children are also trustworthy weather vanes that record almost instantly shifts in life's winds.

There is no therapeutic magic in the case of Georgia M. She came to treatment an unusual combination of the obsessed and the rational, and the changes she effected were more in the nature of self-help than thera-peutic wisdom and guidance. The substitution of love for hate in her life and her attempt to reduce the anxiety of just being alive clearly occurred as a reaction against things she found repulsive in her early life. This de-fense was an expensive choice in the currency of human relations and Georgia continues to pay the price in personal unhappiness. The future is a treacherous one for Georgia M.

Edith Dines

I'll Never Forget What's His Name

–Mac K.

PROLOGUE *At this very moment* it is possible that you—the reader—are in the throes of a dissociative reaction, have amnesia for some period of your past life, and have obliterated your previous identity to assume a new one. Your deep conviction that this has not happened to you and that you know who you *really* are is a worthless piece of evidence, of course, since, in a true amnesic state, you would be the one person least able to testify to its truth or falsity. You would have no awareness of your previous identity and you might even have no part of your past life for which you could not account convincingly. It is the rare person who has total recall for all or even most of the events that occur in a normally busy life. Each of us has memory gaps and imperfect recollections.

Think about it for a moment. Most of us have experienced simple or primitive forms of dissociation from the real world at one time or another. After all, it happens every night when we dream—at that moment the dream *is* real and the outside world an absent memory. Which one of us has never felt isolated and detached from the swirl of human activity or estranged and distant from other people? Who has not experienced a mild form of depersonalization ("I don't feel like myself today") or a sense that the noisy world seems a little unreal, strange, different? Who has not vacationed with the sole purpose of getting away from it all and forgetting the cares of everyday life? This is the material from which amnesic states are constructed. In a very real sense, amnesia victims are simply persons whose life history and habitual patterns of psychological reaction have made them exceptionally good at getting away from it all. The uncomplicated, normal amnesia of "forgetting" past and present painful experiences (the dental appointment, the unpleasant task, the embarrassing faux pas) can be exaggerated for certain of us who have learned to deny the existence of larger segments of our experience when such forgetting seems to be the only way out of a painful, anxiety-laden situation.

Dissociative reactions range from somnambulism (sleep walking), through amnesia, and reach to the extreme of multiple personality. In each of these symptom patterns an adaptive maneuver has partially miscarried since the loss of large segments of one's experience, personal history, and identity can only reduce the effectiveness of a human being already troubled by a growing mountain of unsolved problems. Let us consider each of these degrees of disassociation from the world in more detail.

The forerunner to the onset of somnambulism is the action dream of violent sleepers—those who toss, turn, thrash, and mutter while resting. Sleepwalking is a special kind of dreaming that most often occurs in adolescence, among males under stress. With his eyes partially open, the person arises from a normal sleep and acts out some urge, impulse, or wish that has been denied access to consciousness. The somnambulist is less capable than most persons of keeping a clear distinction between sleep and waking life and of separating fantasy from reality-oriented thought processes.

A related form of dissociation is to be found in nervous mannerisms or bodily movements that somehow get detached from conscious control. Many of us are the victims of tics, twitches, and motor habits that seem to live a life of their own in that they occur without our conscious awareness of their existence. In this respect, hypnotic phenomena (with amnesia for the events of the trance state) are a kind of model of how parts of consciousness can be disconnected from other parts for brief or extended periods of time in assumedly normal people. The hypnotized person performs actions and has

feelings and experiences that seem different in quality
from behavior that is processed psychologically
in the normal waking state.

Amnesia is likely to occur in egocentric, immature, and
highly suggestible persons who cannot accept the notion of a
conscious running away from life yet have learned to blot
out parts of reality when the onslaught of anxiety makes it
necessary. With amnesia, there is a loss of memory for parts
of one's experience or for various aspects of one's personal
identity. If John Smith is having trouble, and one ceases to be
John Smith, then both John Smith and the troubles disappear,
and one can begin a new life designed, perhaps, to fulfill
secret wishes John Smith was unable to express
openly and publicly.

The victim of amnesia has made his life situation more
complex by entering an amnesic or fugue state in which flight
becomes the focus of his attempt at problem solving. One day
the fugue state may lift and he will recall who and what he once
was while he still has amnesia for the period of the fugue.
When a fugue state occurs, one's previous identity is lost
but lifelong habit patterns, likes and dislikes, skills and talents
remain essentially intact. Life can be resumed with the participant
dealing himself a new hand that has in it the kinds of cards
he most prefers to play. Still, it must be a chilling experience
for such a person to awaken one morning with the sudden
realization that he does not really know who he is.

The amnesic, dissociative, or fugue state is a desperate
and destructive attempt to escape from an intolerable
life situation. It is desperate in that it occurs infrequently
in the general population and reflects the last-ditch effort
of a person for whom all other resources have been exhausted.
It is destructive in that it is a psychological maneuver that is
subtractive rather than additive in form—it takes away what
exists, substitutes nothing in its place, and requires that the
engine of life produce full power on fewer than the full number
of psychological cylinders. It is paradoxical, but an inadequate
human being barely able to cope with life somehow insures
his survival by slicing out of his psychological structure
great chunks of himself. The psychic surgery may seem to be
radical but for the patient, anything less would be
insufficient for a cure.

IN DETROIT, the missing persons bureau is a one-man operation that is called 30 times a day about people who have disappeared from their usual haunts. At least 95 per cent of those reported missing have run away from familiar places of their own accord and of the approximately 11,000 who drop out of sight in Detroit each year, almost two-thirds of them are boys and girls 16 years old or younger. The versions of kidnapping the movies so love to dramatize are a true rarity. The bulk of officially listed abductions are children being used as pawns in marital battles, adults engaged in dramatic lover's quarrels, and tavern frequenters who get abused by their drinking companions of very recent acquaintance.

When Mac K.'s wife called me to say that he had disappeared, I was startled but not really surprised. In my hours of conversation with Mac, I had anticipated that he would run if the stresses in his life were to become too severe for his fragile coping mechanisms to manage but I was taken aback that I had not been more sensitive to what, in retrospect, seemed to be clear warnings of his impending bolt from the tensions of life. As I looked back, I recalled that in our most recent hour the expression on Mac's face had matched one that I observed when he described how he had run away from home as a young boy. There is nothing so discouraging to a therapist as the late discovery of an important clue overlooked in the mass of information that floods in on him during complex therapeutic hours. Mac had run because it was the only alternative that seemed attractive and possible at the moment. Mac had run for his psychological life and the problem now was to trace his movements and to try and predict what he would do and where he would go.

I tried to put myself in Mac's place, mentally. What would I do if I were Mac? How would I react if I were suddenly to find life closing in on me and could no longer cope with or tolerate it? How would I go about becoming an amnesiac and how would I execute the necessary complicated maneuvers that would make running away a solution to my problems? If I were Mac K., where would I go, and what kind of person would I become? To begin with, I would remain true to my Scottish ancestry since Mac K. made a particular point of describing in some detail his Scottish origins and the implied nobility of his remote descent from the original Irish-Scottish kings. The "Red Hand of Ulster" borne on the Clan Flag was a matter of no small moment to Mac K. Being a Scot meant something to him. He interpreted WASP to mean White, American, Scot, Protestant and contained within this somewhat idiosyncratic definition was the subtle implication that one inherited authority and superiority by the simple act of regal birth.

A Scot he was, then, and a Scot he would remain in whatever disguise he chose for his new life. Mac K.'s longing for the riotous life was an ill-fated fantasy on his part since neither his well-defined conscience nor fundamental rejection of rabid pleasure-seeking could weather any powerful storm of temptation. I did guess that Mac K. would seek a big city environment—he could hardly be expected to confine his secret urges and impulses to a rural area. Mac K. had to be lionized socially to be happy and he had to find a city in which his pretensions to intellectuality could be satisfied with some ease. If I was correct in this analysis, it would limit Mac K.'s escape to a few cities—San Francisco, Denver, Chicago, and, perhaps, New York. For him, Washington would be too political, Miami too tourist-oriented, Los Angeles too make-believe, Boston too straight-laced, Newark too dull.

Since my guesses seemed largely speculative, I never shared them with the family but waited patiently for a break in the case. There was little I could do, and the thought lurked in the back of my mind that it might be years before I heard of Mac K. again. This might have been a case with a sudden ending except for an unexpected quirk of fate. Mac K.'s brother-in-law was the wrestling coach for a nearby university and he and his team were scheduled for an exhibition match in San Francisco. As a treat, Angus (the brother-in-law) took the team for a night out at North Beach. The team's tastes ran to belly dancers and it was in the second such establishment that Angus spotted Mac K.

There he was occupying a front table vigorously cheering the dancers on. Angus at first thought he was seeing things, but he overcame his initial doubts, approached Mac K., and insisted he knew him. Mac K.'s reaction was predictable to one aware that he was suffering amnesia, but puzzling if he had deliberately and consciously deserted his wife and family. Mac K. reacted at first as if Angus were nothing but an overly friendly drunk. When it became apparent that Angus was really sober, Mac K. paid his check quickly and left with the feeling he had been harassed, and that it had spoiled an otherwise pleasant evening. But, Angus persisted and followed Mac K. in a taxi to where he lived.

When Angus returned to Detroit he called the missing persons bureau and told them the whole story. Mac K. was contacted by the San Francisco police, identified by his wife, and put in contact with both his minister and a Detroit psychiatrist hired for that purpose.

During the ten months before Mac K. was heard from again, his wife and children settled into the routine of a fatherless household. The younger children were told that Mac K. had gone on a long trip and might not be back for quite some time. The oldest boy Mac, Jr., knew what was going on and told his mother he thought Mac "had to go away and think about his troubles for a while." This seemed to be an unusually insightful speculation for a 14-year-old boy so I asked the mother to have him come in and talk to me. I told Mac, Jr., that his view of his parent's disappearance startled me because that was exactly what I thought had happened and I wondered why we both suspected the same thing.

As Mac Jr., said,

It wouldn't surprise me a nickel's worth. He and mom have been arguing more all the time and he has been hollering a lot about how lousy things are at work. For a while I figured it would all blow over like it did in the past but this time he just kept it up and kept it up. I used to keep the other kids quiet and out of his way as much as I could figuring maybe they were getting on his nerves but it didn't help.

I like my dad and I feel kind of funny saying this but, you know, he just up and quits stuff when it gives him a hard time. I thought I was bad but he starts stuff that he never finishes more than I do. I remember one day we were going to fence in the back yard so the dog couldn't get out. We got most of the posts in but when we tried to put the wire up we couldn't do it right and it looked like a mess. All of a sudden he just dropped the wire cutters in the grass and walked into the house without saying a word to me and he never came back. When I went in to ask him when we were going to finish it because I wanted to go play baseball he got mad at me and started yelling. From then on he never said a word about the fence. It was like it never was even started.

Dad was always forgetting things and not showing up places where he was supposed to be. I guess I heard him make a thousand excuses to people and I always got a little ashamed for him. I always thought he shouldn't apologize so much or make up those whoppers about why he didn't do something he was supposed to. I just think he couldn't take it any more and had to go away for a while till he feels better. He'll be back before too long.

I hoped Mac, Jr., was right, but Mac K. had now been missing for five months. With each passing day the odds against his return became greater. Mac K. might simply and deliberately have joined the legion of males who desert their families when the going gets too rough. Yet, desertion was not really Mac's style. He had in the past been gone for a week at most at any one time and then he always called home to tell them he was all right but needed some time "to think things out." When he returned, his wife reported that he would then be an almost model husband. He would stop complaining and feeling sorry for himself for several weeks or months, and he would spend a lot of time with the children trying to make up for abandoning them for a while. He always expressed a great deal of guilt about these episodes and felt he had let people down.

That was another curious thing about Mac. He seemed to be very anxious about pleasing people and doing the right thing, but he always managed to maneuver himself into a spot in which he let others down. If he made a solemn promise to do something, and he frequently volunteered to take on unappetizing chores, it was almost certain not to get done. This quirk predictably produced a great deal of anger and resentment in his relations with others. It seemed to me Mac always followed the same path and ended up in the same place over and over again. He would volunteer to be responsible for something and fail. Then, people would be angry with him, and he would apologize, acting terribly guilty about failing to keep his promises. I concluded that it was as if Mac were never sure of getting unconditional love from others, or that they could accept him even when he misbehaved, as a mother does a child. Unsure that he was really loved and accepted by everyone, Mac had spent the greater part of his life running tests or experiments to find out. Mac literally provoked others to see how they felt about him when he was being "bad." Misbehavior and rejection were twin facets of Mac's view of life and he had to keep checking the relationship between them to feel comfortable.

One additional bit of evidence occurred to me. Mac K. was an enthusiastic amateur actor in the local civic theater group. And, he was very good. This is not to say that all thespians are potential amnesia victims. It is, rather, an observation that the ability to cast off one's own personality easily and thoroughly and to assume accurately the thoughts, emotions, and reaction patterns of another character is not a capacity that has been learned equally well by all of us. Mac seemed to "become" the character he played. Not just "act" like him but "become" him. His wife, in a half-amused, half-serious manner, related that this sometimes was annoying because she would never know which Mac K. was going to come home from play rehearsals. During the run of a play the family and Mac K.'s business colleagues had to suffer his apparently altered personality and character. In fantasy, Mac K. became totally absorbed in the life of the character he was to play. It seemed obvious that Mac frequently wished to be someone other than himself, and play-acting was the closest he could get to it while still leading his customary life.

In combination, Mac's resentment of his position in life and his feeling that he deserved much better, his predilection for ignoring unpleasant reality, the harassment he felt he was suffering in life, and his proclivity for losing himself in the personality of make-believe characters all added up to a readiness to run away from life by dumping his former self and beginning all over again. He had practiced running and hiding throughout his life and had simply become more and more adept at getting out from under when the pressure mounted beyond his capacity to manage it.

This time in Mac's life proved to be the culmination of a series of events, and he assembled, through amnesia, a final and complete portrait of a man whose psyche plays tricks on him when these tricks make him feel less pain. A part of Mac's consciousness separated from the whole of his awareness and he actually became two persons. One Mac K. had memories that included a wife, children, a job, friends, and a mounting

pile of troubles. The other Mac K. had all the recollections of self except
those that would remind him that he had failed in some important way to
become what he thought he ought to become. Mac No. 1 had been unable
to achieve what he ought to and was reminded of it at every turn. He
was a man beset by difficulties, shortcomings, limitations, and awareness
of failure. Mac No. 2 was a new man reborn without recollection of
hurdles never mastered or tasks sloppily and only partly accomplished.
He was still young enough to run more successfully the same race he felt
he had lost before, and he was a man unencumbered by responsibility
that would limit his capacity to exercise his talents. He could play-act, for
example, without returning to home and family. In his new life he could,
with clear conscience, idle away the early hours of morning discussing
with great seriousness the fine points of technique with novice actors who
hung avidly on his every word. With his flair for fantasy Mac had little
difficulty filling the missing years with romantic deceptions and half-
truths that described his life as he wished it to be rather than as it really
had been. The gap in his existence could be decorated with events and
happenings that would make his person more attractive, mysterious, and
romantic than it really was.

What happened to Mac was an extreme version of what is a part of all
of us in miniature. With Mac it achieved proportions beyond what most
of us could manage comfortably. Mac did what many of us do in fantasy
but few in real life. Mac K., however, had adopted a solution to his problem that was destined to fail, primarily because Mac was only partly ready
to drop his past for an unknown and shaky future; he was uncomfortable
with the solution that he had chosen, but it was this or nothing at all for
him.

The reunion of Mac and his family was an eerie event to witness. It was
an odd mixture of relief and resentment. Mac seemed bewildered by the
flood of reminders of his previous life; reminders that were being forced
on him before he was really ready to accept them. Mac K. seemed to me
to find himself squeezed into a mold that was part Mac No. 1 and part
Mac No. 2 and he was uncomfortable with this new third person that was
constructed of an odd assortment of bits and pieces taken from the conscious and unconscious selfs of both.

Mac remained somewhat confused following the reunion, and this bewilderment lasted for several months. I anticipated that Mac would sooner
or later descend on one or the other of these personalities and become a
reunited person, whatever the form it would take. The months to follow
let Mac slowly work out his problems. Some adjustments were made in
his external environment—for instance, he left his job and found work
more compatible with his nature that allowed him a more flexible command of his working time. The joy of the family over his return was unmistakable and pleasurable to Mac.

The amount of acceptance and support Mac got contributed materially to his recovery or, perhaps, reconstitution of his life. Mac became a person who was a kind of compromise between Mac No. 1 and Mac No. 2, and he achieved this by conscious effort. Mac came to understand why he had run away and he learned to reconcile his conscious impulse systems with those of his unconscious. I was convinced that to the degree that Mac learned to know himself, he would be happier and less subject to the dangerous extremes of reaction based on impulse and need to escape from problems left unsolved. Mac really had to learn how to deal with life as it presented itself to him and to achieve some reasonable resolution of the difficulties he faced. Mac had to learn not to dodge and avoid trouble or to deny its existence in the hope that it would go away. He is still engaged in the process of learning how to resolve difficulties, but my feeling is that he is a ready learner who discovered that running away is the least productive path to follow—that it solves nothing and eventually produces more difficulty than it eliminates. I think he is beginning to learn and that is the best sign so far.

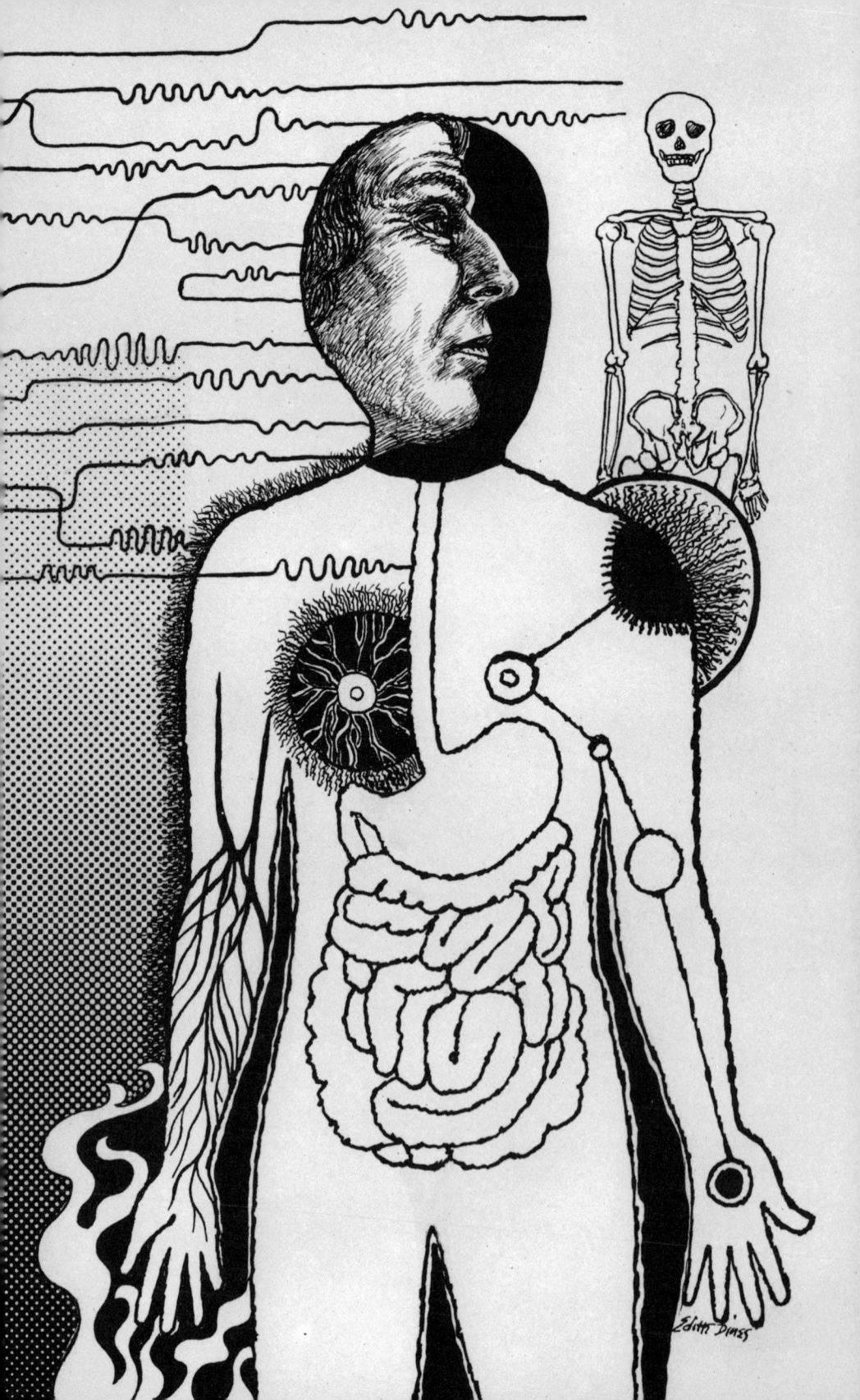

Edith Dines

I Told You I Was Sick

–Grace H.

PROLOGUE   *I have always* been particularly fond of the
syndromes of hypochondriasis and neurasthenia and recall
with some nostalgia the days in which they were psychiatrically
more fashionable. Neurasthenia in times past literally suggested
that the patient suffered from "weak" nerves and although
such a complaint was anatomical and physiological nonsense,
it was a perfect symptom, psychologically. It was vague
and all-embracing including irritability, headaches (or aches
anywhere), insomnia, indigestion, lassitude, constipation
or the possibility of having any or all of these complaints.
With the simple addition of anxiety to this mixed bag of
symptoms you have all the needed psychological components
for hypochondriasis. These once were fascinating diseases
caused, it was thought in the early days, by excessive
masturbation or by a damming up of one's sexual energy
by celibacy.

   Hypochondriasis was never better described than as a
condition in which the patient "enjoys poor health." As you
might imagine, the hypochondriac in all of us is the prime target
of Madison Avenue and its talented advertisers who teach us
in graphic detail how to worry about being almost but not quite
sick with some strange disease. The list of social and personal

diseases man is potentially heir to is incredibly long and
each of them suggests that it is the forerunner of its fatal
counterpart. A pervasive anxiety about one's body learned in
childhood may lead to a desperate concern about the state
of one's health and the condition of the body and its functions.
Health can become the obsessive focus of all
one's waking attention.

Throughout written history the hypochondriac has been
described with amused tolerance by observers. Frightened by life
and its inevitable dangers, made "sick and tired" by life,
the anxious victim seeks a real disease to justify the chronic
whining and complaining that have characterized his life. Being
a hypochondriac has at least three distinct advantages:

1. Anxiety about health can be used as a substitute for the
anxiety one really feels about the self and its relation to life
and the people and social problems it contains. This bodily
anxiety is manageable since it is focused and circumscribed
by the limits of the envelope of skin that confines each of us.
Anxiety about disease and death frees us of the even more vague
and frightening experiences of anxiety
that has no discernible target.

2. Chronic illness from some unknown, unspecifiable,
and incurable disease requires that everyone in close contact
with the victim give him sympathy, extra attention, nursing care,
and special consideration with respect to the demands of life.
The unusual arrangements that often must be made
for the comfort of the hypochondriac might include
the preparation of special foods, the scheduling of specified times
for rest, or the control of social life to fit the state of health
of the patient. Undefined sickness of this sort becomes,
obviously, a tyrant of the household and gains for the patient
a tender loving care that any infant would envy.

3. Hypochondriasis provides a beautiful and foolproof
escape from the race of life. After all, who asks someone
who is crippled to compete on an equal basis with the normal
and healthy? Being sick takes one out of the competition of life
with a reasonable amount of honor. The fact that a sick person
competes at all amounts to a heroic display of fortitude and,
at the same time, problems of inadequacy, inferiority, and failure
can be neatly sidestepped. The delicate health hypochondriacs

feel they have acquired in childhood has become a weapon to be used in the contest of life.

When hypochondriasis blends subtly into neurasthenia we have the housewife's common complaint of continuous exhaustion, fatigue, restless sleep, low energy level, and all-encompassing lassitude. This physical fatigue has its psychological counterpart in feelings of inadequacy, low tolerance for stress, a high level of anxiety and fearfulness, a continuously alert system of tension and readiness to defend the self against anxiety, plus a seriously disturbed set of interpersonal relations marked by egocentricity and concern for the self first and others second. The victim of neurasthenia is blind to the feelings of others since the bulk of his energy is devoted to avoiding further deterioration of his personality organization.

A physical machine subjected to continuous tension and readiness to react defensively is bound to feel the effects of this stress and to begin to produce alterations of bodily function designed to meet the threat. So it goes with the hypochondriac and the neurasthenic. The body becomes a burden to be nursed through life. This burden becomes tragic when it leads to useless surgical and medical procedures that produce pain and bodily damage while they overlook completely the psychological nature of the problem the physician must deal with. When the illusory illness is used as a tool to control the lives of others in interpersonal orbit with the victim, then the disease is best described as infectious and crippling.

GRACE H. CATALOGUED in excruciating anatomical detail a full range of symptoms—past, present, and future—to which she was heir. She had "almost" had a series of exotic diseases, has suffered for years from a strange collection of symptoms that fit no known malady in humans, and was about to come down with something certain to be nearly fatal. I resisted the invitation to feel her pulse, but I did listen sympathetically to her extended tale of physical horrors. Probably the most startling aspect of the scene was the obvious and absolutely noncontroversial fact that Grace H. looked as healthy as a horse. The fact that she was 72 years old had to be some kind of testimony to her hardiness in the face of plague, pestilence, and, as she viewed it, the perversity of the medical profession.

Grace H. was not really my client, but she was the primary problem of the daughter who had asked me to see her. She was all the hypochondria-cal mothers rolled into one whose potential heart attacks had produced generation after generation of guilty sons and daughters tied tightly to mother's apron strings. Grace was a controller, a manipulator, a manager, and a user of other people. It was as if she gained her life's strength by preying on other human beings. She had reduced her husband to a quiver-ing mass of soft-spoken compliance, and she had whipped her children into line as effectively as a Marine drill instructor. Her training program was almost perfect since it began in infancy and covered the lifetime of her children.

According to the children, Grace's histrionics had been in evidence for at least the last 40 years. The eldest son who was 50 years old, recalled that his mother had been ailing when he was just a child. As he said, "Sometimes when I was in school, I would get worried that mother would be dead by the time I got home. I knew she was sick when I went to school and I was sure it would be all over by the time I got home. I had a hard time concentrating on my school work because I was always worried about her health. Now I have heard her complaints for so long that I just shrug and talk about something else."

The daughter, Ginny, was nearly 26 years old and unmarried. She was engaged but, after her father died, she had twice postponed her marriage for fear that her mother's health would be affected in some unrecoverable and probably fatal way. Her fiancé was losing patience, and, between his urgings and her guilt and concern, the engagement period had become a running battle between them. Ginny—under pressure from her fiancé—finally asked her mother to come and see me and talk to me about her health. Grace was ready, willing, and eager. She had nothing to fear since she knew she was sick and if doctors disagreed with her, the only logical explanation was that they were wrong. Grace was starkly and madly in love with an extended audience of medical men who could barely write fast enough to record the full range of the ills she had experienced.

Ginny recalled vividly the half-dozen instances when she had informed her mother of her marital plans only to be treated to a maternal display of exquisite enjoyment of extremely poor health and the bare hint that it might be fatal. At 18 Ginny decided to take a job as a secretary in the oil kingdom of Kuwait. Her mother's reaction was violent. As Grace sank slowly into a fatal malaise, Ginny abandoned her plans and took a job typing in a local insurance company. She never talked to her mother about her job and her boss because her mother was always full of advice about how to rise in the world of finance without really trying.

When Ginny quit her job and went to college, it was a time of family catastrophe. Grace H. knew all about "those radical professors" and the "beatnik" types she would be exposed to and insisted that Ginny call her twice a week and tell her how things were going. Ginny went to college and dutifully called home twice a week, but every phone call was like taking an emotional bath from which she emerged exhausted and limp.

After college, Ginny came home to a joyous reunion with her parents, but she didn't know what to do next with her life. At 23 she was in between everything and she regretted instantly her decision to come back to home and hearth. She had the feeling she had deliberately and voluntarily put her foot back into the same bear trap that had pained her so much before. She took a new job—secretary to the French Consul—and this was fascinating and fulfilling to her for a while. She met glamorous people and broadened her academic grasp of the French language. It was there she met Richard R. After a classic romantic courtship, she decided that married bliss was perfect for her. Two years passed and the triangle of mother, daughter, and potential son-in-law was as lively as it had been at the beginning. Potential sons-in-law traditionally have only forced affection for mothers-in-law and Richard was no exception. He played the game for a while but soon lost interest and began to be bitingly sarcastic about Grace's physical condition. At times it seemed to Ginny that he picked on her mother and baited her into an even more serious set of symptoms. Richard was fed up and Ginny was getting nervous. It was an act of desperation on her part finally to call me and ask me to see her mother.

The fundamental question for me was what to do. The mother was an artful specialist in hypochondriasis who had practiced all the arts of being sick while staggeringly well. She seemed to be totally free of anxiety until asked about her health and at that point she disintegrated into a mass of nervous energy. I contemplated working with the mother to alter her pattern of life but decided it was hopeless. I decided to deal with Ginny in terms of *her* reaction to her mother's behavior. Ginny was still young and flexible enough so that there was hope of altering her perception of her mother's many illnesses. Grace became a kind of half-patient seen on a supportive basis and Ginny became the focus of my concentrated effort.

As Ginny and I traced the outline of her life, I was at once puzzled by how rarely she mentioned the existence of her father and how brief and unrevealing those comments that she made tended to be. To hear Ginny talk would lead naturally to the assumption that her father had died or deserted the family some years ago. Emotionally, Ginny's father had done just that. He had deserted his post as male parent under a barrage of withering fire from his wife.

Ginny knew little of the relationship of her father and mother in the early days of their marriage but it was apparent that the wedded battle had been lost at almost the first marital skirmish. Neither Ginny nor her older brother could recall a time when their father's reaction to Grace's demands had been much more than silence or sullen assent. When Grace

began a familiar tirade, they all knew they were in for a performance that
had at least three acts with as many scenes as were needed to complete the
production. Grace would begin discussing things "rationally and logi-
cally" for Act I. For Grace, this was nothing more than an assortment of
argumentative assaults on the irrational and illogical positions held by
everyone else in the assembled group. "All right, let's be intelligent about
this," was her signal to begin the debate. By the end of Act I, the "debate" had degenerated into a loud and emotional diatribe in which she
interrupted everyone and proclaimed her disagreement at greater and
greater length. As Ginny acridly observed, "Her mouth was open but
her mind was not."

During Act II Grace regularly sabotaged the lingering remnants of
logic by diverting the argument into an irrelevant rehashing of past injustices committed against her by each and every member of the family. No
imagined injustice was too microscopic for repetition and her staggeringly
accurate memory made each recounting an exact replica of the last time
she brought up the subject. Her gestures became more expansive and her
voice rose measurably during Act II until they reached the fever pitch
that set the stage for Act III—Sickness unto Death. There was never an
intermission between Acts II and III. At the height of her agitation, Grace
would lapse suddenly into an acute attack of whatever malady suited best
the issue that needed resolution. She not only writhed in sudden pain but
blamed the stubborn intransigence of the others for the suffering she was
undergoing. She would shout hysterically,

> See? See what you are doing to your poor mama? I could die
> and you wouldn't care! None of you would! This is the thanks
> I get for sacrificing my life so my children could be happy!
> When I'm in my grave you will all be happy that you have
> killed me. Nobody wants me! I'd be better off out of your way.
> Then you wouldn't be bothered with me. You wish me dead!

When these words were accompanied by sobbing and shrieking, the
effect was exactly as she hoped it would be. The father would then
become enraged at his own inability to cope with the situation and his discomfort at arguing with his wife, and would turn his wrath on the innocent children. Siding with his wife he would shout, "See what you are
doing to your mother? Why do you torture her this way? Is this a way
to treat your mother? Is this the way children treat their parents nowa-
days?" After subtly including himself as one of the victims of the ingrati-
tude of modern day children, he would storm out of the house (conveniently removing himself from any further controversy) and stay away
for several hours. By this time Ginny and her brother would be frantic
with concern about the trouble they had caused for their parents and
would devote the next several days to being quietly helpful around the

house. The subject matter that provoked the original battle was, of course, a totally dead issue never again referred to openly. Grace H. had, by default, won again.

It took some weeks before Ginny could comprehend the complementary role her father was called on to play in these maternal scenes. Ginny, when she first discovered this seeming parental plot to cow the children, was violently resentful that her father was not "more of a man" who would "stand up to his wife once in a while." As we explored in greater detail some of the emotional reaction Ginny experienced when being flayed by her mother, sympathy, and understanding displaced the criticism she at first expressed toward her father. Ginny learned her father was feeling the lash just as she was. Her father Arthur had frequently described his own mother in terms that fit his wife exactly, but he never made a logical or emotional connection between the two most important females in his life. Arthur had unwittingly aided and abetted the process of making his children into the same kind of guilt-ridden adult that he had become.

When a crisis developed in her relationship with Richard R., Ginny also began to learn that she was more her mother's daughter than she at first suspected. Richard had been offered a new and important job with a publishing firm in the East and he asked Ginny to marry him at once. Ginny was panicked by the suddenness of the arrangement and insisted she would need more time to make so important a decision. The argument raged back and forth for several days and culminated in the uncompromising insistence by Richard that they get married and move to New York or just forget the whole thing.

What was fascinating to hear in her recounting of the argument was that at exactly this moment Ginny began to have sharp chest pains. Her sudden discomfort postponed any further angry exchange between them and for the next two weeks Richard R. was very concerned with Ginny's health as she underwent a thorough medical checkup. As her mother said of their doctor, "He's a heart expert and very famous. You can't be too careful with something like this, you know. Remember your Aunt Rose? She was perfectly healthy and then one day she just fell over with a heart attack and—God rest her soul—died on the spot. It's better to be safe than sorry."

When the family doctor told Ginny he could find nothing wrong with her, she described him to me in quite a disparaging and insulting way. As gently as I could, I suggested that it seemed to me that Ginny was acting and talking very much like her mother and that Ginny's "chest pains" had been very convenient, coming as they did at the height of a continuing argument with her fiancé. Ginny got so angry that she stormed out of the room and failed to appear at her next hour. As I reviewed the notes on her case, I was convinced that I had been on the right track and that the vehemence of her reaction to my interpretation suggested that I was closer to the truth than Ginny was ready to admit. I decided that if Ginny returned to therapy, I would start where we had left off and pursue this line of reasoning as far as she could tolerate.

When Ginny did return she displayed what has been called a "flight into health." She was symptom free, unworried, and reported all was smooth in her life. I refused to accept this portrayal of placid life as a valid reflection of things as they really were and reviewed the sequence of events that had led to this break in therapeutic contact between us. What I said to her, roughly, followed these lines:

> Ginny, in our last hour it seemed to me that the sudden appearance of chest pains at the high pitch of your argument with your fiancé and your unproductive contact with your family physician was exactly the kind of pattern you have complained about in the behavior of your mother. I realize that this suggests you are more like your mother than you can comfortably acknowledge right now, but I think your anger at my observation and your "accidental" forgetting of the next therapeutic hour cannot be chalked up to happenstance alone. What I said bothered you a great deal, and I wouldn't be surprised if you stormed out of here last time and said some very uncomplimentary things about me to other people. But, we must start again where we left off. You should not be surprised that you are your mother's daughter, and that in many ways you have learned from her and resemble her. Is this really so hard to understand?

At this point Ginny began to cry with great gusto and, for the first time we began to make measurable headway in her understanding of herself and her relationship to her family. We discussed the pros and cons of marriage to Richard R. and what leaving her mother and moving to New York would entail. Ginny suggested it might be an appropriate time for me to see her fiancé and discuss the condition of their engagement. I felt she was ready to withstand the rigors of such an encounter and calculated it might stabilize their view of each other and reduce the amount of friction between them if I were to help the two of them look with greater dispassion on the plight of having Grace for a relative. The issue to be discussed was not just the advisability of the impending marriage but the technique of handling Grace in the future. She was healthy enough to live forever and this meant that the young couple had to learn how to cope with the inevitable interference and attempts at manipulation that Grace was certain to make. When Ginny married, it would seem to Grace that she had indeed not lost a daughter but had gained a son. Ginny and Richard also needed to establish a set of ground rules for interacting with one another when the inevitable chafing of double-harness occurred. Their marriage had, unfortunately, become a triangle with one corner fastened down firmly by Grace.

After several months of discussion of possible hazards to their impending marriage, the date was set (by Grace) and the preparations begun. That month of getting ready for the wedding was a harrowing one. I began to feel like a professional wedding counselor as I was called upon to settle endless disputes about almost every aspect of the wedding. A wedding can be the occasion for an emotional free-for-all between parent and child and this was exactly the case with Ginny and Grace. They fought about whom to invite, what flowers were appropriate, how the wedding gown should be fitted, the reception, etc., etc. As Ginny noted wryly, "She will be with us on the honeymoon if we don't do something." I tried to make each of these mother-daughter encounters therapeutically profitable, but I did not always succeed. I tried to keep Ginny focused on the basic problem of how to deal with a mother who was startlingly similar to her in many respects. Ginny and Grace were equally matched in the weapons they preferred to use and their battle was rapidly becoming a stand-off in which both were being injured but neither could quit the field of battle.

Several times during the preparations for the wedding both Grace and Ginny were sick with headaches, stomach upsets, or "nerves." It was painful for Ginny to entertain the notion that she was managing no better than her mother to solve the problem of how one gets married. Grace began what looked to me to be a long-range plan of erosion of her son-in-law. Ginny overheard her mother discussing Dick and the content of the conversation perturbed her. Her mother first lavished effusive praise on Dick and described, in glowing terms, all of his sterling characteristics. Then, subtly, she stirred into the conversation a number of doubts and pointed questions that undermined all that had gone before. For example, Ginny reported that Grace mentioned Dick's generosity and then wondered aloud why it is that he earns so little money in his job. Ginny found this insidious character assassination of her husband-to-be offensive but she never quite developed the proper means to combat it.

The wedding finally took place despite all its trials and tribulations, and Ginny and Dick have moved to New York. Since her last child has left her "alone and helpless" Grace has been a more frequent visitor to my office. Grace wonders constantly how Dick and Ginny are getting on and she plans to visit them as soon as they are settled down. For a lady her age Grace is certainly not senile but she is a practiced trouble maker. In her visits with me I have practiced a more direct and vigorous confrontation in my interpretation of how she is behaving and why she is feeling the way she does. Nothing fazes Grace, however. She seems to love verbal combat of this sort and obviously enjoys what she takes to be arguing with me about what is right and wrong. She treats me somewhat as though I were a not-too-bright son who is being impertinent to his mother.

I enjoy my time with Grace (she now sees me twice a week) and have become suspicious that we might even be making some progress.

Sometimes, when Grace is feeling low, she skirts dangerously near to in-sight and some realization that she is not a perfect person or a perfect mother. Whenever these moods overtake her I must confess I move in with heavy artillery to take advantage of the moment. Grace's visits have become a kind of low level experiment in the degree to which ancient ladies can be made to acquire new insight so late in their lives. I have been pleasantly surprised by the amount of flexibility and new learning Grace is capable of and am beginning to think that my original judgment of the hopelessness of her case was in error. Grace is a woman who loves to talk and a woman who waxes eloquent whenever she has an audience worthy of her performance.

I am planning to continue to see Grace on a regular basis. I even dis-suaded her from visiting the newly-married couple for at least a year or at their invitation, whichever occurs first. Grace has begun to talk about her husband and their early married life together, and she has startled me sev-eral times by noting things about him of which only an insightful person would be aware. I don't often accept older persons as clients but Grace could change my mind.

With astonishing perceptiveness Grace recalled the look in Ginny's eyes when they buried Arthur. "I knew what she was thinking," said Grace with a slow shake of her head. "She was thinking I had never let Arthur be a man and have a proper part in deciding things about the family. But she was a late baby and Arthur was an old man before she was old enough to know him. I wanted Arthur to be a man but that wasn't what suited him. He tried at first but it didn't last long. After a few years I not only took care of everything around the house but managed all the money and decided everything. Arthur got so that he wouldn't answer the telephone or the door and he never liked having people over to the house. He was always a quiet man and one day without even talking it over he announced that he wasn't going to drive the car any more. I've been driving ever since. Ginny doesn't think about these things, so she blames me for taking away his manhood."

Describing the impact of Ginny's arrival so late in their life, Grace could at least give lip-service to the possibility that she had overprotected her from the beginning. Grace had always felt more like a grandparent than a mother toward Ginny and reported that throughout the pregnancy she was embarrassed by her condition and had been kidded constantly by close relatives and friends about beginning a new family so late in life. When Ginny was born, Grace lavished every attention on her and "wor-ried herself sick" over the many perils life held in store for a young, growing girl. Grace and Arthur drew up the drawbridge of life and re-tired within the walls of their castle to raise a princess all their own.

Grace felt guilty more often than she was capable of admitting to any-one close to her. Since she feared ever letting others get the upper hand in what she took to be the struggle of existence, when she experienced the disquiet of guilt she crushed the life from it at once by piling atop it a weighty mass of incontrovertible evidence of the rightness and propriety of her actions. If this was not sufficient, she would insist that her case be judged by its durability in time—one day "they" would all understand that she had been right from the beginning. Her fantasies of future vindication were satisfyingly soul-filling but they never blossomed as naturally as she hoped, so she fertilized, pruned, and force-grew them until they appeared despite themselves. She repeated her predictions whenever the original decision was called into question, and in those instances in which time did indeed tell she would broadcast her original correctness. Each such success eased the pangs of guilt yet to come, because she could then stand firmly on her almost flawless record of accurate prediction.

The unseen difficulty here is depression. A woman of Grace H.'s age has for too long played the game of complaint and manipulation to abandon it easily. Beneath the aggressive assault on others must lie the fundamental feeling that she, as a person, is not very acceptable to others nor much loved by them. Thus, she has had to take recourse to vengeance rather than affection and acceptance of others. If this secret and insecure Grace were suddenly to appear on the scene the truth might hurt a great deal more than help. Youth holds the promise of time—time for reorganization and time for the second effort. In old age one is crippled by the years that have vanished so rapidly and denied the grace of doing again what one first did badly.

Grace can be helped but the truth may be so savage that it is injurious to her. I sometimes weary of the elaborate and detailed recital of things in which she seems so to delight. She will not brook interruption, she remains more lodged in the past than in the present. Time will tell.

Edith Dines

Look Out Below

–Caroline W.

PROLOGUE   *Q.* What is illogical, unreasoning, not inherited,
"normal" in children, widespread among adults, and has existed
since ancient times? *A.* Phobic reactions.

The pathological fear called phobia indeed bears all
of these characteristics and quite a few others. Phobias are fears
that are always irrational but never groundless; fears that are
not subject to the influence of logic or reasoning. Phobias can be
constructed around anything that does exist and a great many
things that do not.

Many adult phobias are based on severe infantile fears now
long forgotten. Fear of all sorts is the "normal neurosis" of
childhood. Young and inexperienced minds, incapable of
applying logic to the stimuli of life are filled with an unreasoning
terror of bugs, the dark, predatory animals, and ghosts.
The "scairdy cat" child may become the phobic adult who,
through a complicated psychological defensive maneuver,
attempts to master these fears and anxieties in a way calculated
to assuage anxiety and maintain peace of mind
in a still frightening world.

It is perfectly obvious that the newborn infant does not have
a full comprehension of, say, the fear of falling (acrophobia).
If he had an awareness of fear, it would not be necessary

for parents to watch so carefully over the creeping child
wobbling to injury or destruction unaware that things have edges
and brinks that cause pain. Before long the child learns the
lessons of gravity, balance, and concussion and pays for them
through a long series of aches, pains, cuts, bruises,
and miles of band aids.

Day by day throughout childhood each of us learns about
fear and phobia. We learn directly by traumatic experience,
as in the case of a child suddenly and unexpectedly confronted
by a big dog that barks savagely at him, or by imitation of a
model, for instance, the mother frightened witless by electrical
storms. From these beginnings can come adult phobia among the
great, the near-great, the young, the old, the bright, and the dull
among us. Chopin was terrorized by the possibility he would
be buried alive, and Schopenhauer so feared sharp edges that he
singed rather than shaved his beard. The recognition of phobia
stretches back in man's history at least as far as the Greeks
and the golden age of humanity.

The dynamics of certain forms of phobia follow
a distinctive pattern.

First, the person senses that his or her personality may be
disrupted or destroyed by an increasingly threatening onslaught
of anxiety and terror.

Second, the phobic person discovers that this anxiety
cannot be dealt with successfully by defense mechanisms
usually effective in handling anxiety.

Third, the anxiety being experienced is transformed—
in desperation—into a set of fearful fantasies that need some
concrete expression in one's daily behavior if the experience of
anxiety is to be avoided.

Finally, these painful anxieties get transformed into a
collection either of diffuse or focussed external fears that may be
the symbolic equivalent of the internal anxieties
one experienced previously.

In each instance of phobic avoidance the victim shuns
the anxiety-laden object or situation in order to escape the severe
anxiety attack which might result from confrontation. Think of
what you fear most, for example, and imagine what reaction
you would have to a sudden, unexpected exposure to the dreaded
object. What do you fear? Height, filth, rats, snakes, spiders,
darkness, crowds, fire, closed areas? How would you feel,

for example, sitting in a room full of ravenous rats
or poisonous snakes? In all this it is almost impossible to draw
a hard and fast line between normal and pathological fear since,
like an allergy, the response one has is most often determined
by the degree of success one has in avoiding the allergenic
substance.

Most of us live fairly comfortably with a number of minor
phobias and never undergo the stark terror phobic victims
experience. Each of us is made slightly apprehensive about
great heights but few of us have been made physically sick
by looking out the window of a tall building or have been
rendered helpless emotionally at the possibility that we might fall
and be killed. In some cases, anxiety about falling from great
heights is compounded by the gnawing, frightening feeling
of wanting to leap when too close to a precipice or open window.

The paradox of these mixed self-destructive feelings and
terrors of an accidental fall is that they are not shared equally
by all people and are not "sensible" in ordinary terms. A phobia
may be a neurotic compromise in which the original but
inexpressible fears are repressed because they are psychologically
threatening or unacceptable to the self and to others and
displayed toward other less dangerous objects and situations.
Phobia represents an attempt by the individual at curing himself
of his private frights, but it is a cure that is costly. It impairs
personal psychological well-being in that it restricts the
victim's freedom to move comfortably in the world, and it may
generalize and spread to areas of life previously uncontaminated
by these anxieties. A full-blown phobia can cripple as effectively
as a physical injury when it spreads to encompass one's whole life,
feeding on itself until it attains a massive and crushing size.
Exaggerated fears are a common burden in a frightening world
and more of us are phobic than we care to admit.

WHEN CAROLINE W. walked into the office I hadn't the faintest idea what
was bothering her. This was surprising since the process of making a first
appointment is usually marked by the patient's telling my secretary something about his troubles. Caroline knew what she wanted, asked no questions, did not ask to speak to me, made an appointment, and hung up. I
mentioned this departure from usual events to Caroline when she appeared for her appointment. This is what she told me:

I have such stupid and unreasonable problems that I have stopped telling people about them. I used to tell close friends how I felt and sometimes I would confide in what seemed like a sympathetic ear (after a couple of martinis) but then I found out that their interest was totally phony. People to whom I had never mentioned my problem would casually mention that so-and-so had been telling them I was frightened to death of heights of any kind and that it was beginning to disrupt my married life. I guess I had to learn the hard way, but I began to keep my mouth shut so the vultures couldn't feed on me.

Now my so-called friends don't "just happen to drop in" for a little extra feeling of superiority by asking me how bad my fears are. I tell them it was just a passing phase that's better now and change the subject if I can. They always look a little disappointed to learn that I haven't gotten a lot worse since they talked to me last. It seems to me there is nothing other people enjoy more than discovering that you have worse troubles than they do. It's like when I was a kid. I was fatter than the other kids and sometimes it seemed to me the other kids went out of their way to come over just to call me Fatty. It was like a group activity when they got bored, I guess. It must be that these kids grow up and turn into adults who still enjoy other people's misery so much. But, I have been lying to them. I'm not better. I'm worse. And, it's wrecking my life. My regular doctor said he couldn't help me any more and told me to call you and try to get this settled once and for all. It has been bothering me for years but it was never as bad as this before.

It became clear, in the hours that followed, that Caroline W. had been a prime candidate for a phobia from very early in her life. She was (by her own admission) a "scairdy cat" when she was a child. She hated bugs crawling on her, was frightened senseless by spiders, and shied away from dogs. One of the most horrible experiences she could recall was having a snake thrust at her by a boy at summer camp. The list of similar ancient but still surviving fears stretched to a great length.

She had always feared violent weather, for example. She would scream in frenzy at nearby bolts of lightning followed by thunderclaps. When storms began, she would retreat to the bedroom and cover her ears with pillows. No amount of common sense, persuasion, or bold example of fearlessness on the part of her husband, Jim, could stop her trembling at each new roll of thunder. The vibrations would make her quiver with panic and she would often pull the covers over her head in an additional futile attempt to ward off her expected destruction.

Caroline not only listened religiously to weather reports on the radio, but she bought an expensive portable radio that gave her marine weather forecasts and made it possible for her to tune in a nearby airport which broadcast a continuous weather report for private pilots. When network television programs were interrupted to broadcast a local tornado alert she would run around the house frantically disconnecting all of the lamps and electrical appliances. She nagged Jim until, with some embarrassment, he constructed a tornado shelter in the southwest corner of the basement. However, he refused to enter it every time weather conditions suggested the remote possibility of tornado conditions. He thought it was bad enough to sit in the dark on summer evenings till the tornado alert was over, but as he told me,

> I'll be damned if I'll go underground like a mole every time the wind blows. The kids think it's a big joke and I always tell them we are just practicing in case there is a real emergency. She's going to make those kids scared to take a deep breath at this rate. There's no talking to her when she gets like that. If you try to calm her down it only bugs her more and she starts to get hysterical and holler.

Jim and Caroline agreed that many of her fears were shared by other people, but they both knew that the extent and intensity of her upset were clearly beyond the bounds of normality. Caroline's heavy weather horror was difficult but not impossible to live with. After all, it was a private anxiety limited to the confines of the immediate family. When the weather was threatening, they could not leave home and had amassed, as Jim noted, a mammoth collection of unused tickets for plays, concerts, recitals, and lectures plus an astounding repertoire of last minute excuses to be handed out when friends had invited them to supper.

A more pressing and bothersome problem was Caroline's growing fear of heights. Caroline recalled that when young she had never felt really comfortable high off the ground but these feelings had seldom posed much of a problem to her since she simply avoided such situations. She remembered that when she was four years old she and her older brother had climbed a ladder to the top of the garage when her father was re-shingling the roof. As she told it, her adventures in climbing ended when both her mother and father shook with fear at her escapade. She recalled dimly that her mother discovered them on the roof and carried on hysterically, and that her father had given both of them a stern lecture about the dangers of high places. She also recollected that she was incarcerated in her bedroom for the rest of that afternoon to think over the seriousness of her deed but she didn't feel that this had anything to do with her present anxieties.

As I suspected, Caroline's fear of heights was a complex affair. When she and Jim were in New York on their honeymoon they had pursued the traditional sightseeing path which ended, inevitably, on top of the Empire State Building. Caroline had agreed reluctantly to this part of their

trip and tried to explain to Jim how scared she had been on her one and
only experience with a roller coaster. But, Jim pooh-poohed it all and,
feeling very masculine, dragged her along with him. All the way up on
the elevator, she was nervous and wondered "why they had invented
husbands and honeymoons," but she stuck it out and tried not to communicate the state of her mounting fright to Jim. As they reached the wind-
swept reaches of the observation platform she could taste the fright like a
lump in her throat and prayed frantically for a face-saving way out. With
her hand covering her eyes and her head drooping, she told me about it.

> I felt like my period had started suddenly. I was scared but
> couldn't admit how scared I was, and I think I never did tell
> Jim what I felt like inside then or any other time since we have
> been married. It was like you were going to throw up but you
> were in a public place and didn't see any way to get to the john
> to do it unobtrusively. It is a physical thing that is hard to de-
> scribe but I can remember I was panicked and thought I might
> wet my pants if I had to step out of the elevator. I did go out,
> though, and tip-toed over to the edge without looking down. I
> closed my eyes and clung to the balustrade but I still began to
> feel dizzy. The worst part of it was not the possibility that I
> might faint and fall over the edge, it was the terrible urge I felt
> to run to the barrier, jump, and kill myself. It was like the
> Sword of Damocles that hung by a thread over the head of the
> King. I found myself thinking it would be better to jump and
> get it over with than to worry that I would fall by accident.
> When we got back to the pavement I was so shaky I started to
> cry but I couldn't tell Jim what it was all about.

Caroline's frightening experience took place on her honeymoon in New
York. She could recall no other time in her life when she had undergone
quite so violent an upheaval triggered by height alone. As further details
about her honeymoon became apparent, I began to be curious about why
her most vivid recollections were focussed on the early years of her marriage. I talked with her at some length about her reactions to sex and
marital experience and was startled by the fact that she seemed to be two
different persons contained in the same body. In some hours of therapy
she exuded an aura of primness and propriety about things sexual; during
other hours she spoke quite forthrightly, and with intense feeling, in a
very direct and euphimism-free way about the sex act. The terms she
used to describe sexual parts and the sexual experience ranged from prissy
to prurient and they varied in what at first seemed to be a random fashion.

When I mentioned that sometimes she was raw and earthy when speaking of sex and at other times so intellectual about it that I could never tell
what mood she was in or which Caroline she was at the moment, she
sighed despairingly and commented, "That is the story of my life." Her

parents, she recalled, had displayed the same ambivalence about sex. Most of the time it was treated like a filthy thing that should never be mentioned publicly but then every once in a while they would deliberately talk about sex as if it were "lecture time." She never mentioned it to her brother but she was sure both of them felt that parents ought to talk to their kids about sex without such pained expressions on their faces.

This uncomfortable program of sex education taught Caroline the following series of "facts."

1. Men will molest you sexually every chance they get.

2. Sex is a filthy and sinful practice that is not to be thought about by nice girls.

3. After marriage, sex magically becomes transformed into the most beautiful, spiritual, and rewarding experience any two human beings can have.

The first two lessons Caroline learned too well. The violent difficulty she experienced came with lesson number three. Sex in marriage was not something you could try out when young to see if it worked, since it was held to be filthy and part of the animal nature of man. You just had to wait and try to imagine what it was like. And, as vivid as Caroline's imagination was, it was totally incapable of manufacturing even a faint semblance of what the first night was really going to be like. To begin with, all their friends were addicted to horseplay and practical jokes and, after the wedding ceremony, they unceremoniously accompanied the bridal couple to their room in a hotel. Until 5 a.m. these so-called friends proposed a seemingly endless round of champagne toasts of an increasingly drunken and meaningless sort. When their rough and ready friends finally departed, Caroline and Jim found their suitcases were filled with clothing that had been carefully knotted into a hopeless tangle.

Jim, like many newly married males, felt called upon to consummate the marriage despite fatigue and the late hour. His attempts, consequently, were fumbling, frantic, ill-advised, badly-timed, and productive of sexual catastrophe. The promised beauty of married sex never materialized for Caroline; sex was sex, and it seemed awkward, vulgar, animalistic, and rarely contained pleasure. The next day, as they packed to take the train to New York, they were both crabby and out-of-sorts and it seemed a poor way to begin married life. Perhaps the French had the right idea when they proposed that the newly married couple should retire gracefully to the marital bed in the family home for the first intimate experience of one another.

At any rate, this dredged-up recollection of the ancient past seemed, to Caroline, hardly relevant to the present difficulties she was experiencing. As she said, "I don't know why I remember this. It has nothing to do with anything." The trouble Caroline faced now was that she was not only frightened of extreme heights but she had become terror-stricken at the remote prospect she would even unwittingly come into close contact with the potential threat of height. Jim and Caroline had lived in a traditional two-story house, but she persuaded him to buy a modern one-story ranch house in a different section of the city. Jim complained at first about the costs of such a move and the practical adequacy of their present house, but he became convinced when Caroline decided she could no longer stand the upstairs bedrooms of their house and took to sleeping on the couch in the living room.

The new house relieved Caroline's fears for a while but she seemed to be nervous all of the time now. This split-level housing did little to remedy the sexual difficulties they were having since Caroline was so involved in the necessary chores of moving and resettling that she had little time for him. When stability seemed close to achievement, Caroline decided they needed more room and called in a contractor to redo the basement. This, predictably disrupted their lives for another four months, and Jim began to lose patience. They argued more and Caroline became totally homebound. Going downtown was too much for her, and essential shopping never seemed to get done. They were always out of everything Jim wanted at the moment. At this juncture, Jim demanded that Caroline get help. He threatened her with vivid descriptions of the physical charms of his music students with whom he had sensed an increasing attraction. That did it. She called me immediately and displayed an interesting combination of frenzy and calm during the first hour of our contact.

In the hours that followed I came to know Caroline a great deal better and I began to feel sorry for the unfortunate blows that fate had dealt her. I could understand her anxiety and feel sympathetic about the difficulties she was undergoing, but I knew that her life could not continue as it had in the past. It was exactly the time for a change if she was to survive as a whole person.

What Caroline found most frightening was not the implicit threat Jim had made about having an affair with one of his music students. She knew he was upset and had been through a lot with her but, as she said,

> He's gotten pretty fat over the years and he would rather sit with a can of beer and watch TV than dash around town in hot pursuit of some female half his age. After all, he was no world-famous Lothario when we were dating in our home town.
>
> No, what's bothering me is that my fears of high places and tornadoes were bad enough but now its spreading and making life even more miserable for me. Lately I have begun to feel a terrible and unreasoning fear that the food I am preparing for Jim and the kids is going to poison them or make them sick in some way. It's not really that I think it is poisoned but that it is spoiled or rotten in some way and will give them ptomaine poi-

soning. When I shop I check everything four or five times and pick everything over before I buy it but I still don't feel right about it by the time I get home.

No one knows about it but it is driving me batty! Jim has no idea why our food costs have risen so in the last few months and he blames it on the government and the high cost of living. What he doesn't know is that I have been throwing everything out after I have had it in the house more than a day or two. For instance—I'll buy a dozen eggs and use about six of them. Then I'll start to worry about how fresh they really are. I think of how easy it would be for some farmer to slip in some old, rotten eggs just to get rid of them or how the supermarket might not sell many eggs for a week or so and I might be getting really ancient eggs and not know it. After I have worried about this for a while I crack open an egg and smell it and it always smells funny to me. So, everything that has been around the house even for a few days gets dumped down the garbage disposal.

Worst of all I am getting afraid to eat and I watch the others secretly to see if they look funny or taste anything unusual in the food. If Jim ever finds out about this he will kill me and I'm becoming a nervous wreck because it is on my mind day and night.

This confession that Caroline's phobic pattern was expanding into even more sensitive areas perturbed me for several reasons. To begin with, a phobia that spreads to so fundamental an aspect of living as the preparation and consumption of food is like a distress cry rising in intensity and desperation. The spread of the symptom tells us of an extension of the disorder to deeper reaches of the personality and warns of a crumbling ability to cope with the problems and anxieties life presents.

In addition, Caroline's anxiety about food coupled with her report of things looking, feeling, smelling, and tasting bad distressed me since it seemed to occupy a kind of twilight zone between the moderate disturbances of neurosis and the more severe disorders of psychosis. Caroline's reactions seemed from her report, to go beyond the usual anxiety about food or finickiness about eating so characteristic of a neurotic disorder. I began to fear Caroline was in more psychological trouble than she had appeared to be at first. Finally, Caroline's fear that she might unwittingly poison her family was irrational considering the number of years she had been preparing food for them without any hint of illness or injury to them. Her previous anxieties had been unreasonable in a reasonable fashion.

These most recent anxieties were not only unreasonable but they introduced a new and worrisome aspect to her case. Hidden beneath this transparent facade of concern for the well-being of her family was the opposite side of the coin—her resentment of them and unconscious wish that they would die. By being upset about the possibility of poisoning her family, Caroline effectively denied her impulse to kill them. Perhaps, really, Caroline wished only to have them gone, "out of the way," or "out of her hair" so she could pamper her phobia and not be pressed constantly to abandon it and to venture into areas and experiences that paralyzed her with fear.

As it turned out, Caroline proved unable to navigate the rising tide of anxiety that was her lot. She became increasingly agitated and convinced that sooner or later she would injure or kill her family through negligence in food preparation. Her state of collapse became apparent to Jim after an incident in which the youngest child got sick and threw up after supper (it turned out he had measles) and Caroline became hysterical shrieking she had killed him and that she ought to be executed as a criminal and a child-murderer. Jim called me an hour later when he found he was unable to console Caroline or to calm her down by explaining that nothing was really wrong. Together we decided it was necessary to admit Caroline to the hospital before her agitated behavior produced even more upset in her children.

Caroline calmed down following sedation in the ward and was easier to talk to the following day. At that time she was informed her child had measles and that she had not injured him by her cooking or by contaminated food. This information had little impact on her since she now appeared deeply depressed and could only shake her head and insist that she was such a horrible person and had made others suffer for so long that she deserved extreme punishment for her misdeeds.

In the next three weeks Caroline's depression deepened and the seriousness of her disorder became manifest. Caroline had been phobic about heights, was terrorized by the possibility that tornadoes or lightening might strike her, had been disenchanted with the joys and pleasures of sex, and, now, was convinced that her urge to be free of responsibility had caused her to make a mistake that might have resulted in the death and destruction of her family. Caroline had progressed from anxiety about her own welfare to concern about the possible involvement of those she said she loved best.

It was in this last phase of her disorder that the ultimate secret of her life was bared. Caroline was a hater of other human beings who throughout her life wore a mask of solicitude and concern for them. The mask was unnatural but this was apparent neither to Caroline nor to those closest to her emotionally. Having worn this disguise for so many years, it became more real than the face it concealed. Caroline's fears of storms and heights were essential features of the mask she wore because, as long as these were the prime focus of her attention, she could safely ignore those deeper lying parts of herself that were potentially much more dangerous to her well-being.

I wish I could report that this case miraculously came to a happy ending but this is not possible. I have high hopes for the eventual restoration of Caroline to a fully productive and happy life, but this is a hope rather than a confident conviction. Caroline has left the hospital to return to her family and has a part-time maid to do the cooking. Her symptoms are less prominent than they were. She is making therapeutic progress in uncovering that part of her life in which she learned, defensively, to resent those who caused her anxiety by requiring that she stop concentrating on herself in order to give to them.

As it turned out, Caroline's fear of self-destruction was, in part, a mask for her urge to destroy others. Her unconscious logic seemed to be, "better me than the ones I love." The therapeutic task lay in understanding the source of these impulses and converting them to some socially useful form. We are currently both hard at work at the process, and I think we will succeed.

There are those who are bound to quibble that Caroline W. has a phobia whose roots are so deep that it might better be classified as a psychosis rather than a neurosis. I think this is a matter of optimism and taste. The depth of Caroline W.'s disorder reaches beyond the usual confines of neurosis, but I am convinced that this adjective best describes the long-term run of her life. The dynamic basis of her symptoms is by no means clear and consistent to the practiced diagnostician. She is a strange amalgamation of superficial and serious distortion. I hope I am right in an optimistic view of her case.

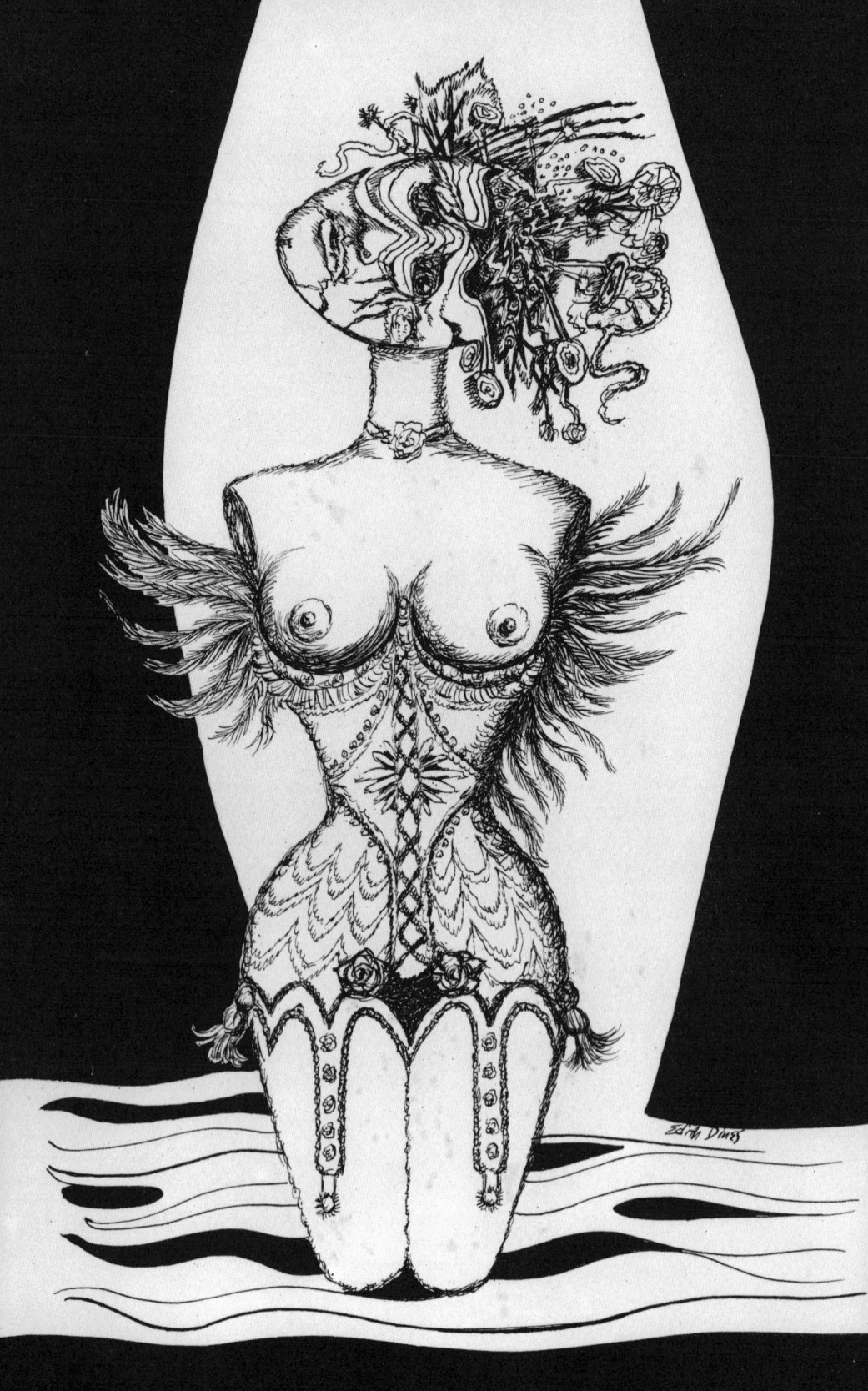

I've Got a Splitting Headache
–MARGE S.

PROLOGUE *Musculoskeletal reactions* that take the form of
headache occupy a special niche in the study of psychopathology,
primarily because of the frequency and regularity with which
"headaches" influence the lives of so many of us. Our culture
regularly excuses the physically sick from full participation
in society and a headache is a legitimate excuse for such
nonparticipation. Frequent headaches can be a specific form
of reaction to anxiety or an expression of an obsessive concern
with bodily processes.

   Why are headaches so often the illness of choice in civilized
society? To begin with, a splitting headache makes most people
so miserable that they are almost totally incapable of interacting
successfully and meaningfully with other human beings.
When sufficiently severe, headaches are exalted by the title
migraine and the sufferer may writhe for days with facial flushes
pallor, dizziness, visual flashes, and intense pain.

   For many, the body is the primary vehicle by which
emotions are expressed—emotions that, because of learned
patterns of interacting with people, cannot be otherwise shown.
Emotional difficulties learn to travel a physical road, and the
body shouts what the person can only whisper to himself.
We have long known that emotional reactions have physiological

concomitants that can alter basic functions, such as respiration, circulation, digestion, heartbeat, and glandular secretion. The study of psychosomatic medicine was founded on the premise that the psyche and the soma could interact such that: 1) mental events would be mirrored in physical reactions and 2) physical states would alter one's mental condition.

Mind and body are essentially one, but the distinction we make between them, although staggeringly artificial, has been convenient for theoretical and analytical purposes. No one of us has escaped these mental-physical exchanges in the form of blushing, trembling, stomach cramps, urine and bowel urgency, sweating, shivering, and so on. Recall, for example, the physical changes your body underwent the last time you spoke before a large audience, got a traffic ticket, met a famous person, were criticized or challenged in an aggressive manner.

A psychophysiologic disorder is a chronic and exaggerated state of normal physiology occasioned by repressed emotion which, if continued for a sufficient length of time, can lead to structural changes in the affected organ system. Such long-lasting and acute alterations of physical functioning, when they are massive, have been labelled "organ neuroses." Hypertension is a good example. Between 75 and 80 per cent of those suffering chronic high blood pressure are discovered to have no organic basis for their condition. What then can elevate one's blood pressure? The theoretical speculations are that rage, anger, hostility, and hatred that cannot be expressed toward an appropriate target make up the core of emotions that find bodily outlet when other forms of expression are dangerous or forbidden as a means of release. In some respects, the psychophysiological reaction is similar to the kind of response that typifies an infant's reaction to stress. Faced with stimuli he cannot comprehend or adjust to, he thrashes about wildly and physiologically reaches a fever pitch of vain and random response.

People suffering psychophysiological disorders appear normal in almost all other respects. To the careful observer, it is obvious that even when they are having a good time they seem poised on the edge of pain or discomfort and that, under stress, they display disintegration and decay in the functioning of their organ systems. Passive-receptive relationships may characterize the interactions they have with others, so that they seem to be quiet, unexpressive, sit-in-the-corner types. Meanwhile, the body becomes an instrument for demonstrating their repressed rage and resentment.

Musculoskeletal reactions produce the same benefits as hypochondriacal affliction. Those in close contact with the victim give increased attention, affection, care, and support to the sufferer and can, as a consequence, be controlled and manipulated in the name of the disease. Social competition is, of course, reduced for the sick person, and he is freed of some feelings of inadequacy and low self-esteem. The primary and secondary gains of illness are pleasurable in the extreme. The splitting headache, for example, excuses the victim from participation in a dreaded social event, and at the same time, it assures him of an almost unending supply of tender loving care by others. The case we are about to consider focusses on the manipulative aspects of psychophysiological disease—using functional sensations of illness to control those who must interact with the patient and maintain an affectionate relationship with him. Ours is a culture that seems overly sensitive to physical distress, at least among members of the middle class. In our own pioneer days and in a number of current economically marginal cultures, pain and deprivation are common, and they are responded to with considerably less solicitousness and concern than can be afforded by a more affluent society. The retreat from life in the name of pain is a luxury that only the most industrialized and civilized society can afford.

Everyone learns of the resonance between body and mind, but only a few capitalize on it and make it a way of life. Suffering is a weapon available to all, but it is selected for interpersonal combat primarily by persons without more mature resources for adaptation.

MARGE WAS GOING to have that headachey feeling again. She knew it because she felt "blah" when she woke up that morning. She knew it because it was going to be hot and sticky that day and she didn't feel at all rested when she woke up. Besides, she remembered they were supposed to go out that evening with some of Tony's business friends. She decided she was not up to getting out of bed to make breakfast. Tony mumbled something she didn't quite hear as she rolled over and dropped into a fitful sleep. She woke up when the telephone rang at 10:30. She did not want to answer it since she had no idea who would be calling, and she was not in the mood to talk to anybody. She knew she would worry all day about who had called and why she so often did not want to talk to people but she buried her head in the pillow and waited in agony for the ringing to end.

She regularly kept the draperies drawn in the living room so that, when the doorbell rang, she could peek out secretively to see who was intruding on her life. It really did not make any difference who was there, of course. For Marge, answering the door depended on whether she was psychologically ready for people—most often she was not. It even upset her if Tony went to work and forgot to put her car in the garage and close the door. When he failed to do this, people knew she was home and she would have to hide in her own house until they went away.

The list of household responsibilities Marge neglected was a lengthy one, but it was evident that the most overlooked were those that could be accomplished only by a person who felt comfortable with fellow human beings. Two things bothered Tony the most. As he left for work each morning, he found himself the bearer of a long list of things he could pick up on the way home from work. These lists got longer and more complex day by day, and now he had to plan on leaving work early every day to get his shopping done if he wanted to get home before 6 p.m. As a mild rebuke to Marge, he would complain about the parking problem in town and detail how much time he spent shopping for her. Marge then, ritually, reminded him that "after all, you're the man in the family."

Tony was particularly impatient about shopping for feminine things. Buttons, thread, bias tape, hair spray and deodorant were bad enough, but buying tampons really irritated him. He had difficulty deciding whether to go to one drug store each time where there was an understanding pharmacist or to go to different stores so no one would realize how henpecked he was.

Tony was particularly annoyed by Marge's postponement of shopping for what seemed like weeks at a time. He never sat down with Marge and discussed the problem or insisted on a fixed schedule of weekly shopping because he sensed in advance that whatever they agreed to would be violated shortly. Having reasoned thus, Tony waged a guerrilla campaign that faithfully followed a familiar script. The script called for the spontaneous use of an assortment of related interpersonal gambits calculated to make a point without seeming to do so.

Scene 1

TONY. (*After carefully examining the contents of the refrigerator.*) Marge? Where's the coffee cream?

MARGE. I forgot to leave a note for the milkman.

TONY. Well, why didn't you buy some when you went shop-

ping today? (*Tony is fully aware Marge did not go shop-*
ping today.)

MARGE. I'm going to go shopping tomorrow. (*Marge knows*
she will not shop tomorrow.)

TONY. You said you were going to go shopping today. (*Marge*
knows what she said.)

MARGE. I was so busy doing the laundry, I didn't have a chance.
(*It took Marge exactly one-and-one-half hours to do the*
laundry.)

TONY. (*Knowing he is losing ground.*) Then I can wear that
blue-striped shirt tomorrow? (*Tony knows there is not the*
remotest possibility of it.)

Scene 2

A classic argument focussed on the theme of neglected house-
hold responsibilities. The script allows invention and impro-
visation for both actors as their mood moves them.

TONY.

   1. "Why the hell didn't you at least . . ."

   2. "You said you were going to do that yesterday . . ."

   3. "What about the   X   you were going to take care
of . . ."

   4. "You always say you will but . . ."

   5. "No other husband has to . . ."

MARGE.

   1. "You always want to start an argument . . ."

   2. "You always pick on me . . ."

   3. "Why can't you help by doing a few simple things . . ."

   4. "You act like I didn't do anything all day . . ."

   5. "I've been sick and you don't care . . ."

In the third scene, Marge lies on the couch with a cold cloth
on her forehead suffering from an excruciating headache obviously caused by Tony's bad disposition and continual deprecia-
tion of Marge.

Tony mutters half-intelligible imprecations as he sulks and
slams the kitchen cabinet doors. He has cleared the table and
started the automatic dishwasher. He is noisily mixing himself a
large after-dinner drink. He prolongs this process and increases
the volume of noise hoping Marge will start in on him about
drinking too much and give him more reason to drown his sorrows. Marge studiously avoids rising to this obvious bait.

Meanwhile, Marge changes into a revealing nightgown. She
carefully ignores his boisterous mixing of an unwanted drink,
asks him to bring her three aspirin and a sleeping pill, and

prepares herself for a seductive-yet-sick demonstration on the couch followed by a display of great pain before she heads wearily for bed.

Tony drinks enough to make him groggy as he watches television, lurches a little as he drops sleepily into their king-size bed (Marge said they needed more room so they wouldn't be "on top of each other all the time"), and would, as he always did lately, feel lousy in the morning.

Marge, still awake when Tony flops into bed, is relieved to see that he is drunk. She rolls over to contact Tony, stroking him sensually, and says she feels better now. Tony can only reply, "That's nice," and he drifts immediately into a comatose state made up in equal parts of weariness and alcohol. He hates the thought that she is ready and he is not, but it is hopeless. Marge returns, hurt, to her own distant side of the king-size bed, but her hurt is mixed with a sense of vindication. Whenever she is ready, he is too tired or drunk. Marge sleeps soundly and peacefully—the sleep of the righteous; the sleep of the winner of a regularly repeated fight to the finish. She does not have to worry about getting up early tomorrow to get breakfast—it is going to be another hot day and Tony will be sheepishly guilty about the scene he caused.

The lack of sex bothered Tony too, but in another way. When he was going with Marge before they got married, she was the most provocative female he had ever encountered in his life. She promised sexual adventure in her every gesture, her every movement, and whenever she spoke. Marge, before they were married, had been a conversational fondler of men. Whatever she said was punctuated by an arm squeeze, a nudge, or a small but spontaneous hug. She greeted casual acquaintances with a warm kiss on the lips and a great deal of *double-entendre* conversation underscored by eyebrow raising and the subtle suggestion that were it not for the public setting she would lose herself with reckless abandon.

Then, they were married. At a cocktail party she remained a magnet to other males and, when sufficiently irritated at her attractiveness, Tony would mutter, "All talk—no action." Cocktail parties posed no real problem for Tony since they seldom went to them any more. Marge was usually sick, so Tony would phone the host and make up another version of the same old story he had been telling for four years. For a while he thought she might be fooling around with one of her cocktail-circuit friends, but, he mused, "it would have to be home delivery and she probably wouldn't answer the door." As far as he was concerned, it was like being married to a nervous nun. He knew he provoked her more often than he should, but, somehow, it was more than this. It was as if she could predict when he was eager for sexual encounter and planned that moment to be sick. She never delivered a fraction of the promise she held out for him during courtship and this discrepancy always lingered as a resentful half-thought in the back of his mind. He felt he had been cheated but didn't know quite how to complain about it. He would have trotted the problem out into the open and complained, but he was not nearly that confident about his own masculine performance. The thought kept recurring to him that perhaps she *was* running around with somebody else because he wasn't very good in bed. He felt lousy when sex didn't work out right, and he often thought it was his fault for being too ready.

Marge—as her male admirers learned—was all talk and no action, indeed. She had been that way since junior high school days when she first learned the relation of sex to social success. Faced with the perpetual problem of being attractive sexually while avoiding a sense of guilt, Marge had unconsciously learned to be the epitome of what every male desired and the model of what every male feared he could not manage.

Marriage, for Marge, was a serious threat. In a way she knew that she would be inadequate since she was secretly so acutely conscious of her fears and anxieties that she could not comfortably tell anyone about them. Marge was a fake but Marge had "been around" in an odd sort of way. She had again and again found herself in compromising situations in which she could not live up to what males obviously expected of her. She learned every glib reason to excuse her from delivering what she promised so graphically, and it was rare that she was accused of being phoney or a "tease." In those instances, she dismissed her partner as an "adolescent boor" or, when feeling guilty, accommodated him in a way that insured her continued virginity.

Clearly, Tony and Marge had to evolve a different pattern of relating to one another if their shaky marriage was to survive. Marge was becoming a hermit and Tony was becoming less patient hour by hour. The word divorce was never mentioned by either of them at any time despite the fact that their marriage resembled a fighting separation more than an example of togetherness.

The serious problem, I concluded, was Marge's. It was not that Tony didn't fit beautifully into the marital play they were acting out—did not, indeed, perform his role incredibly well. It was, rather, that, of the two, Marge was more incapacitated by her life's pattern than was Tony. So, I concentrated on Marge and tried to trace the tangled web that comprised the design of her life. It was not an easy task since, for some weeks, Marge denied that she was anything but what she thought herself to be—an innocent victim, plagued by a husband who did not understand or appreciate her. When we managed to get past this obvious distortion, we began to make some progress.

Marge, who had been extremely seductive in the first hours of our contact, finally gave up and began to have insight into her contribution to the mutual unhappiness she and Tony had been experiencing. As she described her early years and detailed her encounters with the male of the species, I began to visualize an almost unbroken chain of panting males who failed to recognize that Marge was "not that kind of girl." As I interpreted the highly apparent course of her relations with the opposite sex she at first became angry, and developed headaches that conveniently appeared when I pressed too close to the truth of her condition.

Marge's problem was that her body spoke more eloquently than she ever could. The rage and resentment she regularly felt seldom reached consciousness and rarely was openly expressed toward me. This was significant since I tested the limits of her ability to feel one emotion while she was expressing quite another. In a sense, I provoked Marge S. into developing bodily symptoms in exchange for the resentment she felt toward my exploration of the motives for her baleful view of men. In everything she did, Marge invited male attention. The bathing suits she wore were bikini in style, her dresses were form fitting to a generously endowed figure, she crossed her legs with provocative abandon, and she casually caressed males in ways that suggested a physical paradise. It occurred to me that the last time I had seen so sexy a demonstration of total availability was in a ward of a neuropsychiatric hospital where four hysterical females were patients. One could not say good morning to them without being inundated by a powerful wave of sexuality. Marge was similar. She exuded sex but she never delivered what she advertised.

Marge S. was perpetually offended when suddenly confronted with her handiwork. She was totally unaware, consciously, of cause and effect in her relations with men and was always startled when they sought the natural outcome. Marge S. was a tease. She was all promise and little substance, but she enjoyed immensely the pack of admirers she always attracted when she exuded signals to anyone in range.

There were several related items of behavior to account for in the psychological make-up of Marge S.: her hermitage from the world of relations with others, her seductive facade in the company of males, and the bodily distress she experienced when confronted with unpleasant or demanding events in her life. Her hermitage and her headaches had a history that dated from very early in her life and could be traced with greater ease than could the development of her pulsating promise of sexual paradise.

Having a headache that would force Marge to retire from the world of people had its origin when she learned she could get away with it. Marge's mother had always been overly concerned with Marge's health and would make a great fuss, not only when Marge was actually sick, but even when Marge looked like she might be coming down with something.

Marge regularly had Monday morning sicknesses that kept her home from school. These maladies had a high correlation with academic stresses such as examinations, or scheduled performances of any sort in school. Marge had learned to alert her mother to possible illness early in the game. She would complain of a vague pain or of the beginning of a patterned set of symptoms but would dismiss these as inconsequential as soon as her mother became concerned and began to cross-examine her about her physical condition. This move on Marge's part established several premises: that she was about to come down with something, that she was prepared to suffer it through heroically and without complaint, and that only a severe attack of some dread disease would keep her from meeting her responsibility. Her mother played the game according to these unspoken rules, and Marge soon learned that there was profit in sickness if it was used wisely and adroitly. With practice, Marge became expert.

Once Marge's mother was convinced that she had a sick girl on her hands, the second phase of the illness sequence was launched. In this phase, Marge learned the meaning of seclusion and secondary gain. Marge, at first, faked illness, but, before long, the pains became real and Marge was truly sick. When this happened, she could count on a great deal of anxious attention from both her parents—attention she luxuriated in, attention that made her seem valued, wanted, loved, and accepted by her parents. That it required sickness to achieve this state was something of a commentary both on the nature of her relationship with her parents and on the degree of reassurance she seemed to need regularly of her attractiveness as a human being. Anxious parental concern about her well-being irrigated her self-image and made it blossom and thrive. Marge's chronic headaches provided primary gain through her avoidance of anxious or threatening situations. Being sick she could not be expected to manage what people demanded of her. She gained by escaping, in a legitimate manner, from the problems posed by life. She gained, in a secondary fashion, the pleasure of returning briefly to the days of her early youth in which she was cared for with absolutely unquestioning love. Parental concern and sympathy was an extra added attraction furnished by her illnesses.

Seclusion was another by-product of her sicknesses. Attention was thus one side of the coin and seclusion the other. Having headaches meant retiring to a darkened bedroom and spending endless hours alone with one's thoughts. Sleep is a great time filler at first, but humans can only sleep so long; then, thoughts must occupy the rest of their time. Fantasy can be a very pleasant kind of pseudo-reality since it is totally controllable and, in fantasy, life can be as you would like it to be rather than as it really is. The fantasy world is, basically, without anxiety-provoking problems of any sort. When life proves confusing, seclusion allows us to think things over, to try to find some resolution, and the opportunity to rehearse the management of life. For Marge, seclusion and thinking about herself and others became positively pleasureable events that compensated for the difficulties she found in meeting real life.

Marriage for Marge was very much like being admitted to a private sanitarium. Marriage allowed her to retreat from life whenever it became too burdensome or complicated. Withstanding her husband's resentment and irritation at her behavior was difficult at first, but, having learned how, she could choose to participate in life only to the degree to which she wanted. Her husband provided for all her physical wants and needs as her parents had, and there was very little reason for her to mature, grow up, or adopt a new pattern of interaction with people.

This less-than-perfect adjustment to life could have been accomplished without the complicating factor of her seductive attitude. Her role as temptress, I discovered, was constructed almost entirely of emotions opposed to those she was really feeling. She acted secure when she was insecure, brave when frightened, sexy when disinterested, sophisticated when naive, and gay when depressed. Marge had developed a whole other self as a massive denial of what she really was. When she played out the lie, it was always done with an intensity that an astute observer could recognize as the laugh substituted for the sob. Whistling in the dark, as a wise man once observed, is always a little off-key. Marge's act was convincing if one were not too critical or if one wanted very much to believe that appearances were an accurate reflection of the underlying reality.

This other self was a hollow mockery of everything Marge really was, but her self-view hardly reflected that fact. She saw herself as a socially charming, competent, admired woman who was plagued by physical infirmities that, annoyingly, limited her contact with others. The process of altering Marge's self-view to conform with greater accuracy to her appearance in the eyes of others was not going to be an easy task. I was concerned, as we undertook to labor together, that Marge would need some new source of psychological strength and skill to substitute for the patterns of response she would have to abandon if her disintegrating marriage and dilapidated social relations were to be repaired.

The first task was—as it always is—to overcome Marge's resistance, both to seeing herself as others saw her and to dealing without defensiveness and denial with things as they really were. There is safety in what is familiar and tried. Marge did fight and continues to fight but she is losing some enthusiasm for the battle. While she insists the whole therapeutic process is expensive, silly, and a waste of time, she is unaware that in a subtle fashion her behavior has begun to change. The husbandly complaints that brought her to therapy have diminished in intensity and frequency, and she is getting better. She refuses to admit the reality of these changes but time is on my side. She is getting better despite herself, and she might as well surrender. It is all over but the victory celebration.

Marge S. is a particularly instructive example of the slow, laborious,

and frequently unproductive course of therapy. Marge S. was very difficult as a problem and as a person. The defenses which had served so well
to insulate her from the real world were equally effective in holding me
at arm's length psychologically. Hour after hour in the course of her
treatment I would put away my notes with a sigh realizing that we had
wasted time sparring for an advantage where none was possible for either
of us.

Almost all therapeutic problems present magnificent challenges disguised as insoluble problems and case presentations uniformly report the
steps that forge ahead rather than the much greater number of steps taken
in place with no visible forward progress. These usual months of what
seems like marking time are an inevitable part of the total process of any
therapy. Helping others is arduous, frequently discouraging, and time
consuming. The therapist's optimism is rooted in his awareness that similar
dark moments have given way to the blinding light of insight and the
almost audible "click" when the parts fall into place. Such is the case with
Marge S. The course of therapeutic movement has been long and circui-
tous, but there is hope.

One for Me and One for Me

–Dan F.

Prologue *For the last 150 years* we have tried to pin down the psychopathic personality long enough to learn its nature. At various times in medical history the terms moral insanity, moral imbecility, and constitutional psychopathic inferiority have been used to describe these cases. Popular literature has coined more colorful names, such as liars, swindlers, imposters. The variety of names that have been applied tells us something of the elusiveness of the phenomenon.

The psychopath or sociopath presents a problem of social maladjustment to the rest of the citizenry, but he is not sick in a traditional or classic fashion. He is not usually neurotic, psychotic, or deficient in intelligence. He is, rather, like a walking dead man devoid of the usual notions of right and wrong, and lacking the kind and quality of affectional and emotional reactions that most of us seem to feel. An antisocial or asocial person who is aggressive, impulsive, and free of the restraining influence of guilt is a social monster psychologically two years old while chronologically and experientially an adult. This was the problem posed by Dr. Frankenstein's monster—the social conscience of a child housed in the powerful body of an oversized adult.

The clinical challenge is for professionals to reach agreement regarding who does or does not merit the dubious

honor of being designated a psychopath. Of all the persons ever
labelled psychopath, there is little doubt that most of them
were not truly qualified for the title. The attempt to define
the essence of the psychopath has been plagued by a steadily
mounting confusion regarding the criteria that ought to be used.
Some attempts have been made to bring order to this diagnostic
chaos by trying to describe the essential features of the
psychopath and these descriptive accounts may include
characteristics such as the following:

-lip service to conventional moral standards disguising a
  grossly inadequate development of conscience

-repeated social maladjustment and conflict with authority

-normal or superior intelligence

-unreliability, egocentricity, untruthfulness, impulsiveness,
  and poor judgment

-lack of insight, inability to accept blame or to learn
  by experience

-hedonistic self-gratification without anxiety and guilt

-low tolerance for frustration or deprivation

-charm and social poise without depth or emotional
  commitment to others—uses people to serve his own ends

The list could be extended almost indefinitely, but it then
becomes no more than an elaborate catalogue of the pain
and injury one person can do to another and ceases to be useful
in differential diagnosis.

The diagnostic category labelled psychopath is probably
scientifically useless. It is most often used as a catchall for
antisocial behavior that does not clearly belong to some other
form of disorder.

Perfectly normal persons commit psychopathic acts once in
a while—the key diagnostic phrase is "once in a while." Probably,
under the right circumstances and pressure, no one of us
is so stringently moral that we would not bend the truth a little
with a white lie or cut corners and be less than perfectly honest
or ethical. We expect and forgive such temporary lapses
from ideal behavior in very young children but find intolerable
its unrelieved continuation into adulthood. In this respect, the

psychopath is best described as an adult with a sense of right and wrong suitable only for a preschool child. The psychopath has a conscience but it is atrophied. The psychopath's conscience may operate only part time, may be called into play only when it is convenient or profitable, or may function according to a set of rules unique to himself and not shared by others in the society in which he lives. If man is to coexist in close quarters with his fellow man he must live by rules that make the behavior of others predictable. The psychopath is unpredictable since he plays the game of life according to his own rules and has little regard for the rules of others.

The niceties of categorization will be ignored for the purpose of presenting the case of Dan F., and we will pretend we can distinguish the psychopath from his normal counterpart. He is a fascinating study of a kind of human being who has grown to maturity only partly finished—an incomplete organism that preys on the rest of the human race for his personal pleasure.

DAN F. WAS NOT a patient of mine but he probably told me more about himself and was less defensive than most of the patients I had treated. He was a well-known actor, a "personality" who had appeared on national television a number of times but had never really made it big on what he called the "boob tube." He made a lot of money, had a handsome wife, a big house in an exclusive suburb, drove a beautifully appointed Mercedes, and couldn't care less that there were other people in the world. He was as close as I ever got to what I conceived a psychopath ought to be.

During the time I knew him he unfolded a hair-raising tale of life as he lived it, and it amused him to talk about himself. Most of the details of his conduct had to be taken at face value since I had no way to check their accuracy. Some of the stories were certainly untrue and I was convinced many others were greatly exaggerated. He seemed fascinated by the chance to talk to a "headshrinker" in a social rather than therapeutic setting, and he, in turn, fascinated me. He was urbane, charming, knowledgeable about a variety of subjects, a seeming friend of every nightclub owner and entertainer in the city.

Physically, he was commanding—six feet tall, with curly hair and regular features that were enhanced and somewhat glamorized by his personal fastidiousness in dress and grooming. But it was his bearing that added the finishing touch. He wore arrogance and noblesse oblige like a hand-tailored garment. He was not just bluff and appearance. For ten years he was a disc jockey with a wide following, and he knew popular music so

well that every singer, musician, and entertainer in town would drop over
to pour out all the current frustrations he or she was undergoing at the
moment and to get his advice. He played the therapist with such grace
and smoothness that it was embarrassing. There was a faint air of the cool
and distant in his interactions with other show business types but it became clear that this restrained quality was exactly what the situation demanded. It was a *very* nervous game to be an entertainer and he always
played the part of the relaxed and understanding person who was both
part of it while removed from its strain. He was sensitive to the needs of
others when it was profitable and insensitive and callous about those
who could not do him any good.

He had certain mannerisms that telegraphed some of his feelings, however. Whenever he was going to create a public scene, involving the assertion of "who he was" and "what he had a right to expect," he would tilt
his head slightly to one side, tug at his right eyebrow, look piercingly at
the person in question, and begin a hostile Socratic dialogue. In a restaurant in which the manager toadied to him and flattered him without restraint, which Dan knew instinctively was a sign of fear and weakness, he
carried on one evening about the condition of the Shrimp De Johnge. The
dialogue with the waitress went something like this:

DAN F. (*in a loud voice.*) Is this supposed to be Shrimp De
    Johnge?
WAITRESS. (*half-smiling.*) Certainly, Mr. F., is something wrong
    with it?
DAN F. Here, taste it and you tell me.
WAITRESS. Let me take it back and tell the chef.
DAN F. No! Taste it and tell me if you think this is fit to eat.
WAITRESS. Well, Mr. F., I really can't tell.
DAN F. You could sure as hell tell about this even if you don't
    eat here! Send me the manager and make him eat it.

By this time Dan had a nervous audience alerted for the next scene.
Enter the bowing, scraping, apologetic manager. When a new plate of
Shrimp De Johnge was brought to him, he shoved it rudely aside, refused
to taste it, and ordered London broil commenting in disgust that the chef
couldn't do much to ruin *that*.

The scene he created (I witnessed four such in two years of contact
with him) is less relevent to this account than his reaction when he resumed conversation with me. It had obviously been a contrived and calculated act to establish his presence in the restaurant, and no hint of his
emotional outburst remained when he resumed discussing the previous
subject. He, of course, barely tasted the London broil before pushing it
aside disdainfully.

"Dan," I said, "I have a sneaking suspicion that this whole scene came about just because you really weren't hungry."

Dan laughed loudly in agreement and said, "What the hell, they'll be on their toes next time."

"Was that the only reason for this display?" I asked.

"No," he replied, "I wanted to show you how gutless the rest of the world is. If you shove a little they all jump. Next time I come in, they'll be all over me to make sure everything is exactly as I want it. That's the only way they can tell the difference between class and plain ordinary. When I travel I go first class."

"Yes," I responded, "but how do they feel about you as a person—as a fellow human being?"

"Who cares?" he laughed, "If they were on top they would do the same to me. The more you walk on them, the more they like it. It's like royalty in the old days. It makes them nervous if everyone is equal to everyone else. Watch. When we leave I'll put my arm around that waitress, ask her if she still loves me, pat her on the fanny, and she'll be ready to roll over any time I wiggle my little finger."

He was convincing. I believed him. That's exactly what he did on the way out and there was no mistaking the look in her eye. She was ready any time he was, and she thought he was a lot of man.

Dan F. was brutally frank with his colleagues, and, in a business so fraught with deception, insincerity, and mutual hustling, this was interpreted as refreshing honesty and an absence of guile. In an odd sort of way, his emotional quicksand looked like the Rock of Gibraltar to those more nervous than he. It was a startling state of affairs but, as I said, it was a nervous kind of business.

One night, a colleague of Dan's committed suicide. In my casual contacts with him he seemed like a nice, relaxed guy whose problems appeared to number no more than the average. In retrospect, I could single out personal questions he asked of me that might have signalled a deeper concern with life than was typical of the others, but this was only in retrospect. At the time he seemed pretty much like everybody else.

But, he hanged himself one night. My phone started ringing early the next morning with the inevitable question "Why?" The executives at the station called but Dan F. never did. When I did talk to him, he did not mention the suicide. Later, when I brought it to his attention, all he could say was that it was "the way the ball bounces." At the station, however, he was the one who collected money for the deceased and presented it personally to the new widow. As Dan observed, she was really built and had possibilities.

Dan F. had been married before, a fact he had failed to communicate to his present wife, and, as he described it, was still married only part time. He had established a reasonable basis for frequent nights out since his variety show required that he keep in touch with entertainers in town. He was currently involved sexually with girls ranging from the station manager's secretary (calculated) to the weather girl (incidental, based on a shared interest in Chinese food). The female of the "show biz" species seemed to dote on the highhanded treatment he accorded them. They regularly refused to believe he was "as bad as he pretended to be," and he was always surrounded by intense and glamorous women who needed to own him to feel complete as human beings.

Dan F. had charm plus. He always seemed to know when to say the right thing with exactly the proper degree of concern, seriousness, and understanding for the benighted victim of a harsh world. But, he was dead inside. People amused him and he watched them with the kind of interest most of us show when examining a tank of guppies. Once, on a whim, he called each of the burlesque theaters in town and left word with the burlesque queens that he was holding a party beginning at midnight with each of them as an honored guest. He indeed held the party, charging it to the station as a talent search, and spent the evening pouring liquor into the girls. By about 3 a.m. the hotel suite was a shambles, but he thought it was hilarious. He had invited the camera and floor crew from the television station and had carefully constructed a fictional identity for each: one was an independent film producer, another a casting director, a third an influential writer, and still another a talent agent. This giant hoax was easy to get away with since Dan had read correctly and with painful accuracy the not so secret dreams, ambitions, drives, and personal needs of these entertainers. What was staggering was the elaborateness of the cruel joke. He worked incessantly adding a touch here and a touch there to make it perfect. The television station crew knew enough about Hollywood to be convincing, and the room hummed with grade-B movie dialogue studded with much name-dropping.

Finally, some of the girls caught on to the gag and spread the word to the others. As they stalked out, with some very vulgar descriptions of Dan's sense of humor, he doubled up on the floor holding his sides in laughter.

The list of incidents I witnessed and the long succession of stories he related painted a grisly picture of life-long abuse of people for Dan's amusement and profit. He was adept at office politics and told me casually of an unbelievable set of deceptive ways to deal with the opposition. Character assassination, rumor-mongering, modest blackmail, seduction, and barefaced lying were the least of his talents. He was a jackal in the entertainment jungle, a jackal who feasted on the bodies of those he had slaughtered professionally. He was, for example, the master of the blind copy memo. This maneuver took several forms. He would, for example, write a letter highly critical of a colleague, and send it to the station manager, indicating that a copy had been sent to the victim. The copy was, of course, never sent. The consternation and misunderstanding this caused was considerable, and the outcome often was exactly what he had in mind. Sometimes, the victim got the letter in copy form but the original was not sent to the station manager. His most spectacular device was to enlist the help of A to "get" B and, as the plot progressed, to implicate A to the station manager in a subtle fashion as the culprit: "I don't like to mention this, Mr. Manager, but lately A has been complaining about B behind his back, and I wouldn't put it past him to try to make trouble for B. If they can't get along with each other there may be trouble for you." It always worked since station managers seemed to spend their lives uncovering plots and counterplots on the part of the talent. Managing so many prima donnas without getting injured while an innocent bystander was an ability every station manager had to possess.

Dan told me,

> I can remember the first time in my life when I began to sus-
> pect I was a little different from most people. When I was in high
> school my best friend got leukemia and died and I went to his
> funeral. Everybody else was crying and feeling sorry for them-
> selves and as they were praying to get him into heaven I sud-
> denly realized that I wasn't feeling anything at all. He was a
> nice guy but what the hell. That night I thought about it some
> more and found out that I wouldn't miss my mother and father
> if they died and that I wasn't too nuts about my brothers and sis-
> ters, for that matter. I figured there wasn't anybody I really
> cared for but, then, I didn't need any of them anyway so I
> rolled over and went to sleep.

As we discussed his early life he told me he could not recall a time when he was not "doing everybody I could and the easy ones twice." He remembered that when he was 12 years old he had read a pocket book about "con men." It was then he decided it would be his life's work. They were heroes to him and he "fell down laughing" when they took some "mark" for his "bundle." As he said, "There is a sucker born every min-ute, and I'm glad the birth rate is so high."

When Dan was a teenager he was a model of recklessness and revolt against authority. He pressed for those illicit experiences denied the young and became what every parent feared was the shape his own child would assume. Even at that age he knew in his bones what behavior would comfort the anxieties of "old folks" and lead them to believe that their half-remembered impulses were not typical of the newer generations they now had to confront. He assumed that parents preferred a lie to the truth, so he was careful to be what they hoped him to be rather than reveal him-self for what he really was. He became a skilled small-talk conversation-alist as he submitted himself to the critical scrutiny that regularly took place in the dead time that existed before his date made her dramatic en-trance into the living room.

He was shy, he was humble, he was self-effacing. He was whatever he sensed they needed him to be to pull the teeth of the fears that chewed at them. He was declared "safe" by one parent couple after another but he knew this contrived ease was never communicated between them in an open fashion. He played nice but this seldom interfered with his real thoughts and expectations. He became, in fact, what he described as a "Mom's Apple Pie" favorite for many parents. It must have been an incredible sight to watch him ingratiate his way into the hearts of his elders. He mentioned that he remained tense until that moment when he knew the planned, casual slip of addressing his date's mother as "Mom" would penetrate directly to her anxious and guilt-ridden heart.

Dan F. played with parents just to keep his hand in the game. When I asked why, he replied, "Like, it's how you get to Carnegie Hall, baby— practice, practice, practice." As we talked at some length of these early feelings of resentment toward the parental protectors of feminine virtue among the quarry he had selected for the kill, he expressed a contempt that seemed to match his feelings toward his own parents.

As he said, "I could con them the same as I fooled my own folks. When I got caught by the cops I always blamed the other guys. I would admit to just enough to make me appear to be a slightly imperfect but earnest kid who deserved another chance. They went for it time after time, not because they believed it but because they couldn't stand the idea that I was really a rotten kid. Mostly they didn't want to be bothered by it all. When I figured that out I didn't have to lie so much. They believed anything I told them because they didn't want to hear anything else and that way they got out of the whole messy deal quicker."

Dan F.'s youthful escapades were of the kind that some stable and reliable citizens brag about with a feeling of nostalgia for the lost vigor and juices of their youth. But, for Dan F., nothing had changed. He had aged without maturing and his adolescent depredations against the "square" populace had become only more sophisticated and slick. Dan F. was a teenager trapped in his own lack of development. As a teenager among grown men, little else could be expected of him and he expected little else of himself since he was convinced he had figured out a magic formula by which to lead his life.

Ours was and continues to be a strange relationship. Whenever I see him, he regales me with tales of his most recent depredations against the human race. He is always ready, willing, and eager to argue with me about the historical origins of traditional morality and its current uselessness in modern society. He has recently discovered two allies, the writings of Albert Ellis on sexual freedom and those of Ayn Rand on enlightened selfishness. He reads Hugh Hefner's Playboy philosophy semi-religiously and repeats it with a cultist fervor. His present wife (defensively, I have assumed) pooh-poohs his bold talk as intellectually pretentious and dismisses it as an attempt to impress other people. I am certain she is "whistling in the dark" to gain confidence because I have noticed that at parties she always manages to disengage herself from conversation and drift through the house to find out why Dan has been gone so long from the company in the living room. Invariably, she finds him engaged in a seemingly harmless exchange with an attractive female guest, but she dismisses this as the cost of being married to a celebrity and blames it on predatory women. She is becoming increasingly nervous about him, and the raging arguments they have at home bode ill for their marriage. As a confidant of both of them, I have noticed that she is the only one who has any emotional reaction to their disagreements about his behavior. When Dan reports their fights it sounds more as if he has been playing chess with an opponent whom he can beat at will.

In a strange way, Dan has been brutally honest with me. He has openly confessed shortcomings that others would hide in shame but the appropriate emotions simply never appear. It is impossible to distinguish between emotionally important and unimportant events with him. I sometimes think he has substituted practiced social skill for all emotional experiences. He mixes a perfect martini, he tells an inexhaustible string of interesting stories, he is well read, extensively travelled, and senses like an animal what other people need to make their lives complete. This last talent is the one he wields in a rapier-like fashion. He can "get to people" in such a short time that he is avidly sought-after socially at all levels of society. He is as much at home in the social swim of an executive's twenty-room mansion as he is in a bar where as many women as men are tattooed. He speaks the several languages of class, caste, and occupation with ease and great fluency. He is a chameleon with a sixth sense that few other human beings possess.

What is the most likely fate of Dan F.? It would be pleasing and comforting to most of us if we could believe that one day he will be punished for his behavior. There is very little likelihood that this will happen. Dan is successful in a material sense and doing very well for himself professionally. Canny and jungle-wise, he is firmly ensconced in a business in which being cool produces a profit. He will continue to get fan-mail in great quantity, he will rise to new and greater heights, he will live his life as he always has but will expand its scope and the elegance of its design. He will be divorced again, but it will hardly matter to him. He will continue to see me socially because this is the one flaw in his armor—he feels compelled to parade his personal values before me to demonstrate that good guys finish last. I am certain that I cannot alter his way of life in any meaningful way. I suppose that change will occur only if he gets into serious trouble, and I doubt that he will be sufficiently insightful even then to recognize it when it happens. Dan will always make out one way or another and will get his share even if others go without. Dan F. is a psychopath par excellence. He will always be amusing and charming but one must be cautious.

The triumph of evil over good is difficult to witness not only because it is irritating but because it seems unjust to all of us who, despite our urge to the contrary, toe the line of social and interpersonal conformity. It is unfair that we abstain and suffer while others indulge and pleasure themselves. Dan F. should, if there is any justice, suffer some pain as a consequence of his present adjustment or, at least, have ahead of him a dismal and unpromising future. Perhaps Dan F. will suffer adequate retribution in heaven but it is likely he will only begin to be uncomfortable on earth.

There are signs, however, that all is not well in the life of Dan F. While he pretends disinterest in the probable dissolution of his marriage, I think he seriously miscalculates the degree to which he needs the love and admiration of a female who can live with him and tolerate his flaws yet not abandon or reject him as his mother did. The adage that it takes a thief to catch a thief also holds true here. Thieves of every caliber and variety seek Dan out because they know he has basically defective judgment. Quick-profit business opportunities appealed to Dan and he had unwisely invested large amounts of money in schemes invented by fellow psychopaths whose judgment was equally flawed. Dan smarted under the sting of these losses because they indicated he had been suckered again. Being taken by others was a sharp blow, both to his vanity and his image of himself as a smart operator.

Dan insisted that the absence of normal affectional feelings and sentiment were no burden to him but more than once I detected a wistful quality in his discussion of the state of his emotional affairs. It was very much like the color-blind person who insists that color vision is no asset. The argument sounded hollow since he was hardly in a position to dismiss as meaningless sensations he had never experienced. Those who see color cannot share with the color blind the thrill and wonder of such vision but they know they would feel a sense of loss if deprived of it. Without emotions, something important and valuable in human life is missing and we are less than human in its absence. Dan was a nonhuman whose life was incomplete in a very vital way.

Dan was also victimized by his impulsiveness and inability to tolerate frustration for long. He moved too fast and with too little wisdom when the impulse struck him and the outcome was sometimes painful even to him. He resentfully reported several incidents in which he paid dearly for some momentary transgression that escalated to unpredicted heights and cost him more than he was interested in paying. He never quite knew how he got into these jams and, most often, blamed the stupidity of others for his predicament.

Dan F. got burned more than once but he never seemed to learn much from experience. The same temptations would confront him again and he would be led down the same garden path to personal loss and difficulty. Dan seemed to lack insight about the kind of person he was and never learned that his judgment was impaired by his needs of the moment and that he was truly incapable of adequate long-range judgment. Dan protested that he made more money than he lost and did better socially than most, and I was forced to grant that this was true. He often succeeded where others failed but he regularly failed where a less impulsive approach would have profited him more.

Even Dan's social smoothness had about it a transparent and veneer-like quality. The most astute of his casual acquaintances reported that they saw through it and distrusted him in important matters. These insightful ones reported that Dan was a charming addition to the group but that the fires of human warmth seemed always to be banked in him. An empty and superficial hail-fellow-well-met approach to life is not conducive to long-lasting and deeply unperturbable relationships with others. Dan suffered a critical shortage of warmth and depth. While he shrugged his shoulders and dismissed it as inconsequential to his well-being, I could not escape feeling that he was crippled but hated to admit it. Dan was doing spectacularly well, but the seeds of discontent had grown and were about to bear their very bitter fruit. The first signs of a change in his interpersonal relations were appearing. A great many stars were beginning to fail to appear at parties he designed for them, and some of his long-term associates began to be busy when he needed them to promote his own status in the world. Dan tried hard to explain why his great and good friends never showed up, and I knew it was getting to him more than he could admit.

Dan F.'s days are numbered because he has never prepared himself to accept defeat. In victory he is almost magnanimous; in defeat he is helpless. Dan's demise depends on the insight others have about him, and I am sure the time is close at hand when the mills of rumor and character assassination will begin to grind slowly and exceedingly small. Once the word is out, Dan will be dead in the entertainment business. Yet, he will become only an aging version of his younger self, for he has little capacity to change the way he is.

We know little of Dan F.'s first dozen years, and this really is the key to understanding him. Dan has told me in brilliant detail of every other facet of his experience, but this early gap bothers me. Why did Dan's humanity wither on the vine? What kills feeling in the human organism? We can begin with the assumption that the newborn infant is a purely physiological machine that has yet to learn human feelings and proceed to speculate that cold and unloving parents could make the developing child into a monster empty of human compassion and oriented solely to a profit-and-loss perception of his own kind.

Somehow, it happens. Somehow the semi-psychopaths of the world spawn and rear purer examples of their species—to the detriment of the rest of mankind. Dan F. is one, a product of his early years and further shaped by contact with his fellow man. The shadowy form of his parents is cast wherever he goes and falls, unfortunately, on the living shape of everyone he encounters.

Edith Davis

Crime Does Pay

–Tim C.

PROLOGUE   *With a major crime committed* every 15 seconds in this country and four per cent of our population arrested for misdemeanors or felonies, we have a serious social problem by anyone's standards. With a quarter of a million citizens detained in our prisons and an additional 40,000 youngsters incarcerated in juvenile "homes," it is obvious that we are suffering a percentage of social misfits greater than any society can long tolerate.

Eighty per cent of our juvenile offenders are male. Nearly one million of them have negative contact with the law each year, and 600,000 of them are remanded to the courts for social disposition. Of these juveniles, 60 per cent have records of prior arrest for antisocial actions in the form of crimes against property rather than persons. Burglary, larceny, robbery, and auto theft head the list of crimes committed by those under 18 years of age.

Understanding and explaining away this social and personal phenomenon was easier in the old days when such actions were viewed as the predictable outcome of hereditary predispositions. "Like father, like son" was all the explanation anyone needed. We have become somewhat more sophisticated and now understand that many young people commit delinquent acts, but only in rare cases does the child come neatly packaged

in the form of an identifiable delinquent. Our delinquents
always turn out to be a mixed bag of human emotions, feelings,
needs, and problems. They more closely resemble political
revolutionaries who have no constructive plan of government
to offer the society they violently oppose. Each of us is
delinquent, but in different ways, and our society is most
troubled by one particular form of delinquency—assault
on our property or our person.

For some, delinquent acts are an almost reasonable
adaptation to an almost totally abnormal human environment.
For some young people, delinquencies are blows struck against
the society—they are antisocial actions. For others, delinquency
is an asocial or dissocial act that fits a set of values, beliefs,
and standards that are reasonable in a particular subsociety
but are uniformly rejected by society at large. The various social
classes do not share totally congruent patterns of values, and the
discrepancy between them is a continual source of conflict.

A series of predictable conditions marks the lives of those
judged socially delinquent. They are frequently victims of
pathological psychological conditions such as organic brain
damage, mental retardation, psychosis, neurosis, and physical
handicaps. They have frequently experienced pathogenic family
relationships produced by divorce, desertion, or parental neglect.
Often, this takes the form of rejection by the father and
subsequent domination of the children by the mother or other
female members of the household. The subculture to which
the potential delinquent is exposed is an extremely unappetizing
one filled with all forms of social deviation, poverty, and a
hopelessness that encourages the banding together of sufferers
who have been rejected by society and its educational system.

From such a situation may come group and gang formation
as a means of securing acceptance, approval, status, a sense of
belonging, self-esteem, and security. This produces an essentially
uncivilized (in a middle-class sense) young person who
is defiant, impulsive, resentful of the treatment accorded him,
and who exercises self-control only when he is likely to be caught
and punished for his need-gratifying actions. His psychic
structure has a familiar pattern that includes a low threshold
for frustration, or the inability to manage the emotions that
accompany frustration. The impulses that arise through

frustration disable the individual and destroy his capacity
to make rational judgments about right and wrong. By the same
token, the delinquent, despite his tough façade, has difficulty
coping with insecurity, anxiety, or fear and may attack when
exposed to these threats. Further, his low resistance to temptation
and his susceptibility to group thinking add little to his stability
as a person.

The individual psychological characteristics of the so-called
delinquent may include a host of other forms of damaged ego
apparatuses. These cripple him in the competition society requires
for success and access to its personal and material benefits.
In our society, the delinquent is caught in a trap. There is a
prevalent myth that the delinquent views his conduct disorder
as a suitable and effective solution to fulfilling his social and
personal needs. Nothing could be further from the truth.
The self-image of the delinquent young person is a thing of
shreds and tatters, ugly to the observer and equally repulsive
to the delinquent. His past is a shabby record of failure and
rejection by others coupled with a raging sense of helplessness
and futility. The future holds no promise, and he can foresee
his career ending in the prison cell he is certain he will occupy
for the best years of his life. The delinquent feels he is rushing
to an inevitable personal catastrophe and that he is being
propelled there by an angry unfeeling society.

Tim C. was well built for a 15 year old. At five feet, ten inches and
165 pounds, it was convincing when Tim "leaned on somebody." Although he actually spent very little time fighting, he devoted most of his
energy to talk of toughness, threats, and inducing fear in others. His conversation seldom strayed far from the topic of aggression, and I often had
the impression that he was imitating a gangster movie. Partly, his size was
his problem. If Tim had grown to be a scrawny, undernourished young
man, his dealings with others and his view of the world might have been
quite different, and, perhaps, he would not have been victimized by situations from which there was no face-saving escape.

I first encountered Tim when he was a patient at a fresh air camp one
summer. When the bus arrived at camp from the juvenile detention home,
Tim, who had somehow promoted a cigar, emerged from the bus door
shouting in a penetrating voice, "Where are the broads they promised
us?" He had been in camp exactly 30 seconds, and I had to take him aside
to talk to him about what we could reasonably expect in the way of con-

trolled behavior for the next eight weeks. Even then he played it cool, giving only what he had to in speech laden with vulgarity. As I pointed out at the time: 1) I knew about him from the detention home, and this attitude had been anticipated when I had asked to have him sent to camp, 2) I had heard a thousand tough kids call me names before and was not impressed hearing it again, and 3) our mutual problem was not to fight with each other but to figure out a way we could live together for the summer, have fun, and stay out of each other's hair in the hot months ahead.

Our hour-long talk (if he had really been cool, he wouldn't have let it last for 10 minutes) had an unexpected impact on him. It was not that he became easy to handle, it was rather that I sensed he was ready for help despite himself. When he went into a rage and had to be controlled physically to keep him from hurting himself or others, he never seemed to struggle quite as hard as I knew he could, nor did he hurt me during the many times when he had me in a bad position to protect myself. Once, after a small-scale riot of defiance in his cabin, I entered the cabin to discover Tim behind the door with a metal chair raised menacingly over his head. Then, he recognized me, and his eyes gave him away. The fraction of a second he hesitated lost him the ball game because now I knew he sweated when he threatened people and he knew I knew it.

Not all of Tim's destructive energy was directed toward people. He and his cabin mates stole the waterfront director's car one night and headed out of camp with it. Their judgment was bad, as it so often was. The car had a faulty carburator and broke down in the middle of the only road out of the camp. He and his gang—we had taken the whole gang together—had stolen many a car and bicycle before, and, far from feeling guilt about such actions, they clearly enjoyed a sense of pride in their accomplishment. When the word spread through camp about what they had done, they became camp heroes who swaggered noticeably as they basked in the admiration of their fellows.

This gang-cabin group, under Tim's leadership, was perversely beautiful to watch in operation. They seemed to have group antennae constantly probing the environment for potential opportunities. What one gang member missed, another was sure to detect. I could cover the 300 acres of the camp and never notice a cigarette butt, but this cabin group, without attracting attention, easily accumulated enough resmokable tobacco at a time to equal several packs. They preferred whole cigarettes, of course, and at least once a week the counselors' quarters were broken into with cigarettes the primary loot. We allowed them to smoke a limited number of cigarettes at specified times under adult supervision after meals and before bedtime, but it was the unlawful thrill they sought.

Tim C. was not a model gang leader. He was a negative leader, most assertive when he was stopping the others from doing things that might be pleasing to the adult world. He never thought up much for the gang to do, but he was full of ideas about what not to do. Interestingly, he had no fist fights while in camp. In our mounting frustration in dealing with him, we sometimes speculated about the possibility that he might be defeated in a fight, but we also recognized that he was much too slick to needle a potential retaliator too much. He was beautiful to watch in action but he was still a poor leader according to middle-class standards of constructiveness.

Tim had a crude but nearly perfect control over his gang. When I had found them out in some delinquent act and closed in to induce confession on the part of psychologically weaker gang members, he sensed at once that he was playing a losing game and secretly signalled to the others. From this point on, no one would talk. I would see them watching him for further signals out of the corners of their eyes, and, even when I would interpret what had happened to the group, it availed me nothing. Even separating the gang members for individual consultation with clinical staff members could not break the group adherence to a code where nobody "squeals." They were afraid, they needed to belong, and this was the price of admission to the gang. Their future promised nothing but trouble and despair, but that was all they had and they stuck to it with a desperation.

Tim was ruggedly handsome. He was big and muscular, but he wore his hair long and carried a soft, pink hairbrush in his back pocket. His hair was never mussed up, and even when he required physical restraint, he would battle for a while and then whip out his hairbrush and use it to regain his composure and his cool. The traces of effeminacy in his make-up were typical of those around him and seemed an unrecognized and unconscious part of himself. This mixture of textures—soft and hard—was difficult to deal with since you never knew which aspect of his personality was uppermost at the moment. Girls thought he was gorgeous, and he was always ready to brag of conquests which took place at a very tender age—nine years old, by his account, but certainly by 12 considering the neighborhood in which he lived.

We survived the summer with Tim at the cost of what seemed like thousands of hours of time devoted to his case. He alternated rapidly and regularly between being impossible and reasonable. Tim intrigued me despite the fact that I had not gotten as close to him as I usually did with other delinquent boys. He intrigued me enough to take him on as a private client for therapy for the year following camp. In one-to-one therapy, Tim changed a lot. He still related hair-raising tales of gang rumbles, which I suspected were more fiction than fact since I could never verify them in my contact with the police or his streetcorner worker. However, these horror stories occupied less of our time than did discussing who and what he was as a person and what life held in store for him.

One day, for example, he began to ask questions about the soundproofing of the office and about how far a loud sound might be heard by others. These questions seemed immaterial to the conduct of his therapy, and I was puzzled until he pulled a revolver out of his jacket pocket. Faced with this seemingly deadly weapon in the hand of a troubled delinquent, I remained calm. I examined the gun, noted that it was not loaded, and interpreted to him my view of the reasons why he felt compelled to frighten me with a gun and described to him what my natural reactions were. It turned out to be a highly productive therapeutic hour in which we got down to what was really bothering him and discussed the nature of how he was responding to the multitude of pressures he felt closing in on him. A little later, I realized how frightened I had actually been at my first glimpse of the revolver.

What he told me was typical of many others. His father was a drunk who got mean on alcohol and beat up Tim's mother. Tim's story of struggles to control his father, of sleepless nights when he feared his father would awaken and begin the fight all over again, of his inability to do school work as he sat in class worrying about what his father might be doing to his mother, whom he revered as a somewhat troublesome saint, and of his decision to be tough, independent, and a better man than his father all tumbled out in a rush after he had threatend me with the ultimate injury.

For the first time I felt we were getting somewhere in therapy. Tim had finally cracked and exposed himself as an oversized kid who wore the mantle of the tough hood very uncomfortably. Beneath the façade of the mean and fearsome punk was the kid who found life hard since he had to arise each morning prepared to fight the world whatever the cost. Tim wanted to escape the role life had thrust upon him but every door he tried seemed locked to him. I was offering an open door to another way on a new and alien path. There was no question that I was offering him an unusually bad deal. I was urging him, in essence, to give up his past patterns of behavior and start a new way of life that would be difficult, sissified, inhibited, and emasculating at first but would, in the long run, be better for him according to powerful middle-class people.

I knew Tim faced, uncomfortably, the biggest decision of his life. He had to decide to abandon his past life and to try a new direction, or he had to reject everything we had discussed in the last year and declare himself an official outlaw. Unfortunately, the latter was the one he chose.

One night as he was "ramming-around" restlessly and senselessly in a friend's car he let the revolver make up his mind for him. It could easily not have happened; any change in the circumstances would have deterred him. But, he did it. When the gas station attendant asked for the money to pay for the gas, he pulled the gun and took $28 from the till because he "didn't like the way the guy acted."

He was caught, of course, because he left a trail a mile wide for the cops to follow. At that time of night, a kid in a car on the expressway would have been suspect anyway, and with his license number and description known, he was begging to be picked up. He was sent to the juvenile detention home for an indeterminate term and was soon playing his old power game with the inmates. The kids there described him as the "king of trouble" and they lauded his defiance of adults as much as they feared he would turn his hostile attention towards them. Despite the armed robbery, he was considered prime material for rehabilitation and was placed, three months later, in a half-way house where he was given more freedom and attended the local school. At this point we resumed therapy on a more frequent basis and the story of Tim C. unfolded in greater detail.

You had to live in Tim's neighborhood to understand the real meaning of terror. As I walked down the street to visit Tim's mother (his father had deserted the family and was not expected back), I felt uncomfortable since it was a Negro ghetto typical of sections in every large American city, and the people sitting on the porches along the way stared at me with open curiosity. I was uneasy because I knew there was no way in which I could communicate the fact that I was there to help, not to hurt. "Whitey" was not received warmly at any time on this street, and although I could understand their feelings, I was sorry it had come to this low point in the relation of one human being to another.

The house looked only mildly decrepit from the outside, so I was not prepared for the shock presented by its inner appearance. When the door to the apartment was opened by Tim's mother, I was greeted by silence and suspicious glances from everyone present. An "uncle" was visiting the mother and, after looking me over, he moved silently to one of the back rooms. Five of Tim's brothers and sisters were watching television in the living room and, as if they shared a common reaction, it was turned off in mid-program and the room was suddenly vacant except for Tim's mother and me. Besides the television set, a couch was the only piece of living room furniture. The floors were bare, a succession of cracks crisscrossed the walls, and the window shades had been drawn as if to close out the rest of the squalid world.

Tim came closest to being a totally loving, fully accepting, unfrightened human being in those moments when he and his younger brothers and sisters laughed and screamed with the pleasure of one another's company. Their mutual joys were simple—ice cream cones for all, a mother in a happy mood, some small success by any one of them, or some ludicrous mishap witnessed by all but suffered by someone else. These infrequent moments could happen unexpectedly, like the crash of an ice cream truck whose strewn contents were left unattended in the excitement. Since those frozen and seldom available delights would become shapeless, soggy masses in the sun, there was some logical justice in

the greedy speed with which the children would claim natural salvage
rights to the distressed cargo.

Some shared pleasures grew sweeter with the waiting. Each February
the Shrine Circus came to town. And, annually, some social worker bent
on pleasing the poor people magically provided them with tickets, begged
in the name of social justice from one charitable organization or another.
When the first pop art posters made their appearance in town, Tim and
his brothers and sisters began to savor the joys in store for them by describing to one another how they would feel as each attraction made its
dramatic and flamboyant way around the oval that passed close to their
seats. So close you could pat an elephant—if you dared.

Their excitement mounted to such a fever pitch that most nights in
January they would cuddle together four in a bed and eight in the room
shivering both with the cold and the thrill of it all. Sometimes these
whispered sharings of secrets would turn to talk of how life would be in
days to come and of what each would be when he grew up. Tim reported
that he would help these moments grow by describing fantastically improbable careers for himself. What he would become was detailed spar-
ingly, but an excessive luxuriance was accorded the description of material
joys that would issue from his future position. The fondest dream of each
sibling was to be realized in a measure beyond imagining and when these
pleasures became unbearable there would be the excruciating addition of
even more, and more, and more, and more. Finally, by age and in an almost absolute order, they would fall asleep, leaving only Tim still awake,
slightly distressed about the beauty of the picture he had painted and the
ugliness of what he knew life really to be. The circus ahead was an ever
renewable experience for all and he knew that tomorrow night they
would again play the same game with pleasure undiminished by repetition.

Tim often felt hurt about being older than the others. They were little
kids and didn't know what was ahead. It was hard being older but he
never could explain it to them. They would have to find out for themselves. He hoped things would change and they would have it easier. It
was not likely.

Tim's mother told me about the trouble he was having in the neighborhood and, as was characteristic, blamed his troubles on bad company. Tim
had always been helpful around the house and would take care of his
brothers and sisters while his mother worked, but, as she said, he seemed
like a different child when he "ran with that gang." As she said,

> Them kids is always gettin him in trouble. They steal stuff
> and sass folks who wasn't bothering them at all. They hang
> around that store and mouth off at everybody that's there on
> real business. He goes out after supper and won't tell me where
> he's going, and I never know when I'm going to see him again.
> When his father was here, I used to tell him to whip Tim but

he never would. He was a no-account man every which way, and he never did nothin around the house and he wouldn't work steady. He said Tim was a punk who wouldn't listen to him and had no place to go but Jacktown [Jackson Prison].

Them police is part of it. When those boys ain't doing nothin' to nobody the fuzz gotta come along and bust em just for the hell of it. They ask em questions and tell em to get off the streets like the streets wasn't public. I don't like Tim to be always hangin' around them places either but the fuzz shouldn't always be after them all the time. If a white boy stood on the corner they wouldn't say nothing about it, but they are always pickin' on us. Why don't they leave us alone? We didn't do nothin' to them.

The teachers at that school are just the same. They always pickin' on him too. They never treat him fair. Even the colored git uppity and tell him to do different than he's doing. He is a good boy and he minds me most of the time. If people would leave him alone he wouldn't have no trouble at all.

This maternal transfer of blame for her child's difficulty was not an unusual phenomenon, nor was it a complaint without merit. It was a one-sided view of cause and effect and failed to take into account that 80 per cent of the children in that neighborhood underwent only minor run-ins with properly constituted authority. Some children exposed to an apparently identical physical environment somehow get armored against the pernicious influence of the danger and chaos in which they grow to adulthood. How this happens is not exactly known, but it indeed happens. Tim's mother was partly right in her appraisal of what it is like to be the Negro victim of "white power" but it was necessary to view the same social setting through Tim's eyes to get the whole picture.

Tim was aware of his mother's anxiety about his companions, the neighborhood, and his late hours, but he also knew something she could never quite understand. Tim had no choice in the matter. Sometimes the family moved to a new street every few months when they couldn't pay the rent, but every street in every neighborhood was just like the one they had just left. The "cats" that "worked the street" were always the same and they always played by the same rules.

Tim was particularly verbal one day and told me what it was like to live there. With some feeling Tim reported,

You get kicked out of one place and you move a couple of blocks to the next pig pen. One of my "uncles" gets a truck and we load up all we got and go somewhere else. After we dump the junk in the new joint, I cruise out cool on the street and look out for whose ass I know I can whip. I'm "bad," man. I'm mean. After I drag the street once, I know what' shakin'. I know whose big and who ain't and what's goin' on. I don't

mess with the guys that can beat me till I find out who's
chicken and then I try a couple of them. I move in slow but
hard and the next day everybody knows. Then they know
"mess with me and you die." Nobody pushes with me and nobody says nothin' about my mother. Man, you got to push or
suck hind titty where I live. I don't suck no hind titty. That's
all. They fool with me and they in a whole world of trouble.
You a whitey. You don't know nothin' about it. You can go
downtown any time and nobody says nothin' to you. I got the
color and I can't go nowhere except with my own kind. You
try it and see how you like it.

Tim's account of the form of his life was an accurate guide to survival.
Tim knew what he had to do and he did it in the grand style. There was
little I could say that would magically alter life as it was for Tim, but I
also knew that Tim was not nearly so enthusiastic about his lot as he sometimes pretended to be. Tim was above average in intelligence, and he perhaps saw things in a somewhat different light. He knew that some of the
others would be ground up by the machine, but he had the strange feeling
that he had a chance. It was a mysterious calculation that he could shake
the life if he could learn to talk to me and trust me.

Trusting "whitey" did not come easily to Tim. This basic trust evolved
slowly at first, but one day when he was at camp, Tim's cabin-mate made
a disparaging remark about his mother and called him some race names.
Tim blew up—he had heard the names before but no punk had the right to
say them to him. Tim had been subtly vying for cabin leadership with
this white boy, and he was not quite sure he could take him in a fair fight.
The white boy played it cool when the explosion took place, so cool that
he waited until I was holding Tim to stop the fight, and then he kicked
Tim and kicked him hard. This perverse act put Tim into a blind rage,
and I was hard-pressed to control him. My glasses got broken in the
scuffle, but I held Tim for an hour and a half before he calmed down
enough to talk about what had happened.

Somehow, I had gained Tim's trust after this extended attempt to injure
and insult me for restraining him. Tim was a magnificent spitter, and he
got me twice. That I did not blow up and hurt him physically or lose my
temper was so unexpected that Tim could hardly cope with it. It was
strange for him to see that a white adult could control him without taking
revenge. Even more convincing was the fact that Al R., a Negro senior
staff member watched unconcerned as I controlled Tim C. At first Tim
accused Al of being an Uncle Tom (hardly appropriate since Al was the
local president of CORE) who let "white-folk" push on him. Finally, Tim
learned that control of a berserk child was not a civil rights or racially
tinged issue; it was, rather, a matter of proper versus improper behavior—
of reasonableness versus unreasonableness.

Whenever Tim got into serious trouble from then on he would insist on talking to me. Tim had learned that some adults could control him without counteraggression, rage, or hatred. Tim had learned he could get a fair shake from someone whose skin color differed from his own. It was on the basis of this primitive trust in me that therapy was begun again. If Tim could keep out of serious trouble for the next few years he had every chance of making it and being someone other than what he seemed destined to be. If life were to deal him many more bad cards it would be inevitable that Tim would lose the game.

Tim was nearly 16 now and these years were to be crucial ones. I worked desperately to remove him permanently from his hopeless street and to introduce him to a different way of life. At a half-way house there is hope for Tim because he is bright enough to learn new ways of reacting and new patterns of behavior. I am confident that Tim can make it, but it will require resources that go beyond what I can offer. I hope he makes it because he represents thousands of others trapped by misfortune. Tim had indeed been dealt a bad hand for most of the years of his life but the half-way house offered him a new deal along with lessons on how to play bad cards for all they are worth. I worry about whether Tim has enough time and resources left to make the proper moves but I worry more about the multitude of brothers and sisters he leaves behind him. If Tim makes it, maybe they will too.

Despite substantial evidence to the contrary, I continue to wish that the social refuse of our culture might somehow find its way over the inordinate set of hurdles in its path to become what it is capable of being. There is truly little hope for Tim C., much as I hate to admit it. He hangs perilously by his finger-tips on the edge of a society ready, without mercy, to relegate him to the garbage heap. He must be exceptional, not just ordinary, when he is allowed entry once more to civilized life. He may not have the needed resources for this effort. Brightness and all, he may be incapable of doing what has to be done.

To Be or Not To Be

–MATT T.

PROLOGUE *Homosexual experiences are common,* if infrequent,
among males, especially those of adolescent age. We will limit
our discussion here to male homosexuality. When mature males
find themselves deprived of women, or when immature males
become aware of their ineptness in social-sexual congress, the
urgency of physical and psychological desires drives them to
seek satisfaction with whatever means and objects are
immediately available. The ways in which homosexuality is
experienced may range from not at all or a single homosexual
contact to a life of mixed sexual pleasure or a career of
exclusively homosexual relationships. One estimate lists only
4 per cent of the male population as exclusively homosexual,
but notes that 50 per cent of unmarried males 35 years of age
or older have had such experience.

There is a "gay world" populated by homosexuals in every
major city in America and, on a less obvious level, in every
university in the country. Its members are neither easily
recognized nor marked by the stereotype of the male dressed as a
female and imitating secondary female characteristics. To the
homosexual, another member of the group is immediately
detectable; to the bulk of society only the extremes are apparent.
Categorizing homosexuals as passive or active is not accurate

since such relationships occur in varying degrees and ways for most homosexuals. It is as incorrect as describing heterosexuality in similarly stereotyped terms. It takes all kinds and there are all kinds.

In marshalling social support for homosexuality (or as the Mattachine Society of homosexuals would have it, at least neutrality on the part of society) reference is often made to historical figures known to have been homosexual—Michelangelo, Lord Byron, Oscar Wilde, Julius Caesar, Edward II, Alexander the Great, many of the early Greeks and so on. These historical claims to legitimacy are irrelevant, however, since they constitute a famous, but tiny minority of our population, and seem to suggest that greatness in one field somehow makes deviant sexual behavior acceptable to the majority.

The real problem is that homosexuals are social outcasts who live in constant fear of arrest and punishment, persecuted by a middle-class authority that finds them reprehensible. The avowed homosexual becomes a clinical and psychotherapeutic problem when he is accosted by the authorities or when his feelings of guilt, jealousy, or anxiety become predominant characteristics of his way of life. Becoming a homosexual is no more or less complicated than the process of becoming a heterosexual. It differs primarily in the opposition with which society treats homosexuals.

In Orwell's *1984*, heterosexual activity is punished by measures similar to those taken against homosexual activity today. It is this strange circumstance that presents the clearest picture of this issue in psychopathology.

Imagine, for a brief moment, how you would adjust to and deal with others if heterosexuality were to be outlawed and considered reprehensible. What would you do? How would you feel? Where would you go, and how would you signal other heterosexuals that you were available for this experience? The situation of a fictional outlawing of heterosexuality is not quite identical to the plight of the homosexual. It takes centuries of persecution to provide the guilt and anxiety so often experienced by homosexuals. Their problem is, in part, this persecution, but it is more important to note that they are, almost invariably, unhappy. This unhappiness stems from a basic maladjustment of which homosexuality is a part. Added to this, they do not experience an equivalent of heterosexual love. The predominant and regularly visible fact of homosexual love affairs is that they often resemble the emotional interchange of young adolescents only partly mature. Homosexual love is intense but infantile, and so insecure that it is almost always doomed to failure and disappointment. Man-to-man love is fickle, and two jealous males can seldom work out a stable relationship.

Homosexuality starts in the family circle and there its mold is cast. It may develop through anxiety about sex, immersion in a totally feminine world, and disastrous social and sexual contacts with females. The relationship of mother, father, and male child is the crucial element. A passive father and an aggressive and dominant mother create problems of identification and life patterning. Unable to accept the masculine role and unable to comprehend his feeling of revulsion toward women, the homosexual goes through life a potential victim of an even more gross pathology. His homosexual orientation began at the same moment that he learned guilt and inadequacy. It is in this arcane chemistry that an excessive reaction is formed, and clues to its mysteries still evade us.

ONE AFTERNOON in the fall of the year, Matt T. called me and insisted with frantic urgency that he must be seen *now* and not a minute later. Matt was sandy-haired, and slightly bald but he brushed his hair back in what looked like an attempt to cover more of his barren scalp. While some of his mannerisms were effeminate, they were set in such an overwhelmingly articulate context that the impression was not particularly intrusive or remarkable. His pattern of speech was probably his most distinctive characteristic. He spoke with a forced, driven, explosive quality that reduced me to nodding in a vain attempt to indicate a general state of comprehension of his presentation. The longer I remained silent the more frantic became his verbal outpouring. Finally he ended the anxious mixture of rage and self-revelation with the plea "What can I do?"

As quickly as Matt begged for help, he reversed himself and launched into an extended defense of his homosexual inclinations. Matt flitted from one assumption to another and jumped to arguable and unwarranted conclusions with ease. As he indicated, in mythology the mermaid was half-woman and half-fish, and it was her bottom half that lost its human characteristics. The Medusa, he noted, was described as half-male and half-female, and even Adam was bisexual with one of his ribs becoming woman. Both Bible themes and Greek history dealt frequently with homosexuality, and Matt used this observation as a defense of his condition. At this point I attempted to stem the torrent of words pouring out of Matt, saying,

> Matt, we are wasting a great deal of time detailing the abstract background of homosexuality. As you probably guessed, I am familiar with this information. I can't help but feel that this lecture on the nature of homosexuality is unlikely to change my basic understanding of the problem. It may be necessary for you to go on like this, however, if you really don't want to talk about you and why you came to me. Let's stop discussing sexuality in general terms and talk about what's bothering you. You have demonstrated to me that you are bright, well-read, cultured, and sophisticated. You have also made it clear that you are very upset about something. What is it?

What I had done, essentially, was to interpret his behavior as a defense against revealing what was bothering him. In doing so I had treated him somewhat like a child who was putting up an effusive smoke screen to disguise his real behavior. I had deliberately taken away from him the approach he found most comfortable, and I hoped by this device to get at the basic problem. It worked but I knew I had made no more than a lucky guess about what would be effective at that moment.

Matt's account of his problem was a complicated one and some of the details have been crowded out of my memory by the barrage of words, thoughts, and feelings in which I was immersed during the time of our meetings. Matt's view of his own history and current difficulties went as follows:

> Probably, no one is really, truly to blame for my miserable and distressing condition, but, as I search my available consciousness for some clue to the origin of my horrendous life, I know emotionally that that nun my mother did this to me. She was such a demanding and forbidding person! Nothing seemed to please her! She was a cold bitch as I remember her, and she has become a withered old prune now! She is a dreadful person, and I just hate her!
>
> I could never talk to her about anything, and I always felt she disapproved of me as a human being. ı never had the feeling she was real. She looked like the wrath of God to me always sitting in judgment on others. She castrated my father and made a eunuch out of him, you know. He just sits there talking the sheerest of nonsense and babbles on and on till I could scream. He has become an absolute zero as a person. He was never anything, and I never listened to him. He doesn't know anything about anything but he always has some stupid thing to say about issues he can never comprehend. It makes me sick to talk to him and I swear we have spoken our last words to one another. He is a sorry figure—an imitation really

—of a person and I'll be glad when he is dead and gone.

My real problem is not my parents; it is the beast I am living with. He is shameless and he is terrible. I don't know why I always fall in love with his kind. They are always absolutely unreliable and unbearable most of the time. It is really true that you can't live with them and can't live without them, and they are all the same. He loafs around the apartment and won't pay any attention to me even though I do everything I can to please him. I leave him little presents to open and I cook for him, and then the first new thing that comes along seems to fascinate him and he is off and out all night probably doing horrible things. I don't like to nag him but you would think he could be considerate of me once in a while. He won't even wear his ring and I know he does it just to peeve me. I hate him but I'm afraid he'll leave like the others. I'm not getting any younger and even now I think he is using me until he can find something better. He's nothing but a beast and a psychopath. He doesn't care about theater at all; he just likes to hang around those of us who are real theater.

At this point Matt was describing his lover Eric in the familiar terms of a whining, nagging, neurotic wife whom no sexual object could make happy. I had seen Eric briefly and he was, to my eyes, indistinguishable from the bearded, unwashed, pseudo-artistic hangers-on to be found as camp followers with any theatrical group. The members of this pretentious and self-consciously "different" group earn their keep by shifting scenery, doing walk-ons, and idling in the "green room" discussing acting technique with painful earnestness. They were interns in a make-believe world, and they survived by preying on the good will and favors of those in power. Eric was an emotional parasite who did what he did extremely well—live off others while waiting to discover who or what he was. Eric was also interested in the long-and-stringy-haired, blue-jeaned, sweat-shirted female version of himself. He was bisexual and a taker, not a giver, in both kinds of relationships.

This was the great romance that was tearing Matt T. to shreds. Since the reality seemed so different from the fantasy as reported by Matt, it was evident that the gap between them was being filled by the painful press of Matt's personal needs. What Matt needed from life at this moment in the way of reassurance, emotional support, and a feeling of being wanted was so demanding that it both altered his perception of the truth and made him ready to distort reality to whatever shape his satisfaction required. Love in any form is a kind of very pleasurable illness. Those afflicted by the emotional turmoil of love react in ways that would certainly be described as disordered by either the sexual or professional observer, and Matt T. was a perfect illustration, even if the object of his affection was another male. Emotions are no respecters of convention-

ality and cultural mores—the love of one male for another is subject to all
and more of the trials and tribulations of an intense passion.

Guilt rather than amorousness was Matt's difficulty. His love affairs
were riddled with anxiety because he felt demeaned, degraded, and
shamed by his impulses. He knew he was a social deviant, subject to criticism by others; he resented and was hurt by his status as something less
than a full-blooded, all American male. Had Matt had no regrets and had
Matt never felt the pangs of remorse about life as he led it, he would
never have come to me in the first place. Matt was being torn apart by
his feeling that he was failing to meet the expectations of his parents, his
peers, and those he hoped to impress.

Matt had recently undergone a series of psychological experiences that
had frightened him so much that in his panic, he had insisted on my
seeing him. First, he had cooked a meal that had produced severe stomach
cramps. Fearing that he had fatally poisoned himself, he fell to his knees
praying fervently and begging whatever gods might exist to spare him this
ignominious fate. Second, on a shopping trip for his lover he had suddenly
undergone a severe delusional and hallucinatory experience in which he
was certain he had been transformed into a female. At first he luxuriated
in the experience and sashayed for several blocks feeling "utterly female."
Then, suddenly, he felt he was a bisexual Martian sent to observe earth
life and to report on its quaint customs. Finally, Matt had visions of the
sudden death of his mother and father. He "saw" them being buried in
adjacent graves and himself weeping copiously at the funeral. These
closely packed series of events frightened him, and he felt compelled to
tell me of them.

The evolution of Matt's homosexuality to this final sad state of affairs
was unspectacular and subtle. As a child he had always been very neat and
clean, and he had preferred the company of girls in his neighborhood
because all the boys were rough and dirty. His mother made him stay
away from some of the tougher boys near his home and, after a while, he
felt about them the way his mother did. This preference for the company
of females had a firm basis in his experience. Matt was a frail and a pretty
child much admired by a covey of doting aunts who rewarded both his
natural good looks and his girl-like behavior. His male cousins, envious at
how admired he was by adults, looked forward to the signal that it was time
for the children to go out and play together while the elders talked. This
moment would produce a sinking feeling in Matt since he knew the outcome of this play would be physical and emotional torture for him at the
hands of his revenge-seeking male relatives.

Boys knew almost instinctively that he was a sissy who would not fight
back. In any group of young children, there are always girls who have
begun to evaluate the attractiveness of males according to their toughness,
fearlessness, bravado, and physical skill. Matt became a point-getter for

more adventurous, fearless, and girl-conscious boys. These boys knew that by abusing Matt they enhanced their own status in the eyes of girls at the same time that they nourished their own underfed ego. With each punishment visited on him by other boys, Matt drifted further and further from the feeling that he was one of them.

By adolescence, Matt's attitudes, interests, skills, and patterns of behavior leaned more to the feminine than the masculine side. His status as a social boy-girl was joked about in high school and he, along with the others, came to admire the swashbuckling, all American male heroes each school has. Matt hoped desperately one of them would notice him and include him in the inner circle of those who were admired and imitated. Matt tried to be "one of the boys" but he could never carry it off very convincingly. Matt double dated, for example, with other couples. At these times he engaged in a painful charade of pretense about his masculinity. He treated everything with innuendo and double meaning and played the part of a young and vigorous sex maniac. In the back seat of a car, he acted out the part of a leering, sneering Romeo who was not to be denied by the innocence of his date. Matt's painful and inept attempts to press home his demands met with a predictable fate: girls laughed, boys laughed, Matt was systematically tortured by all his so-called friends.

Once, for example, a group of boys played an elaborate practical joke on Matt in which a local girl of questionable morals was induced to date Matt and to pretend that his wit and charm were so overwhelming that she would succumb to any demand. Matt was taken in by this sudden conquest and pleasured himself at the party with half-realistic fantasies of a masculine attractiveness he had always desired but never had. The moment of horrifying truth came when Etoile reacted aggressively to his pretended masculinity. To the cruel and somewhat pathological pleasure of the other boys, Etoile tried to get him to perform sexually in full public view. Boys who had dates had left the party by this time and Matt was just dimly aware that only he, Etoile, and the stag line were left in the house. While this organized spectacle might well diminish any male's ability to perform, it was disastrous to Matt. He shrieked and screamed in outrage, but this reaction only made the torture more savory for the others. They removed Matts trousers and had Etoile molest him in a number of ways. From then on, Matt maintained a purely platonic relationship with all females, signalling clearly to them that he was harmless and would be undemanding sexually. He was popular as an escort who would be attentive, charming, and not dangerous.

These bitter experiences soured Matt on the cultural definition of masculinity. He gave up and became a male-female visible to all. Matt's native intelligence, good taste, and sensitivity to the feelings of others found its outlet in writing plays and in the direction and production of theatrical efforts. Although he was respected for his ability, Matt never found his success an adequate substitute for being a male. Men who had managed to fulfill the cultural model of masculinity became increasingly attractive to him as a means of vicariously experiencing some part of what he could never be. A seemingly strong, beautiful, self-assured male actor would trigger a wave of emotions in Matt centered on passionate love and an overpowering need for total care and acceptance. Matt would plan his campaign carefully, and he always judged correctly that many virile-looking males were overly concerned with their external beauty. A beautiful façade was exactly that—a façade so no one could see within.

These "apes," as Matt called them, were gorgeous but without a shred of intellectual depth. They needed desperately what he had, just as he needed to be close to what they appeared to be. All in all it seemed to me to be a magnificent matching of weaknesses.

Matt went from affair to affair constantly troubled by the superficiality and impermanence of them. On closer acquaintance, these friendships dissolved because each partner was counting on the other to fill some void in his life. These mutual voids were, of course, unfillable since they had, neurotically, little to do with the realities of life. They were early problems unresolved by the process of growth and maturation. Each entered the sexual partnership with unrealistic expectations of what the outcome would be and with fantasy-distorted notions of how the new affair would eliminate problems long unsolved. With two grossly immature persons seeking frantically for answers to the riddle of life, there was little reason to anticipate that security and satisfaction would be the outcome for either.

Matt's professional productivity deteriorated with his unfortunate love affairs. A talented genius of the theater had the freedom to be socially or sexually eccentric, but a failure did not. As Matt's formerly unerring sense of the original and the creative began to fade, the volume of criticism increased and contributed further to his destruction as a human being. The sycophants and hangers-on whom he thought to be his friends soon deserted him for a new set of rising stars, and Matt found himself alone and friendless again. Matt feared old age and dreaded the time when he would be unattractive to males and would have to take whatever he could get in the way of sexual partners. It was so demeaning to have to beg and to take the castoffs of other more attractive people that Matt tried to stay perpetually young. In this he failed miserably.

Singly and collectively, these anxieties began to oppress Matt and the resilience with which he usually rebounded from them was now lacking a certain snap and vigor. Matt got depressed about his life and began to worry about having burned himself out at a tender age. He talked in a vague but grandiose manner about "going to Europe to write" and of "hiding out in Maine for six months to find myself again." Both solutions involved running away from life and from those who knew him best, but he was not to be dissuaded from this course of action. I felt then that Matt was running scared and had ceased to deal constructively with a world he felt was closing in on him. Matt called his former analyst in New York and had a long and incoherent conversation with him quite late one night. Even later that evening Matt's therapist called me and we jointly concluded that Matt's current difficulties were more grave than any he had previously undergone.

With the help of Matt's analyst I laid out a course of action calculated to restore Matt to a better balance in life. This plan, unfortunately, was never carried out. Matt disappeared (leaving the theatrical company in desperate straits) and was next heard from in New York. Matt's mother called me and said that he had returned home confused and incoherent, mumbling threats against others and spelling out plans to end his own life. I tried to contact Matt by phone but he refused to answer for almost a week. Finally, he talked to me, but it was obvious that his condition had deteriorated even further, and that he was on the brink of some serious turning point in his life.

Matt was last seen alive by a friend who met him in a professional building muttering that all his teeth were falling out and that he thought he had cancer of the mouth. He told his friend that he was on the way to a dental appointment at the moment and that he was planning shortly to write a film adaptation of several plays of Shakespeare.

Shortly after this encounter, Matt was "pushed or fell" from the twentieth story of the professional building. Matt died ignonimiously in the airshaft of a New York skyscraper and brought his life to the only conclusion that would free him from anxiety and guilt. I knew that as Matt fell to his death he had few regrets. Life held nothing but pain and misery for him, and this was his way out.

Where Did You Go on Your Trip?

–BERNIE F.

PROLOGUE   *Statistics on the use* of LSD (d-lysergic acid
diethylamide) are almost impossible to gather accurately.
LSD has, along with marijuana, become the drug of choice for
literate middle- and upper middle-class college students who seek
truth in inner experience rather than outer interpersonal
encounter. Among LSD ingesters are some of the brightest,
most able, and economically privileged of our young people.

LSD is not known to be addictive although a number of
researchers suspect that it is habit-forming and that it creates a
psychological dependence on solitary, personal, biochemical
experience in which the "acid-eater's" attention and energies are
turned inward and away from the outer world. Microscopic
amounts of the drug (300,000 individual doses can be contained
in a single ounce of LSD) are capable of producing vivid and
intense emotional, sensory, and cognitive alterations of conscious
experience. The effect of LSD ingestion has been described as
psychotomimetic (mimics a psychosis) or hallucinogenic
(capable of producing hallucinatory experiences). It is a sacred,
truth-giving biochemical to its advocates who look to LSD
as the mystic means of achieving the millennium of self-insight
for man.

Anxiety about LSD parties on the campus has suddenly

displaced fears of beer blasts, panty raids, and sexual experimentation in the minds of parents, housemothers, and college administrators. What is most worrisome is the sense of defiance and rule rejection that is communicated by the act of drugging oneself and defending the right to do so. The philosophy is negative—withdrawal inside oneself as life's answer—noninvolvement in life to achieve a kind of negative indentity in which it is better to be bad or at the bottom rather than nothing at all. For the "acid heads" life is all style and no content, and it has little need for other people.

Every young person must one day grapple with the issue of who and what he is. LSD offers some the illusion of choice in the discovery of truth. For the college student free of parents for perhaps the first time, LSD suggests a quick chemical answer to this quest for identity. LSD may appeal to the user for other reasons. Its use is illegal, secretive, "in," and antiadult. The movement has its own language to distinguish the "ins" from the "outs" and to bar those over thirty from initiation into its secret rites.

The acid scene is one in which the user can "freak freely" either alone or with fellow cultists. While "making or digging the scene" he feels for perhaps the first time in his life a sense of true belonging and acceptance by others. He has achieved the ultimate in snobbery, a feeling of superiority, and the freedom to express prejudice—the world is nicely divided into two camps, one containing the square majority and the other peopled by the hip minority.

The frequently voiced concern is that LSD most often falls into the hands of those with many problems, those who are least capable of managing it. In state after state, users and suppliers of the drug are breaking the law. The question remains whether such laws can be enforced effectively since this odorless, colorless, tasteless chemical is almost impossible to detect and can be manufactured with a fair amount of ease in any college chemistry laboratory. Since the takers of LSD produce little social disorder and have access to social, legal, and political power, they present a particularly complex problem for authorities to solve.

Listing LSD habituation as a personality disorder marked by a trait disturbance is a decision based on my recent acquaintance with those who have taken LSD and reported the experience

to me, and with those who are the most vocal defenders of
everyone's freedom to drug himself if he so desires. These cases,
without exception, have involved young persons who are
alienated from both peer and adult society and are searching
for answers to barely understood questions. This sample of cases
is undoubtedly a biased one but my experience to date has been
less than reassuring. Even without the frightening experience
of a "bad trip" with LSD, these young persons would have sought
help eventually.

BERNIE WAS an artsy-craftsy type. She dug Origami, esoteric wines, for-
eign movies, anything high-camp, happenings, total self-expression, and
honesty in interpersonal communication. She pitied, but barely tolerated,
her other self, candlelighting, husband-hunting, sentiment loving, well-
scrubbed, well-mannered, but artificial. Bernie was, with obsessive calculation, all the things her other half was not and she was proud but
just a trifle defensive about it. In the first few hours of contact with her
I speculated about the possible psychological consequences of her eventual
discovery that she unconsciously hungered for the very things she most
despised. The tissue separating love and hate is always delicate and easily
torn, and it looked as though, in her case, the thin veil was about to be
ripped to shreds.

Bernie would never have come to see me, but she got scared about a
recent LSD trip that "took her to the dark side of her soul" and persisted
without relief for five days. She was literally and figuratively "in a sweat"
about life, and she presented an odd mixture of hostility toward me as a
representative of the establishment and resentment about her need for
help, support, and succor from a "middle-aged square."

There was, in addition, an evangelistic quality to her description of her
exploration of inner space. As Bernie said,

> Like, you can't understand at all! You've never been turned
> on so it's like talking to a statue about how flowers smell; it's
> like shouting to a tombstone that it's raining outside. It's like
> you can live and die and not live at all. It's how you feel talk-
> ing to a four-year-old about what life is like.
>
> It's like learning about Santa Claus. All of a sudden they let
> you in on a big secret. Everybody knew about it, but nobody
> would let you in on it until you got old enough or began to be
> suspicious. But I found a treasure my folks never heard about.
>
> I never could talk to them about anything real or they
> would make a joke of it and start to squirm. I used to talk
> about stuff at the dinner table that would embarrass them and

then I would pretend I didn't see the looks they gave each other. They figured I would grow out of everything—but everything! One time I told them I was reading the Tibetan Book of the Dead and was studying Zen to make sense out of life. All they said was that before long I'd be married and forget all about that foolishness.

You know, one time I got a C— in English composition from this creepy Professor. He said I wrote like an illiterate Mickey Spillane. I was so damn mad I could have spit. He wouldn't know good writing if it fell on him, the queer. I told him he couldn't find his rear end with both hands if the lights went out and stalked out of there. That night I had a funny dream about how I married the head of the English department and he had to come crawling around me to get ahead. Boy, did I love it as I played it cool and watched him squirm! I remember asking him if he had published anything lately, and in my dream I could see him blush with shame.

The dream was like what I would imagine would happen if my folks found out I was "turning on" every weekend and breathing pot once in awhile. They'd be sorry but I would just play it cool and superior and tell them, "You simply can't understand so there is no point in trying to explain."

At this juncture I pointed out that so far in the hour she had mentioned that I was too square to comprehend what she had experienced taking LSD, that her parents had never taken her seriously, that one professor had suggested she was a pseudo intellectual with writing pretensions, and that her sorority-sisters were sickening and pompous. "With all these strikes against us," I asked, "why are you here telling me this?"

It was then she started to cry, and between swearing and sobbing blurted out how frightened she had become when she couldn't end the last trip she had taken.

"Scared of what?" I asked.

"Scared that maybe there's something wrong with me or that I could get into trouble," she answered.

"What could be wrong with you, and what kind of trouble could you get into?"

Well, part of it has gone a little too far for me. A while ago one of the guys figured it would be cool if we all stripped to the waist and danced during the trip. I thought it was a dumb idea but I didn't want to be square so I went along with the others. I was embarrassed at first so I kept my brassiere on for a while till I started travelling. Then, it seemed exactly right and perfectly natural. I felt free and unrestrained for the first time in my life and I felt like I could dance for a week. We didn't really do anything—like it wasn't an orgy or anything. I felt

weird. I felt like we all belonged to the same fraternity—Lambda
Sigma Delta. My belonging to a fraternity struck me funny and I
laughed for a long time. But, I can't remember what was so hilarious about the thought. Finally, I stripped down to my pants
and the guys were in their shorts. It didn't last long though because everybody started to drift away and stare at this big can-
dle we lit when we began the trip. We always did that as a
kind of "in" thing to signal we were all together and the "meeting" was under way. Lighting candles sounds a little corny,
but it always made me feel better—like we all belonged together and were part of one consciousness, one mind, and one
body.

"And the trouble you could get into?"

Well, it's like I said—going too far. When I get up on the cube
I don't care what I do, and it's only after a few days that I feel
filthy. It's like I haven't taken a shower for a month and I am
crawling with crud. Then, when my friends come around and
tell me when the next bus is going to leave for LSD land I feel
like I'm with it and everybody else doesn't know about Santa
Claus. I look around the library when I get the message and I
feel like I am better than them. Like they don't know the time
of day.

"What's that got to do with trouble?" I asked.
"Well, take Ted for example."

Ted, I learned, was the leader of the local "acid heads," not so much
because he differed in any visible way from the rest of the members of
the congregation, but because he had a friend who seemed to have an
unlimited supply of LSD. It was highly probable that his friend was a
chemistry major who had been displaying a new found enthusiasm for
late night experimentation in the chemistry lab. The only legal distributor
of LSD, Sandoz Pharmaceuticals, Inc, had not only cut off LSD supplies to
accredited researchers, but it had called back the unused portion of ship-
ments it had sent in the past. If you knew the right people, of course,
frequent trips were available and cost only five dollars. Nobody knew for
sure who was making it, selling it, buying it, or using it but it was *de
rigueur* to pretend that you knew all but said nothing.

The whole affair became more exciting with the realization that a
first conviction for possession of LSD was punishable by a year in jail as a
misdemeanor, but a second offense was a felony and the sentence doubled.

Ted moves like he is hoping the fuzz will pick him up and
make a big deal about his traffic with LSD. He looks and acts
like he is ready to be a martyr and can hardly wait till they
get the cross up. He sits like he was a holy man shoved into the
wrong century. He's like an LSD rabbi. He even holds the

cubes funny, like they were a magic potion to be administered
to the unwashed masses and we have to wait around till he gets
through being mystical and blessing the damn sugar. He scares
me because he is not travelling just for kicks, he is pushing the
stuff as a way of life. He reminds me of Raymond Massey.
Remember, they used to say that Raymond Massey had played
Abraham Lincoln so long that he could only be happy if somebody assassinated him? Ted's like that. If they don't catch him
he won't be anything but a perpetual graduate student who
couldn't make it in the academic world. I wouldn't be surprised
if he tipped the cops and got us all hauled in for scandal time
just to be somebody big.

"So," I observed, "you are afraid that the other 'acid heads,' or at
least Ted, are working from a psychological agenda that is different from
your own and it frightens you. Where do we go from here? What do
your close friends think about what you are doing?"

Well, Gerry B., the guy I like most, has gone all the way with
me in this, but he has been bugging me about everything lately.
He's not too nuts about the way I dress and he thinks when I
smoke my pipe that I am trying to kid everybody. He wonders
whether I am phony, but I know I'm not. He's a nice guy and
absolutely honest about how he feels about things. He is going
to be an engineer which is pretty square to start with, and I
know he thinks we are sick. He doesn't get "with it" like
everybody else, but he is tolerant and a good sport. I think he
would try to change me if we got married, and I wouldn't dig
that scene at all.

The second and third therapeutic hours were repetitions of the first
with the addition of a series of details about LSD sessions and a colorful
exposition of the emotional and cognitive effects of LSD ingestion. Her
word pictures were startling and somewhat unsettling since such raw
fantasy material is most often produced by overt psychotics. The difference here was the deepening sense of insecurity and anxiety Bernie F. was
experiencing about the bind in which she found herself. If she found the
ultimate answer it would be too difficult to face squarely without help.

Finally, I shared my impressions with Bernie F. I told her that I thought
she was caught up in a social and psychological set of pressures that she
was ill-equipped to manage. She was experiencing guilt in a classic fashion
and was unable to shake the feeling despite her "cool" philosophy. I told
her that it was my impression that she needed parental supervision more
than she was willing to admit, that she was jealous of her "square" peers,
and was frightened by the way she succumbed to the temptations of the
group to which she had become attached. At first she reacted violently
to each interpretation and resumed her original assault on my personality

and character. In time she softened and became less defensive as she began to appraise her goals and seek something that would give meaning to her life.

The case has yet to be resolved. Bernie F. still sees me twice a week. Now she is a junior and is "turning on less" and studying more, and has removed her academic probation this semester. She continues to attribute these changes to accident and luck, but I suspect she has begun to substitute a more traditional set of values for those she previously held. She has used therapy as a wedge to move herself, philosophically, from one position to another but is not yet ready to admit it. She came to therapy wearing a dress the other day but insisted she had done so only because she was going to a dance later on. She was met with hostility from the members of the LSD group when she informed them about her therapy. Her delight in reporting this hostility is prognostic of even greater changes to come but she is not ready to face the full implication of her feelings.

My guess is that she will drift away from the LSD eaters over a period of time. She has reported that she failed to attend one party because she had, of all things, a sick headache. How much insight she will gain about this period of her young life is uncertain. My suspicion is that she plans to isolate it in her memory in such a way that she can recall the best of it, forget the worst of it, and use it as a badge of a liberated early life. I think she will, eventually, settle for conventionality and the square life but will always have these moments as a hidden treasure. If she marries Gerry B., which seems likely, she will have more to share and less to hide.

I have the feeling that treating her is very much like talking to the flapper of the 1920's. The right girl at the wrong time in history, a victim of a transitional time in our culture.

Bernie wants to be a person in her own right and wishes to be treated as a human being first and a woman second. Bernie wants this desperately, but she has serious conflict about accepting either of these roles wholeheartedly. Torn between the middle-class feminine ideal—prim, proper, deodorized, stylized—and its protest version—masculine, unwashed, defiant, long-haired—Bernie was unable to make a clear choice. She viewed society's response to the female as an attempt to cast her in a role subservient to the male. Bernie rebelled against this image of second-class citizenship by denying that she fit the social definition of the female. She looked like a man, she acted like a man, she thought like a man, but she still felt the deep-rooted twinges of femininity within her.

Bernie clearly overreacted to the problems life posed for her and cast her lot with those who, in one form or another, protested but offered no positive, alternative program. For all its mysticism, the fact remains that LSD ingesters are running away from life and hiding from real problems and pressures. Bernie could have involved herself in any number of active social protest movements, but she chose to run from commitment by turning her psychic energies in on herself to wallow in a world of self-indulgence and introspection. LSD allows its victims to avoid facing problems and this was what Bernie sought most ardently.

Bernie, however, was still attached to the pleasures of being a member of the affluent middle classes. The well-educated middle-class woman is a very desirable marital choice for the status seeking male. He needs a socially appropriate mate, one who knows the rules of social living. By going "beat," Bernie succeeded exceptionally well in keeping at arm's length males who threatened to undermine her protest by approaching her with offers of marriage and a return to the life she thought she had left behind. Bernie's dress and behavior provided her with an immunity from conflict about her way of life. As long as she communicated exclusively with her group of fellow beats, she could casually dismiss the remaining 99 per cent of the population as square and insensitive. She could, thus, neatly divide the world into clear-cut categories of good guys and bad guys. The good guys were identified by their beards and beat costumes, and, with carefully calculated avoidance of the others, Bernie never had to trouble herself with disturbingly contradictory evidence that might suggest that her categories were oversimplifications of the facts of life.

Two other benefits accrued to Bernie by avoiding contact with those not in the cool 1 per cent. For Bernie it meant, first, deliverance from temptation. Bernie really feared that, if she got too close to the enemy emotionally, she would fold up and surrender without a fight. She sensed, somehow, that her rejection of the square world was a temporary phase in her life. She was a "practicing beat" but she needed a lot more practice before very many people would believe her performance and applaud it. Like a drunk who is wisely advised to stay out of bars, Bernie could protect her shaky convictions only by avoiding contact with contradiction.

A second dividend for Bernie was feeling for the first time in her life completely superior to the vast majority of the human race. This feeling of superiority had labels tacitly accepted as accurate by all the members of the "in" group. To be "in" meant one was, by definition, intellectually set apart, creative, original, independent, a clear thinker, and a supersensitive organism. In order to assure one another that this group self-appraisal amounted to something more than a narcissistic and infantile denial of reality, the single topic of conversation among members of the clan was the squareness, hopelessness, stupidity, and inability to comprehend that marked all those not included in the inner circle.

Total, blinding intolerance was the prime characteristic of this group. Membership required massive conformity, so getting in was difficult because one had to adhere to a catechism of proper likes, dislikes, and beliefs ranging across politics, art, music, literature, and so on. The one thing these people could least tolerate was protest against the form, kind, or quality of their protest. Once in, it was still not easy. To stay there required constant attention to the ever-shifting sands of fad and fashion in thought and behavior. "Ins" were in constant danger of finding themselves "out" if they zigged intellectually when they should have zagged. The square world had more constancy about it, but it lacked the thrill of defiance and deviation. There was a ludicrous quality about the whole arrangement of obsessive and nervous conformity to nonconformity.

Prior to therapy, Bernie had not had the capacity to move out of herself long enough to take an objective look at what she was doing and why. She was careful to avoid seeing herself as others saw her, and it was only when she had gone too far for her own comfort that she came for help. As she gained greater insight into the motivation for her protest, and as her view of herself became clearer, Bernie began to behave on a more rational and less grossly emotional basis.

As I reviewed my case notes, I concluded that it was highly probable that Bernie would have found her own way out of this temporary maze. It would have taken much longer and would, perhaps, have caused her to suffer a sharper and more painful set of anxieties but, like so many young persons, she had the psychological resilience to cope even with this. Most of the liberals, anarchists, and nihilists of college age become (perhaps unfortunately) the fairly average responsible citizens who live to deplore the antics of the generations that follow them. Youth is, as it should be, a time for exploration and definition of self. Bernie F. tried to find out who she was by violently altering her chemistry. She combined protest with withdrawal from others, and she had failed. The drugged alteration of the way she was did nothing to change the way life was.

Now Bernie is making changes in herself, and, as she becomes a different person, her impact on the world about her has been altered measurably. The world changes as she changes and it is becoming livable, in part, because she is learning how to live comfortably in it. My feeling is that she has resumed the process of maturation, and this temporary arrest in her development has come to an end. She is beginning to understand that those who work within the framework of social organization can do so productively and effectively without drugging themselves into disconnection from the world and the people in it.

Not Too Full. Just to the Top

–NICK L.

PROLOGUE *In* Othello, *Shakespeare described* the effects of
alcohol by noting it seemed strange ". . . that men should put
an enemy in their mouths to steal away their brains." Addiction
to alcohol was preceded by the discovery of the grape and its
effects. According to one legend, when Noah was planting his
vineyard, he became a partner to the devil who killed a sheep,
a lion, a monkey, and a pig and let their blood flow freely on
Noah's vines. As a consequence, when the sheep-like man drinks,
he feels like a lion, chatters like a monkey, and finally wallows
on the ground like a pig. Alcoholism is the most popular
and prevalent form of chemical addiction.

Incipient alcoholism is marked by certain signs. The
occasional, social drinker may find that an increasing tolerance
for alcohol leads him to drink surreptitiously. For example,
he drinks before social engagements to warm up and then gulps
down the first few drinks when he gets to a party to keep his
glow. He worries about a sudden shortage of alcohol, and a
pocket flask may be his solution.

The victim begins to have more frequent and long-lasting
blackouts in which he is amnesic regarding events and his
contribution to them. His drinking then becomes continuous
as well as conspicuous, and he begins to lose control over his
behavior. He alienates an increasing number of friends and begins

to feel that he is misunderstood. His consumption of alcohol starts earlier in the day—"a pick-me-up" or "the hair of the dog that bit me." As he becomes a chronic alcoholic, he is willing to drink with anyone ready to furnish uncritical companionship. At this stage, he has prolonged bouts of steady drinking. Alcohol has become a drug, not a beverage, and he will drink anything with alcoholic content.

Alcohol is a depressant rather than a stimulant. It acts on that part of one's psychological structure that normally controls and inhibits impulsive behavior. This loss of inhibition provides relief from gnawing anxiety, and at the same time, it impairs one's perceptual and intellectual functions because of a substantial loss in sensory capacity, musculative coordination, and adequacy of judgment. The feeling of alcoholic well-being corresponds to the loss in efficiency that actually takes place. A final pathological intoxication may result in a totally confused state matched with amnesia for the events of that time.

Alcohol acts by entering the blood stream and displacing the oxygen in red blood cells. Just a three-tenths of 1 per cent concentration of alcohol in the blood stream can disarray the composure of its human container. As far as the bloodstream is concerned, the rate of intake is as important as the total amount consumed since the rate determines the speed of absorption into the circulatory system and, in turn, the degree to which the brain will be deprived of oxygen.

The typical alcoholic finds that liquor releases him from the clutch of anxiety, and this sense of well-being is all that is needed to establish dependency, habituation, or addiction. The unconscious needs and impulses of the individual are likely to make themselves apparent once inhibitions are dissolved in alcohol. There may be as many as five million alcoholics in America who cannot stop drinking once they have started. Such persons tend to behave one way drunk and another way sober. Understanding the whole person requires a consideration of both sets of behavior.

For many, alcohol, used sensibly, is a relaxant and a pleasant diversion from life's stresses and strains. For some, however, alcohol is a poison that destroys their ability to relate to people and to achieve gratification in a socially approved fashion. The onset of alcoholism is insidious, its development often seen

only in retrospect. Warnings are viewed as a foolish concern
on the part of others. Most alcoholics have a lingering conviction
that they can control their drinking if they try. The problem is
that they never try until they are far past the point when such
a decision can be effectively executed.

In addition to psychological damage, chronic and prolonged
alcoholism can cause serious physical debilitation. Food acts to
soak up alcohol and slow the rate of its absorption into the
blood stream, so it is often avoided by the determined drinker.
An unbalanced, vitamin deficient diet produces the severe
liver damage of which many alcoholics die. Alcohol is a mixed
blessing. It heals and it can also kill.

WHEN THE DRINKS CAME Nick's eyes lighted up, he grinned, and rubbed
his hands together in high glee. He downed the martini in one gulp and
with a smooth, uninterrupted movement raised his eyes to establish the
whereabouts of the waitress and lifted his empty glass to signal his needy
condition.

For a moment it was as though I had disappeared and he sat alone at
the table. All of his attention was focussed on restoring his glass to its
previous state of fullness. That done, he suddenly realized that I had not
yet touched my drink. Nick pointed to it, smiled broadly, and observed
that there was no such thing as a strong martini, only weak people. I
used this opening to move in on the issue that had brought me to the bar
in the first place.

"Nick," I said, "that's what I want to talk to you about—martinis and
people. I've known you for six years and in the last year the only times
we have had a chance to talk have been in a bar or cocktail joint of some
kind. A couple of days ago your agency called me and asked if I knew
where you were. They told me you haven't been in for a week. That's
why I came. What's up?"

Nick's response was, at first, full of venom. We talked for about two
hours, and the conversation was a not unfamiliar mixture of resentment
about other people's interference in his private business and complaint
about how much pressure was on him all of the time.

Several weeks later I again arranged to run into him. By this time I had
had several conversations with his wife and had been in contact with the
agency where he worked. The picture they painted was even more grim
than our recent meeting had suggested. Nick had been drinking heavily
for the last two years. His wife was about to divorce him and move out of
the state and the agency had decided to replace him with someone more
reliable.

Nick was always less than the dominant, aggressive, assertive, decisive male he fancied himself to be. He devoted more than the usual amount of time to cocktail conversation of the "I really told him off" variety. When he did take issue with someone's view of the world, he was careful to hobble each hostile word with apologetic modifiers led by a smile that pleaded for acceptance. Nick hated disagreement of any sort almost as much as he hated to say no to anyone. Nick could only be comfortable saying no if he functioned exclusively as an innocent messenger bearing ill tidings. Even then it would cross his mind that kings once executed those bearing bad news.

Nick's job at the agency was suited perfectly to his needs. He was one of three assistants to a manager whose greatest talent was hoarding authority and responsibility. Like a watchful and concerned father, the manager conferred favorite son status on Nick and wisely assigned him responsibility only for those tasks that did not threaten Nick's essentially passive and dependent makeup. The manager resembled Nick's barely remembered father and Nick even called him "big daddy" when in a joking mood.

Then, without a hint of warning, winter came to Nick's happy, comfortable nest. The manager moved up the ladder and away to the home office and took, as a traveling companion, the assistant Nick had pegged as the least likely to succeed in the corporate structure. The manager said all the right and encouraging things to Nick but his final handshake was just that, final.

Nick began a frantic search for shelter from the angry winds of business relations when he felt them full force, unbuffered by the mountain that was the manager. He spent less and less time at the agency, coming in late and leaving as soon as he could gracefully do so. The new work demands he had fallen heir to required him to take an unaccustomed initiative with others and his palms began to sweat each time he reached for the phone. He martinied more at longer and longer lunches at which less and less business was accomplished. He tried to mold the new manager in the image of the previous one but the great dissimilarity of the two made it a hopeless task. The office began to feel as uncomfortable as an abandoned house containing nothing but memories of better and more protected days.

At home it was the same. He drank before, during, and after supper with a steady, unbroken rhythm punctuated only by brief, bitter exchanges about how much he had already consumed and when he was going to stop. But the phone could still reach him at home. Its ringing seemed incessant and it was like being executed little by little each time he answered it. Before long he took his drinking to where the phones never rang for him.

Nick was alcoholically effusive in his greeting—he seemed to be hunting for someone with whom he could drop his façade of gaiety without criticism. So, I became his "buddy" for as long as it took to get to more serious issues. I felt I could make greater headway if he had some food, so I ordered an hors d'oeuvres tray as if he were a patient who required medication. It failed, of course. He talked and drank, but he studiously avoided eating.

I told Nick what I now knew about the kind of shape he was in and offered to help in any way I could. This approach was summarily rejected as being unnecessary, impertinent, and, probably, ineffective. He was having a good time; his wife had always been a drag anyway, and the agency had never given him what he needed to do a decent job. I was told politely and impolitely that it was none of my business. The rest of the evening's conversation was a repetition of what had gone before.

"We're still pals, aren't we?" Nick asked when I left. We were, but as I drove home, I retraced the conversation and became convinced that it was hopeless. I recalled how Nick said good-by to me in the lobby. Nervously eager to race back to the bar that we had just left, he was less concerned with my impression of his deteriorated condition than about the legal closing hour.

The next day, I talked again to his wife and to his employers at the agency. I passed on to them my pessimistic view of Nick's probable behavior. It looked to me that he was on a slide that was headed downhill and the events of the next half year bore me out. Nick began to drink at an even greater rate and had to be ejected from bar after bar in the downtown area. He would drink until he staggered badly, then wander out to his parked car and sleep just long enough to restore some semblance of equilibrium. He slept between the hours of 4 a.m. and 8 a.m. and was the first customer each morning when the bars reopened. About three months later I saw Nick in the "drunk tank" of night court. He looked ghastly and was so drunk he was incoherent. He was deep in conversation with the moth-eaten group in the tank and treated the whole affair as a lark that had gone awry. I talked to him for a few moments but he barely knew who I was.

When I next saw Nick, he came to my office at 3 p.m.—totally sober —and discussed what had happened to him recently. A stay at a city hospital had dried him out, and he had then been contacted by a member of Alcoholics Anonymous. He had no place to go when he got out so he decided to attend one of the meetings out of curiosity. He said with great earnestness and conviction that he had finally seen his life as it really was in that meeting. As Nick said, "They were talking about me! That was my life when booze had me on the ropes! I knew what they meant when they talked about how liquor can turn a man into an animal!"

Nick had become intense, humorless, and driven by the insights he had acquired in A.A. His old charm had been replaced by a rigid and demanding kind of personality that seemed to be the exact opposite of all he had been before. He told me about his previous life and of the "sins" he had committed while he was a drunk. It was an ugly story, but it seemed to me that Nick took more than a little pride in filling it with elaborate and graphic detail.

When drinking steadily, for example, Nick would not even leave the bar long enough to go to the toilet, partly for fear that he would stagger or fall and have his liquor supply cut off by an observant bartender. More often, it was because he was confused about time. Time was an irrelevant reminder of the cold, organized world and he chose to ignore its passage as an unwelcome intrusion in his life. Finally, staggering to his hotel room, he would stop and urinate against a corridor wall.

Unlocking hotel room doors was a great problem. When desperate, he would drop to his knees, lean against the doorjamb and unlock the door with both hands, closing one eye to correct his double vision. On several occasions Nick fell into the room bruising himself severely. Then he staggered to his knees, disrobed as he weaved across the room, and flopped on the bed leaving a trail of clothing behind him. More than once he missed the bed and ended up sleeping naked on the floor with the door wide open.

Nick's hangovers were spectacular. As he said, the first sensation is blinding pain. Its like what I imagine a brain tumor would feel like. Your head hurts so bad that you cannot even open your eyes. I go to the bathroom and swallow some aspirin but they always make me throw up. I go back to bed and wait till I get sick then I rush to the john and have the "dry heaves" for nearly an hour. My throat is raw for the whole next day and the first drink I take nearly kills me. Then I go back to sleep but I don't sleep long because I have nightmares and wake up dying of thirst. A bloody Mary in the morning is the only solution. When I can get one I nearly choke on it, but in about five minutes my head comes back to my shoulders and my eyes start to focus again.

The hardest part about being a drunk is that you have to pretend you aren't. Acting steady is difficult when everybody is staring at you. You have to watch not to fumble your money, or laugh too much, or do things you know you can't manage. I got so that I would hang around in bars where a lot of guys got crocked and nobody paid any attention to them. The trouble with those joints was that somebody always wanted to fight or some queer would sidle up to you and proposition you. Being steady in public was not nearly so hard as trying not to look drunk in front of your own kids. That was rough because I think they always knew something was wrong and that their daddy was "sick" again.

It was difficult for Nick's children for several reasons. To begin with, Nick would be away from them on a binge for as long as a week at a time and the children were too young to comprehend the reason for his sudden appearances and disappearances. Nick's slightly drunk return to his family always started a violent argument between him and his wife, and the children would be awakened by the shouting and screaming. Feeling guilty, Nick always armed himself with expensive gifts for the kids, gifts calculated to win their approval and acceptance. The children were cornered. They loved the presents and hated the mother-father combat that always accompanied them. Within the year, Nick's homecomings had soured and the children were frightened when they saw him coming up the front walk. It was particularly difficult for them to manage the continual experience of separation from their father. It became easier for them to reject him totally and pretend they had no father than to deal with his unpredictable presence and actions.

Nick was, at times, a crying, dependent drunk. He would burst into tears and cover himself with shame, self-accusation, and recrimination. He became, at these times, a model masochist who insisted on punishment for his multiple sins. He vowed that he would not only compensate for his past neglect but would never again touch a drop of liquor. These extended periods of self-abnegation were convincing at first, but since they were regularly followed by a sudden reversion to alcohol, they soon had little effect. Nick's tears and vows of reform worked only on those who did not know him very well.

Certain reformers are always convinced that they have the cure for this alcoholic disease. The cures range from religion to physical therapy through vitamins, food, a shave, and clean clothing. Female "reformers" often pursue a therapeutic program that involves sexual relations as a sure cure. They see alcoholics as needing the love of a good woman. When Nick would now and again abuse these bar therapists, they would become even more understanding and long suffering. Nick's hostile attitude toward them was really anger directed toward himself.

Nick was startled by the behavior of these women and sought to understand why they seemed to enjoy the suffering he visited on them. I tried to explain the complex process of masochism and passive aggressiveness to him and the deeper I got into the explanation the more I realized that I was describing his wife Antoinette. She had many of the needs and inclinations of the women with whom Nick regularly associated. Antoinette looked and acted different, but, in an analysis of a series of her actions, I became convinced that she needed Nick to be a weak, dependent, alcoholic as much as Nick needed to drink.

To begin with, Antoinette's maturity dissolved rapidly when Nick dried out and stopped drinking. At first it was a general disagreeableness that marked her regression to less mature behavior. Before long, Antoinette began to taunt Nick. She raged at him regarding his admitted marital infidelities, she accused him virulently of having wrecked the psychological well-being of the children, and insisted he had worried her until she had become a lifeless and broken woman. Nick's new religious insight bothered Antoinette particularly and she argued with him about it incessantly.

What was happening to Antoinette was clear. She could be healthy and whole only when she had someone to whom she felt superior, when she had a ready scapegoat on whom she could blame all her failures and her feelings of social and personal inadequacy. When Nick drank, everyone felt sorry for Antoinette. She luxuriated in the role of a downtrodden and abused but heroic, long-suffering female. She used Nick's drinking problem as an excuse to become a much pitied cripple herself. The wife of a healthy, untroubled husband must meet demands that are never asked of the wife of a drinker. As long as Nick drank, Antoinette was in a perfectly protected psychological position. Any flaw in her emotional well-being was insignificant when contrasted with the massive difficulties of an alcoholic husband.

Marriage is so complex an interpersonal arrangement that if you tamper with one aspect of the relationship, you will induce change in other parts of the system. Nick and I worked together for several months trying to consolidate the personal and psychological gains he had made in becoming independent of the drugged alcoholic state. I labored to help him to be both a sober and less rigid human being. It was hard work because it almost seemed as if sobriety went hand in hand with a rigid, inflexible, aggressive, and demanding outlook.

As Nick found he could stay sober while relaxing his grip on life, he began to see his wife more clearly for what she really was. He began to be aware that in marriage he had sought exactly those qualities in her that most contributed to his drinking. As he learned to recognize the irrationality of some of his own behavior and saw how he had sought out punishment when feeling guilty, he at once recognized the complementary nature of his wife's symptoms.

The timing of this insight has been more than a little unfortunate. Antoinette seems to get more disturbed in direct proportion to Nick's success in understanding himself, and she refuses to enter therapy since she continues to view her difficulties as exclusively caused by Nick. I am trying to get Nick to assist me in having Antoinette realize how serious her situation is becoming, but it is not going well. Nick is clinging perilously to his own newly found strength and has little to spare for others. Nick has broached the question of divorce, and I know he has firmly decided in his own mind that this is the path that he must follow.

When they were first married, Nick reported, now and again Antoinette and he had gotten drunk together and had a good time. Before long she had become critical of his drinking. Then she became a teetotaler and spent her time disapproving his drinking habits and predicting he would become a drunk. Now that Nick was an abstainer, Antoinette had begun to drink again, and, according to Nick, she was drinking heavily. Nick had become extraordinarily angry one night when he arrived home to discover her really drunk, and, in a rage, he had beaten her up. I am certain that an important part of his uncontrollable rage is directed at himself and his past life rather than his wife, but she is its current victim.

I am not very optimistic about what can be salvaged in this case. Nick, I think, will survive and reorganize himself into a new, if somewhat damaged, personality. It is likely he will divorce his wife and get custody of the children. It is also likely that Antoinette will begin to live the kind of deprived life from which Nick has so recently emerged. Fundamentally, Nick and Antoinette had the same problem. It would not surprise me if the two of them were to change places psychologically and act out the other half of this drama of disordered life in a kind of reversal of their married relationship. If this happens—as it seems it must—I may find myself back at my original starting point.

There is one ray of hope. Nick recently reported that Antoinette has begun to blame me for her current situation and has threatened to come and "give me a piece of her mind." If this threat is, as I suspect, a sign that she is aware of the severity of her difficulties then, perhaps, we may yet salvage a marriage headed for disaster.

The children of this marriage worry me most. I have the feeling that they are the truly innocent victims of an accident of encounter between two problem-laden people. Whatever the outcome of the therapy, the children are slowly being crippled by the same disability from which their parents suffer.

Physician Heal Thyself

–HY R.

PROLOGUE *Ours is a drug-oriented culture* in many ways. We
have medicines that sedate us, tranquilize us, stimulate us, and
produce delirium for us. Narcotic drugs—opium, morphine,
heroin, demerol, methadone—relieve pain at the cost of impaired
consciousness. Hypnotic drugs—barbiturates such as amytal,
nembutal, seconal and the nonbarbiturates including paraldehyde,
chloral hydrate, and the bromides—are sleep inducers.
Stimulant drugs—cocaine, the amphetamines, benzedrine,
dexedrine, methedrine—alert and sometimes produce a false sense
of well-being. Deliriant drugs—marijuana, mescaline, psilocybin—
alter our consciousness in unpredictable ways. Taken alone or in
various combinations, these drugs allow man to alter
chemically the experience of being alive.

These drugs of joy and relief should, theoretically, be a
blessing to mankind since they offer him the freedom to be
what he wishes to be at the moment he wishes to be it. Drugs
give choice and, in equal measure, they take away choice.
With drugs come addiction, habituation, or dependency and loss
of freedom. Taking drugs is a search for escape, that,
paradoxically, becomes an escape from freedom. Parenthetically,
those least free in our society, members of the lower
socioeconomic classes and of minority ethnic groups, most

often lose their freedom of choice and become the slaves of chemistry. Many more men than women reach the condition in which they can only feel "normal" with drugs coursing through their veins.

The underground world of the addict is populated by immature, childish, demanding, emotionally inadequate, sexless human wreckage, committing slow suicide as they drift further away from any relationship with their fellow human beings. The addict population is composed of persons who have found themselves incapable of establishing enjoyable, stable, and socially approved experiences in daily life. Dissatisfied, and without the inhibitions and restraints that protect most of us from the dangers and illegality of drug experimentation, the addict-to-be seeks escape from conflict and anxiety at the cost of his life.

The drugs hold increases as the victim's body adapts to its narcotized state, develops a tolerance for the drug, and demands an increasingly higher dose if it is to respond with a satisfying physical reaction. The drug becomes the life of the addict and he seeks the company of other addicts in order to be certain that his form of self-destruction will not be denied him. His body will no longer tolerate the drug's absence and symptoms of withdrawal remind the addict that he will be punished painfully and severely if he finds himself in short supply of the needed drug. When the volume of drug in the blood stream drops too far, the victim begins to be restless and nervous, to sweat and shiver, vomit, have diarrhea, and suffer agonizing cramps of all the muscles in his body. Even if he can tolerate the physical and psychological horror of this experience, the addict knows full well that he will then become only the drug-free inadequate and anxious person that he was before and that he will once again travel the familiar road back to addiction. His only reason for detoxifying his body—aside from unrealistic notions that he will become a different and more adequate person—is that it will allow him once again to get "high" less expensively on a smaller jolt of the drug.

The complex personality structure and organization that brings a man to drugs is no respecter of age, education, or social status. It requires only a need for a way out, access to the means for achieving it, and sufficient pressure to overcome any natural reluctance. Drug addicts are acutely aware of their

alienation from the rest of humanity and their self-image
is one of deterioration and worthlessness.

Not all addicts are scabrous and shifty members of an
underground of social outcasts. The world of the junkie has been
described graphically and endlessly. It is a colorful but overly
romanticized way of life that has frequently been exploited
for its shock value. There are few accurate portrayals of the
silent addicts who have the wherewithal to afford their habit
and need not engage in criminal activities or associations to
insure their drug supply. However, in some ways the silent
addicts have a more difficult time of it. They are addicted long
before they are capable of recognizing the addiction for what it
really is, and they must suffer alone without the social and
emotional support of others similarly afflicted. The silent addicts
have more to lose in that they must maintain a normal life while
their secret drug life haunts them. There is comfort in
companionship even in a sinking ship. Going it alone exacts
an unusually high price from the addict.

Hy's HAND TREMBLED SLIGHTLY as the needle pricked the vein. He hardly
felt it. With his eyes tightly shut, he concentrated on detecting the first
signs of the relief he knew morphine would bring. As the surges of re-
laxation hit him, he shuddered, laughed inwardly, flopped into a chair,
and visibly began to unwind muscle by muscle. After a few moments he
doctored the drug records so that the missing ampule would not be detected. He mused that although Judy was an excellent office nurse, he was
just as happy she was pregnant and would be leaving her job in two
months. He didn't think she was suspicious yet, but she was smart and you
never could be sure. Maybe he would go up north for the deer season and
get some rest. Then he could lay off the morphine. Or, at least, cut down
on it for a while.

It was 10:30 and the last patient had finally left the office. Hy turned
off the light in the treatment room, but as he headed out through the
waiting room to the front door something nibbled at the edge of his consciousness. He paused wearily at the door trying to figure out what it was
he had forgotten. He turned back to the treatment rooms and turned on
the lights in each as a final check. To his horror, he found he had left the
syringe and the ampule on the table and had not locked the drug cabinet.
Judy would have found it in the morning, and he would have been hard
put to explain why it was there. It had happened once before a week ago
and he recalled stammering and stuttering as he tried to explain it away.

He dropped into the chair again and started to worry about his increasing sloppiness in the last few weeks. He had been caught in a number of oversights that could have been dangerous. He had covered them up, but he knew that the floor nurses at the hospital had begun to give one another meaningful glances when they thought he was not watching. He smiled and noted that while doctors might be heroes to their patients they could not fool a working nurse for two minutes. They always knew, and all the charm in the world would not change their minds. He knew too. They thought he was a lousy doctor.

Well, he had never been a brilliant doctor in anybody's book. But, he figured, most of the people who came to him needed more tender loving care than they did medicine. He worked hard, seldom took a vacation, always answered night calls, and put in longer hours than other doctors. What did they want from him anyway? It seemed as if everyone was on his back. With a sigh he thought again that he never wanted to be a doctor anyway.

He had had little choice in the matter. His father was a doctor and his older brother was a doctor. His uncle was a doctor and his grandfather was a doctor. It seemed when he was growing up as if everyone of any importance in the family was a doctor. It was not that people told him to be a doctor. They always were careful to assure him he could be anything he wanted to be professionally—it was assumed that he would be a professional of some sort. But, it was also perfectly clear that the only thing the whole family really admired was a doctor. When his older brother decided to go into medicine and applied to medical school, they threw a party for him. His father beamed with paternal pride and told everybody in town the good news. From then on, brother and father talked nothing but medicine, medicine, medicine. Hy recalled being tempted at supper one night to announce to the family that he had decided to become a plumber, but he thought better of it.

There really was no reasonable alternative for Hy. He couldn't count the number of times he wanted to quit, but he knew he was afraid to tell the family. He usually thought about quitting when he got into academic trouble, and although his record was pretty bad (his brother, Simon, had graduated second in his class), it somehow could be patched together well enough to get by, if just barely. When Hy graduated he knew all the prestige and the big money went to specialists, but the thought of three years of training as a resident really chilled him. Simon specialized, of course. Simon always seemed to do exactly what would please his parents, and he always did it beautifully. Hy supposed he liked Simon—after all he was his brother—but he did not like Simon's wife and the brothers seldom saw each other except at family gatherings. Even then, Hy resented the way his mother and father fell all over Simon. He felt guilty, but he exaggerated about how well he was doing just to keep up with Simon.

He figured the worst was over when he set up offices across the street from the hospital. He even liked being a doctor. He liked the feeling he always got when people at a party asked him what his work was. There was something pleasant about saying, "I'm a doctor," and seeing the glimmer of respect that always lighted up the eyes of those surrounding him.

Hy married reasonably well. She was a nice girl and his parents approved of the match. It was a big wedding, smaller than Simon's it seemed to him, but, then, Simon was the eldest son. Hy and Mary had the standard number of children, two boys and a girl, and life settled down to a steady routine of long hours at work coupled with the inevitable demands of home and family. Mary seemed to have everything she wanted in life— a nice house, beautiful furniture, cars of recent vintage, a fashionable social circle in which to travel, and a host of socially approved community activities in which she was involved. Hy sometimes thought, ruefully, that his wife had wanted a doctor for a husband and did not care who it was. She never talked to him about anything but the things she "needed"—for herself, for the house, for the kids. When she asked about his patients, it was only to find out who was having a hard time in life. Sometimes when he was hard at work he had the feeling that if he swabbed one more throat or prescribed one more tranquilizer, he would throw up. It all seemed pointless and when he tried to picture his life twenty years hence, it was identical to yesterday, today, and tomorrow. People depended on him, though. What could he do?

He pushed himself wearily out of the chair. It was 11 p.m. and he had tonsils to take out in the morning—early in the morning. He knew that Mary would be asleep when he got home and that she would be asleep when he headed for the hospital tomorrow. He could not even remember when he had last spoken to her for more than a couple of minutes, and he had not seen the kids long enough to know what was happening to them. He barely knew his kids when it came right down to it. Hy felt like a pack horse carrying supplies from one place to another without knowing why he was doing it or what the supplies were. Maybe if he had a coronary, he thought, he could cut down on his office hours and spend more time at home.

Hy was tired and feeling sorry for himself. He did not know how he got himself into these boxes in life, but he could not remember a time when he was not being pushed by somebody to do things, achieve, accomplish, and get ahead in the world.

He unlocked the drug cabinet, took out another ampule of morphine, and dropped it into his bag just in case he needed it for tomorrow. He would feel better tomorrow, though. He had to. He could not feel much worse.

As Hy observed later in an embarrassed manner, "Tomorrow wasn't better; Tomorrow was worse." He made more mistakes than usual and, as

usual, took it out on other people. He complained about the condition of
the operating room, he carped at the nurses in the recovery room, he lost
his temper when Judy announced that she was planning to leave two weeks
earlier than planned, and he had a major blow-up with his wife when he
got home late and found that she had not yet done the dinner dishes.
It had been a bad day and it was what he spent his time talking to me
about. My contact with Hy was accidental. Trying to open a stuck
window in my office, I had mashed a fingernail.

I had known Hy when he was just beginning practice and at the moment I could think of no one else to call. He said he could see me at
once, so I walked the few blocks to his office. As he examined my swelling
finger, he began to pour out to me the doubts and problems he was facing. Then he asked if we could talk about some of his problems. I assumed that his problems would not be serious ones, so I agreed to see him
and "shoot the bull" as he described it.

I never received a professional bill for treatment of my finger and discussion of this with him proved fruitless. After our first hour I finally
insisted that his failure to treat me as a patient was part of the problem he
faced of wanting to be a patient himself. At the same time, he wanted to
deny it. When this issue was finally resolved, our relationship became more
firmly footed and therapeutic discussions were begun. Interestingly, it
was some weeks before he casually mentioned his use of morphine. His
primary concerns until then were: 1) the monotony of his life, 2) the
competitiveness with his brother Simon of which he was now conscious,
3) the lack of understanding and sympathy from his wife, and 4) how to
escape the trap that was slowly squeezing him to death.

When I pressed Hy for details of the amount and regularity of his
drug use, he was at first evasive and, finally, abusive. As he put it, he was
not a back alley hophead hooked on drugs; he used morphine only when
he was so totally exhausted that it was the only thing that could keep
him going; and, he knew the symptoms of addiction better than I did and
he wasn't even habituated to it much less addicted. We were at an im-
passe regarding his drug use for at least two months. The more I pressed
him, the more he found himself too busy with a succession of "emergen-
cies" to be able to keep his appointments with me. It was just after a
calculated confrontation about the motives behind this sudden set of emer-
gencies that Hy began to stop running and take a close look at what was
happening to his life. Behind the façade of a successful and competent
physician was the face of another person, and it was, to him, an ugly
face.

Hy had three mental portraits of himself. One image was of himself as
others expected him to be. It was a romanticized blending of all that is
the best in man. Every virtue was excessive, overstated and extreme. Hy
always hoped that one day he would grow to resemble it more closely

than he did at the moment. The second image was a scaled down, more human version of the first. Its imperfections were apparent, but they were ordinary failings that made it seem more natural. It was the third image that disturbed Hy. It had much more truth in it than the others, but arranged in an ugly and discordant jumble. The total effect was one of imbalance, chaos, and decay. Hy's problem lay in his feeling about this image, which he considered his real self.

All three were correct in one sense. Each of them reflected reality filtered through one or another person's eyes. Everyone is a collection of different portraits, each resembling the next but differing in a few details. In a stable, well-organized person, there ought to be a high degree of matching and similarity from one picture to the next. In Hy's case, his view of himself was seriously and grossly different from what the average person saw, it differed even more from what his mother thought he ought to be. The problem was complicated by the fact that Hy tried incessantly to disguise his inner self so it would resemble his mother's fond hopes for him.

As we talked, Hy made it clear that there never seemed to be a moment in his life when he was not engaged in trying to do those things that would please his parents. As a child, he had constantly competed for assurance that he was loved and highly valued by them. He had never quite succeeded at it; he always felt that he was doing and being less than he ought. Hy worked harder, worked longer hours, sacrificed himself for the sake of others, and felt very sorry for himself. The treadmill of life was exhausting him and disappointing him with its sameness and its futility, but he could figure out no alternative.

Hy began to realize when he was very young that both his mother and father saw in him a picture of future success and eminence. As Hy failed to achieve as well and as distinctively as his brother Simon, his mother remained faithful to her fanciful image, but his father began to focus all interest in successful Simon. Hy's father then added the worst possible touch to Hy's self-image; he began to expect Hy to be only second best and to anticipate failure even before it took place.

What Hy thought his real self was became clearer and clearer as he translated it into other terms for me. As a little boy, he had never liked the process of growing up. He had entered one competition after another in which, inevitably, he had failed. The certain expectation that he would fail began to be a self-fulfilling prophecy. Expecting the worst, Hy would do little to prepare himself. While in school, for example, Hy had mononucleosis which confined him to the student health center for ten days. When he was released to return to classes he found himself quite a distance behind and though he told me he made a valiant effort to catch up, he was certain his exams would be a disaster. Convinced his situation was hopeless, he stopped studying four days before exams and then went meekly to the intellectual slaughter. Hy was slaughtered again and again during his growing years and he always went quietly. It was what he deserved, he thought, and he felt pride in taking his medicine like a man.

Hy was a more dependent person than he could admit. He found it burdensome always to have to bear other people's problems and worries. He had always been impatient with recitals of how others were suffering since he experienced a great need to pour out a detailed confession of his own problems and worries. He never really did this, of course, despite his powerful urges. He took the admission of problems, difficulties, and limitations as a sign of weakness, and for his own sake and those whose picture of him was one of strength, he kept his turmoil to himself. It was unusual for Hy to communicate anything of his personal self to others. He felt uncomfortable telling his inner doubts to his parents because he knew they were too busy admiring their fanciful portrait of him to allow him to repaint it in truer colors. Similarly, Hy's wife became anxious and upset if he talked loosely of getting out of medicine or reducing the number of patients he would accept in the future. She was too busy padding and feathering her own nest to listen calmly to comments that would suggest that the branch on which she was nesting was beginning to crack.

For all Hy's vehement denial that his drug taking was dangerous or a sign of emotional deterioration, he knew he, as a physician, must eventually face the truth. As I pointed out to him, it must have taken a fairly high level of anxiety for him to reverse his usual pattern and talk to me of his personal problems when I visited his office. As I pressed the point home by suggesting a host of alternative means of handling the pressures of a growing practice—means employed by many of his colleagues—he found no reasonable answer. Finally, we discussed what his professional reaction would be if I were to come into his office and tell him the same story of fatigue, public responsibility, and the harmlessness of the narcotics I felt I needed.

Hy's denial that he had problems was not easily dispelled. Even after he was able grudgingly to accept the possibility that things might be less than perfect in his life, our conversations were interrupted again and again by sudden resurgences of the original denial. It was painful for Hy to admit once and for all that he had a problem and needed help in solving it. He felt he was a failure, but others saw him as a success; he was torn between these two versions of the truth and was unable to accept their compromise. Once Hy was willing to accept the notion that he needed help, the worst of the battle was over. His resistance prevented any real progress for an extended period of time.

At my suggestion, Hy agreed to keep an accurate record of his use of drugs for a single week. He agreed to give me an honest count and then admitted he had already done so, and that the total amount was more than he really thought it would be. He acknowledged that he would be worried if I were to tell him that I used this amount on a regular basis. I

asked Hy to cease completely his use of any drug as long as he was seeing
me for help. This was accomplished at once, and we then undertook the
harder task of reassembling Hy's disordered life.

For some months Hy maintained that he could solve his problems without informing anyone else that he was having difficulty. When I insisted
that it was his inability to admit others to the intimate parts of his life and
to have them understand both his strengths *and* his weakness that had led
him to the use of drugs, he agreed to confront his wife with this new
image of himself. We agreed that this task was one that Hy had to labor
through on his own so that future pressures would drive him toward
people important in his life rather than away from them and into the
chemical relief of a drugged state. One pitiable aspect of Hy's case was
that, in his slow self-destruction by drugs, he was acting very much like a
little boy who threatens to go out in the garden, eat worms, and die. With
every injection of the poison Hy was crying out for the world to hear,
"Look what you have made me do. I am killing myself all on account of
you and you are not even sorry!"

The hurt little boy in Hy was well hidden from the outside world, but
when he responded to the adult world as though he were still a little boy,
he got into as much difficulty as any child would.

To say that today Hy has matured fully and that his life is free of
complications would be unrealistic. To begin with, his somewhat immature wife has not responded very well to Hy's problems. Instead of offering sympathy or accepting the necessary changes in his life, she pouted,
pooh-poohed the idea that much was wrong with him, insisted it was only
a temporary difficulty, and argued against the logic of the plans he made.
Hy decided to join forces with a newly graduated M.D. and to shift a part
of his practice onto the strong and willing shoulders of this young man.
He explained carefully the wisdom of this move to his wife, and she
agreed it might be better if Hy could be home more often. Then, this
sensible move was delayed for some months because she haggled over the
details of the financial arrangement and found an unending series of reasons why this particular young man was not an appropriate choice for
joint practice.

Hy's mother, father, and brother do not yet know that Hy sought the
solace of drugs, and I suspect it will be some time before he feels confident enough to tell them. They have viewed his recent addition of a partner as a sure sign that he will not be a very successful doctor—expand his
practice, charge more per patient, and move into more prestigious quarters.

Despite these obstacles to progress, Hy is getting better. He is making
decisions with greater insight and recognizes pitfalls that he would have
plunged into innocently in the past. He may be one of those who grow
more mature in the wake of disorder.

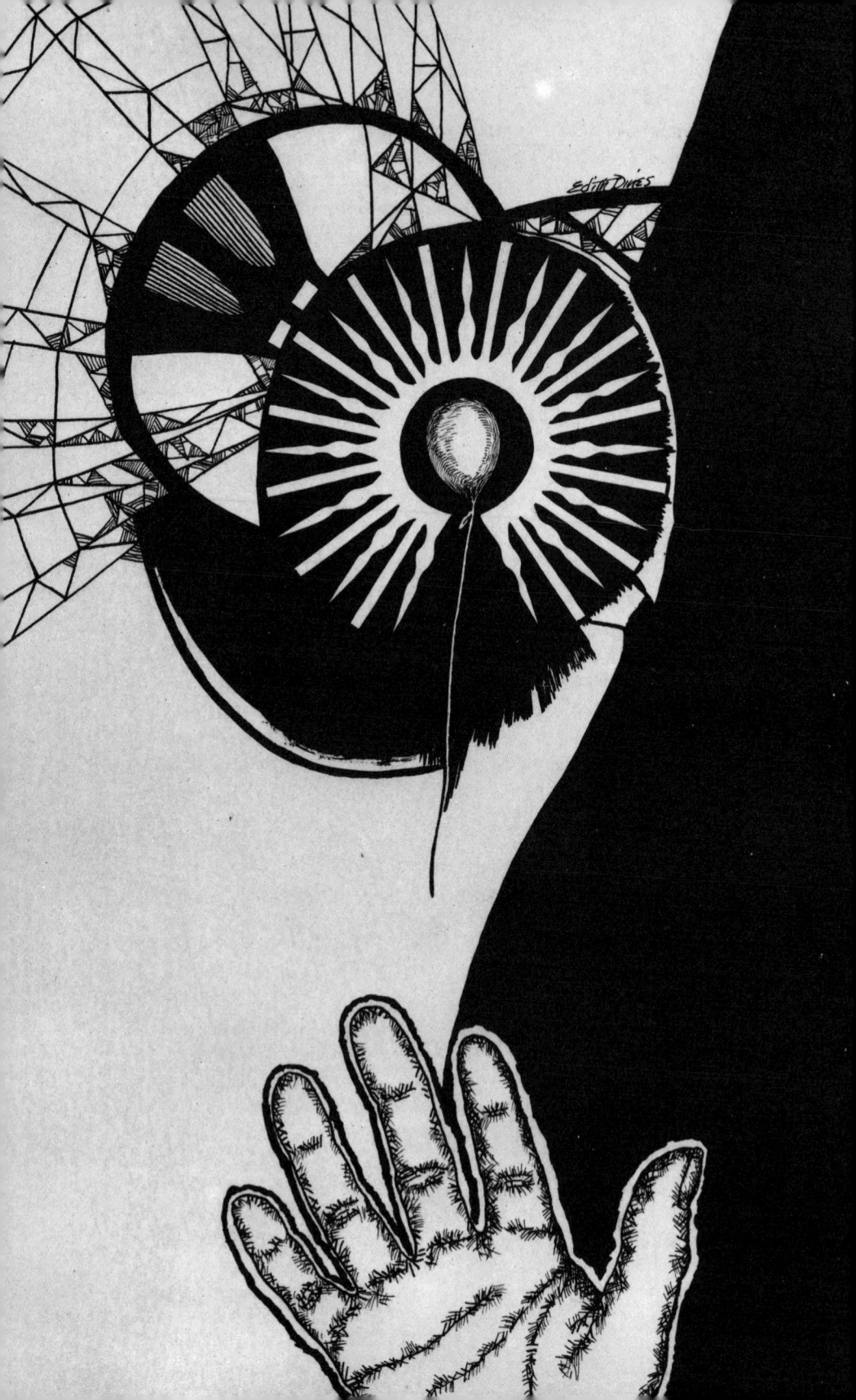

Tomorrow the World

–Joe A.

PROLOGUE *Someone once said* that a fanatic is a person who
redoubles his efforts once he has lost sight of his goal. In the
manic phase of manic-depressive reactions, the patient finds
himself confronted with an anxiety provoking situation so intense
that it threatens to crumble the defenses that have successfully
protected him in the past. Made frantic by internal signs of
impending psychological disaster, he begins a frenzied pattern
of activity designed to save himself.

At first, manic activity may not be recognized as
pathologically disturbed behavior because it mimics a role that
is considered desirable in culture. The American social and
professional ideal is regularly described as dynamic, forceful,
and on the move. He is an aggressive, assertive, confident, active,
hustler who will not take no for an answer. When such a person
achieves the accolades of material and social success,
he is applauded not hospitalized.

The victim of deepening mania is a caricature of our
cultural ideal. In the subacute stage (hypomania), the rate of
heartbeat and volume of blood pressure rises. Muscle tone
increases as does alertness and the degree of physical activity.
As the victim becomes more active, he sleeps less, eats
irregularly, and begins to lose weight.

These physical changes are accompanied by a speeding up
of mental processes so that there seems to be an increased free
and easy flow of thought, a flood of new and original ideas,
a pressured, driven quality to a now rapid-fire speech rate, and
a sense of elation and optimism. The view of the self and its
capacities becomes exalted and the world begins to appear
to be moving at a snail's pace.

As the manic disturbance becomes acute, what had
previously been only moderately impaired judgment and
speeded up physical and psychological action become a
disorganized flight of ideas having little to do with reality,
and a disconnected frenzy of movement and activity. The patient
becomes short of temper, domineering, critical of others, and
unable to brook interference with his lofty plans and schemes.
He has little insight into his condition, explains away the evidence
of a collapsing empire, and denies reality by increasing his
activity. As the disturbance becomes hyperacute, he may become
delusional, hallucinatory, and run loose like a wild animal. In
these days of sedatives, this state is rarely reached if the victim
comes to the attention of the authorities.

Manic behavior is related to the attempts many people make
to forget their troubles by plunging headlong into a whirl
of social activity or by immersing themselves in a mountain
of work. Reality is denied by an attempt to force it to be
different through sheer force of increased activity. It is a
desperate attempt to restructure the way things are so that
greater satisfaction and security will come to the threatened
individual. Manic disorders reflect a denial of what the patient
most fears in fantasy. The appearance of being capable,
independent, and happy may be an attempt to hide an acute
feeling that one is really incapable, dependent, and grossly
unhappy. These negative feelings, long held in check by
repression, break through into consciousness and trigger a pattern
of defensive and compensatory activity. In persons otherwise
stable and well adjusted, this redoubling of effort may actually
succeed if it leads to success and approval. In such cases, the
anxieties which originally threatened are quelled and a shaky
adjustment is possible. For others, however, agitation of this sort
leads to complete disorganization and depression.

THE DAYROOM of the ward was empty except for Joe A., but he was pacing back and forth so quickly, touching every article of furniture, and delivering an explosive oration at the top of his voice, that the room seemed filled with his presence. The police had delivered Joe to the emergency entrance of the hospital in an agitated, disheveled, and wild-eyed state. The police were gentle with him and kept nodding, smiling, and trying to soothe him. Joe wasn't really violent just then since he was busily engaged in presenting a rapid-fire commentary on his life to the police in the squad car. Joe was going to do this, and Joe was going to do that. Joe had connections. Joe knew people in high places. And Joe was going to make both officers full partners in a new enterprise that would make millions. I caught the tail end of the conversation as they urged him into the hospital and it sounded—at a speed of delivery barely intelligible—approximately like this:

> . . . You look like a couple of bright, alert, hard working, clean-cut, energetic, go-getters and I could use you in my organization! I need guys that are loyal and enthusiastic about the great opportunities life offers on this planet! It's yours for the taking! Too many people pass opportunity by without hearing it knock because they don't know how to grasp the moment and strike while the iron is hot! You've got to grab it when it comes up for air, pick up the ball and run! You've got to be decisive! decisive! decisive! No shilly-shallying! Sweat! Yeah, sweat with a goal! Push, push, push, and you can push over a mountain! Two mountains, maybe. It's not luck! Hell, if it wasn't for bad luck I wouldn't have any luck at all! Be there firstest with the mostest! my guts and your blood! That's the system! I know, you know, he, she, or it knows it's the only way to travel! Get'em off balance, baby, and the rest is leverage! Use your head and save your heels! What's this deal? Who are these guys? Have you got a telephone and a secretary I can have instanter if not sooner? What I need is office space and the old LDO [long-distance operator] . . .

As we maneuvered Joe into the ward, I talked briefly with the police officers before the ward physician and I went in to assess what steps needed to be taken.

The ward attendants who had been assigned to watch him were a little nervous about what Joe might do. Joe was agitated but not yet destructive. We feared it was only a matter of time. So, with the help of two attendants we administered a fairly potent sedative injection. I don't think Joe even felt it when the needle plunged home. He was shouting that he did not need a shot, that no one could give him a shot without his permission, and that it would do no good because he "was a ball-of-fire that no squirt gun could put out." The sedative was finally administered, and we waited but it was about 45 minutes before Joe began to slow down and look a little punchy. Finally, we got him to bed and left special instructions for the night nurse.

We then discussed a plan of approach to the patient and allocated responsibility for the diagnostic tasks that lay ahead. What help we could be to Joe depended on what psychological resources he had left and what capacity he had to regroup those forces. Joe was pretty far gone and his problems were part of a lifelong attempt to meet challenges with the least effort on his part. The next day we would begin the slow and painful process of unraveling his life.

In a series of interviews with Joe A. during the next week, I was able to reconstruct somewhat the events that led to his arrest and hospitalization. Joe remained quite euphoric during that week and was perfectly willing to be interviewed by everyone around. Moving quickly from place to place, he accosted every official looking person who passed through his ward. He made innumerable demands that the floor nurses get in contact with various doctors and have them see him at once. Despite Joe's readiness to pour out information, it was almost impossible to distinguish truth from fantasy. He exaggerated everything, skipped rapidly over what he considered to be irrelevant detail, and bounced swiftly from past, to future, and back to past again.

In order to untangle Joe's sense of compressed yet scrambled time, I functioned both as psychologist and social worker in this case. I not only interviewed Joe's wife and parents but asked also to see friends who had witnessed the changes in his behavior over the previous six months. I talked to eleven persons, and from their accounts I pieced together a rough chronology of Joe A.'s breakdown.

April 12: The respondents all reported that on this day, six months before his hospitalization, Joe's behavior was noticeably different from what it had been before. The occasion was his wife's thirtieth birthday and Joe had planned an elaborate surprise party for her. Grandiose rather than elaborate might be a better way to describe it. Birthday celebrations are traditionally limited to family and close friends, but Joe had invited, among others, the janitor in their apartment house, customers he contacted in business, his office staff, and an airline stewardess who had told him she lived in his town. The respondents reported that there were a number of people at the party whose identities were never discovered. Nobody knew how many other people Joe had invited who just did not appear.

The party was a fiasco, of course. Since Joe had lost track of the number invited, several trips to the delicatessen and liquor store were necessary to provide proper party viands for the horde of visitors. Joe had a reputation for being effusive, enthusiastic, and overly friendly, but this was ridiculous and inappropriate, even for him. Joe took it all as a big joke despite the fact that his wife was embarrassed and his sister infuriated. With shouts of "the more the merrier," Joe whirled from person to person carrying on boisterously superficial conversations. At one point he tried to quiet everyone down in order to play some parlor games, but, despite frantic efforts, he failed to get this scheme off the ground.

Everyone at the party thought Joe had simply had too much to drink. No one was aware that he had not touched a drop. When a reasonable time came to end the party, Joe insisted that no one be allowed to go home. As guests headed toward the door, Joe bounded across the room, restrained them physically, removed their overcoats, and pressed drinks into their hands. Protests by the victims that they really had to go home were overridden by boisterous horseplay that irritated them even more. As the crowd began to thin out, Joe began phoning all over town to locate some people who would keep the party going. When Joe's wife pointed out that it was midnight and time to give up, Joe airily waved her away shouting "plenty of time to sleep in the grave."

April 13:   When Joe's wife arose at 8 a.m. to clean up the mess left by the party, she found Joe seated in the middle of the living room poring over charts, outlines, and diagrams he had been constructing all night. Shoving aside party remains, Joe insisted that his wife listen to what he had devised. He had decided to form a national company to computerize the process of dating and mating for people from 18 to 80. Branch offices in every major city would collect data on the personalities, interests, and preferences of subscribers, and, for a fixed fee, the computer would match them with compatible types not only in their own area but all across the nation. As Joe pointed out,

> This is the age of jet travel and the whole country is on the move. Modern morality is shifting and males and females should have equal freedom in courtship. With my plan, either can call up the other and make a date. Your personal date list of compatible people can be used in all 50 states. A guy goes to Boston, for instance, and wants a date. He reads over the handbook of personality code numbers in the Boston area and calls the local office to get the address and phone number of the girl. He pays a flat fee for every matching code number he gets from the local office.

His wife had a headache and dismissed the whole idea thinking he was still drunk. Joe had always been full of weird ideas, but he usually dropped them after a few days, attracted by some new and equally unworkable notion.

April 14–June 14:   During the next two months Joe pursued his project with enormous vigor. He buttonholed everyone he met and expounded on it at length. Four telephones were installed in his office so he could make two outgoing calls while he awaited the arrival of two incoming calls. Surprisingly, Joe A. accomplished an almost herculean feat of organization and finance. His euphoric state and his absolute conviction about the feasibility of this new enterprise was infectious—even staid and conservative financiers were carried away by Joe's enthusiasm. He borrowed enormous sums of money using as collateral nothing more tangible than fast conversation.

It even seemed possible that Joe might succeed. He had managed to overcome incredible obstacles and now he pressed forward to financial victory. Joe believed that he had arrived as a business tycoon ready to challenge the great minds of the financial world. He shouted victory too soon, however.

June 15–August 15:   The two months to follow were catastrophic. Perhaps the impulse level of our society is deficient or perhaps the novelty of the idea held people back, but the result was high overhead and little income. Joe tried desperately to shore up his tottering empire—a staff of 92 in 23 cities—but the odds were mightily against him. Joe could not meet his payrolls. Branch offices failed one after another as Joe's long-distance telephone bill mounted. Joe, of course, was unperturbed by this turn of events. In response to chaos, Joe simply redoubled his efforts, shortened the periods of rest and sleep, missed more meals, and grew ill-tempered with the few staff members who remained loyal to the original idea.

August 16–October 16:   Joe fought heroically to stem the tide of destruction. Hounded by creditors, Joe began to shift his headquarters to increasingly obscure and less elegant quarters. He eliminated food, sleep, and trips to the toilet. With each disaster he became more frantic and hostile toward those whose faith and courage faltered. Swearing, babbling, proclaiming, shouting, and dialing long distance frantically, Joe was finally given a police escort to the local mental hospital.

October 16–March 16:   Joe remained euphoric and grandiloquent during the first two weeks of his institutional stay and helped us very little in our attempt to understand him and assist him to regain his composure. Joe raved and ranted but furnished us with little information beyond an awareness that he was quite manic and was rapidly becoming delusional about his stay in the hospital.

Joe then became depressed and reported over and over that he must pay for the many mistakes and injustices he had committed. For a brief period of four days Joe was almost lucid and yet at the same time regressed and childlike in his behavior, giggling at everything. Now he is delusional and convinced that he is being persecuted by confinement in a mental institution despite a) the great financial loss he incurred with every moment and b) the obvious truth that he was as sane as the next fellow.

Joe has made some new and even more grandiose plans about the actions he will take as soon as he leaves the hospital. He insists that his previous efforts suffered most from a lack of scope and breadth. The fact that he is wanted for issuing a number of bad checks is a detail he shrugs off easily.

Joe's world has collapsed, and for an indeterminate number of months or years he will continue to be a patient in the institution.

Everything Stinks, Including Me
–RALPH R.

PROLOGUE   *Much of our popular literature* and music deals with
the "blues" that all of us experience at one time or another. Both
the well adjusted and the neurotic get depressed, but, in the
psychotic, depression goes deeper into the substructure of the
personality. It is more rigid and unforgiving, and it can reach
delusional levels that go beyond any simple disorder of mood.
The neurotic may use his depression as bait to hook those around
him into denying the truth of his self-accusations, but the
psychotic fully believes in his own total worthlessness
and seeks no conscious solace from others. His absolute
repulsiveness to others is, for him, a fact, not a question.

Since psychotic depression seems so little an attempt at
adaptation or defense and is so little connected to reality, some
theorists have concluded that it can only be an effort to stave
off total disintegration. Psychotic depression resembles regression
to an infantile level of adjustment, a fixation on a primitive
set of responses.

The severity of the disorder ranges from simple depression
to an acute and stuporous state of gross depression. In its simple
phase, the patient may be anxious, discouraged, pessimistic,
and convinced that there is little chance of improvement for him.
His normal level of activity slows down and his ability to
initiate change or new patterns of response is seriously weakened.

As the depression becomes increasingly acute, minor frustrations take on added weight in oppressing him, and bodily functions are abnormally retarded. He may think of suicide. If the depressive process cannot be checked, the victim may fall into a stuporous condition—motionless, unresponsive, uncaring. He is filled with grief, remorse, hopelessness, and an obsession with fancied sins or imagined fatal illnesses and is no longer in meaningful contact with others.

The depressive usually has a history of poor adjustment that finally breaks down under the strain of living. The flawed and barely manageable self he was able to adjust to in his early years bursts forth as a hostile, angry critic of what he has made of himself. Every departure, however slight, from a strict and unrelenting moral code now returns to torment him. Perhaps by suffering he can atone for the discrepancy between what he ought to have been and what he actually is; perhaps death is the only answer. The depressive's inordinate rage is turned on himself and he becomes both torturer and the victim. Self-destruction may be set off by a sudden assault on his sense of security, the loss of a primary source of psychological gratification, an upsurge of guilt long hidden, or a breakthrough of denied and forbidden impulses.

Pessimists, rigid perfectionists, and those who have spent their lives demeaning their abilities and feeling inferior to those who surround them are prime targets for this mood disorder. Depression can also result from overambition if the steps taken to reach a goal cause anxiety to mount. An awareness of negative emotions produced in others by assertion of the self can produce profound guilt if one has been taught that hurting others, even accidentally, is an unforgivable offense. Gross depression is a disease of the conscience—a conscience that is harsh and unremittingly punitive about the slightest deviation from perfection.

RALPH WAS SINKING SWIFTLY into what he called a "blue funk." Nothing much had happened worth getting upset about but Ralph knew he was going to feel bad the moment he got out of bed. He woke up thinking, "Something is missing; something is wrong." He opened his eyes and sensed a great emptiness, but it was only what he deserved. He had made a mess of his life and had failed everyone who had ever had confidence in him. He had failed them miserably and it was all his own fault.

Ralph was both sad and ashamed because he knew it was happening again. He recognized how grim he was feeling and that it was worse to-day than yesterday. He had felt it coming and he dreaded it, but it was like the bad dreams he had regularly in which a building was toppling down on him while he was able to run only in slow, slow motion. This dream alternated with one in which he was driving an automobile on a crowded thoroughfare when suddenly he was unable to see out of the windshield or stop the car. This night fantasy of rushing to automotive destruction would end when Ralph awakened screaming and thrashing just before the actual crash. His heart would be pounding, he would be in a cold sweat, and his hands would tremble for twenty minutes as he sat in the living room smoking to calm his nerves.

What Ralph hated most about these frequent nightmares was not just the fright and anxiety they caused him or, for that matter, the aftereffects of trying to work the next day while exhausted. It was his inability to get back to sleep. Alone in the early hours of the morning he always began to brood about his life, the kind of person he was, his weaknesses and many failures, and the generally miserable condition of the world. By the time he got to work he was deeply depressed and could barely manage the day's tasks. His biggest difficulty was concentrating. He would begin a task, knowing it had to be completed in a certain time, and with a sudden "start" realize that he had again become lost in thought and had not even begun to work. Ralph's depressive episodes were not uncommon, so his fellow staff members had learned to recognize the symptoms and give him a wide berth for the day.

The details of the events leading to Ralph's hospitalization had repeated themselves year after year. As Ralph became increasingly depressed, his whole relationship to life, his work, and other people deteriorated rapidly. His energy would wane, and he would become obsessed with the idea he was a worthless, hopeless, useless person leading a meaningless life. He knew himself to be a grossly sinful human being whose evil behavior ranged from hypocrisy to mental lechery. Ralph's depressive reactions had little to do with actual sins he had committed, but rather with the urges, impulses, needs, and desires that seemed to be his constant companions. As he cried and mumbled to himself about how rotten he was, his behavior came to the attention of his superior officer who personally escorted him to the neuropsychiatric institute in a near-by town. In all, Ralph had been hospitalized five times in seven years and each stay lasted a little longer than the one before.

Ralph settled comfortably into the now familiar hospital routine, but this time the security of the hospital setting and its protective personnel seemed to be driving him deeper and deeper into a regressed depression. The closing and locking of the ward doors behind him signalled vividly that once again he had failed to make it in the outside world, and his psychological disintegration rapidly increased. It took all the chemical magic of tranquilizers and energizers to dredge his personality up to the surface again so that we could discover why it broke down with such regularity.

Ralph was a deputy sheriff in a county populated by nearly half a million people. He had spent 22 of his 45 years rubbing shoulders with what he called the "seamier side" of people. In a county so heavily populated, Ralph was exposed to every human quirk as well as a great variety of "social losers." Ralph was, in his own words, so disgusted with the human race that he was ready to throw up. All day, every day, he was forced to deal with the "filth, the garbage, the degenerates, the diseased, the liars, the cheats, and the murderers." He hated them, was repelled by them, and harbored secret thoughts about the social need to kill all of them for the betterment of the human race. In his more agitated moments he would insist that sudden death was too good for them, that they ought to be "made to feel pain in the same way that they have hurt other people."

Ralph had been involved in police work ever since he could remember. He played cops and robbers when he was young and always insisted on being the cop. Otherwise, he would leave the game and go home. He recalled that he would feel a welling sense of superiority as he headed home, superiority because he had refused to be the evildoer, even in a game.

Ralph was in the ROTC in high school and was one of the best cadet captains in the history of the school. He took his duties so seriously that it was a joke among his peers and a cause for grudging admiration by the high school faculty. Ralph wore his uniform to class more frequently than protocol demanded—he was proud of it and thought other ROTC members should do the same—and was pleased that he had enlisted rather than been drafted in World War II. He asked for assignment to the military police, and, by extending his enlistment, he served as an MP both in Germany and in an area prison in the Philippines. Ralph liked police work because it gave him satisfaction to see that wrongdoers were punished and that the unsavory segment of the population was being controlled.

But, Ralph was a disillusioned man. The good and bad were harder to tell apart than they were when he was young. He saw people pushed around because they were poor, not because they had done terrible things, and he saw people he had once respected arrested for dreadful crimes. Ralph was absolutely convinced that the average human being was a rotten and corrupt form of life.

Interestingly, this was not Ralph's problem. If the sad state of some human affairs were to provoke unmanageable resentment and disgust in everyone who is in contact with it, the police forces of our country would be depressed and ineffective. Somehow, most police officers find a way to keep criminals in some kind of reasonable perspective, to comprehend that they constitute a tiny percentage of the total population, and to have hope for the rest of mankind. Ralph's problem was unique and his crushing sense of despair could be accounted for only by other factors.

A clue came when he described his experience as an MP in occupied Germany. Because he was a first sergeant with experience in the Philippines, Ralph was sent to organize military police stations throughout Germany. Ralph was obsessed with a flaming rage at the atrocities Adolf Hitler had committed against Jews during his reign. Ralph was not Jewish but he caused considerable consternation in the ranks of Army Brass by insisting that he had a right to select whatever religion he preferred and to recognize and abide by the religious holidays of that group. So, Yom Kippur, Rosh Hashona, and Seder suppers became a part of his life. He knew that his beliefs were unorthodox but he preferred to go it alone with his convictions.

Ralph's rage at Hitler and Germanic atrocities took a peculiar turn. He had managed to collect an astounding mass of Hitlerian memorabilia. He had photographs of every concentration camp showing the ovens, grotesque bodies in mass graves, and instruments of torture and harassment. He had, for example, stumbled on an autographed copy of *Mein Kampf* which he displayed with great pride alongside Nazi flags, original execution orders, medals, awards, helmets, lugers. If one were to sum up his collection the term grisly could best apply. It was the grisly quality of his collection that began to disturb me and led me to the clue I was seeking.

Somehow I sensed enjoyment in the care with which Ralph had devoted his free time to such a pursuit. Why not a pattern more typical of the enlisted man in an alien land? Why was the Nazi flag in so prominent a place in his den; why were the most grisly photographs pinned on a bulletin board; why did the room look more like a carefully tended museum than an indictment of a society gone bad? I decided to delve deeper into his voluntary contact with crime.

Ralph described events in his childhood that were revealing to me even if they seemed casual, irrelevant reminiscences to him. His stories of choosing "cops" when "cops and robbers" were the alternatives had more to them than a simple identification with the virtues of law and order. Ralph was known to be a super-nice boy even when young. He came at once when his mother called him and this "at once" had a terrible and recognizable urgency to it. He had even committed the most unpardonable of play sins. He had given up his turn at bat in a baseball game at the sound of his mother's piercing and strident call to come home.

He was the neighborhood model of what a nice boy ought to be at every stage of his life. This image of perfection engendered a natural resentment among the members of his more flawed peer group. Ralph was too good to be true, and his friends viewed this as a challenge to their ability to sully his image in secret if not publicly. Ralph did as many illegal and forbidden things as the others but he was rarely suspected and never convicted for waywardness. He looked true-blue but was fully aware that others thought better of him than he thought of himself.

Ralph had a "thing" about rules. Rules organized life and made it bearable. They seemed to have a godly force all their own, a force of rightness that could not be corrupted by the less than reverent impulses of his friends. It was true that Ralph had fight after fight in an effort to establish clearly the necessary inviolability of rules of conduct. When he fought he always felt that he had right and good on his side and this tightened his muscles and increased the ferocity of his counterattack. He fought and fought well to establish some semblance of justice in the world.

One other fact of Ralph's early character ought to be mentioned here. Pure as he was, he was a torturer of lower forms of life. He pulled the wings from flies and made pets of them, lifted goldfish from their water to watch them gasp in agony, and loosed dogs to beleaguer cats passing by. He was never apprehended in these pursuits not was he aware of why he felt such pleasure at the suffering of other forms of life. He only knew he felt a compulsion to hurt and that this compulsion was exciting to him in every way.

As a child he was pleased most by "tying games" in which the only partly willing victim was rendered helpless by being bound hand and foot and was then subject to the variety of tortures invented most often by Ralph and executed most often by others less thrilled with the game than he. In his father's bookcase he once found *Fox's Book of Martyrs*. This graphically illustrated volume became his personal diagram of how flesh could be torn asunder in the name of justice.

Ralph was obsessed by notions of justice, fairness, and retribution from his very early years. I can only speculate about the source of these feelings but my suspicion was that his experience as a less than favored child exposed him constantly to a situation in which others got rewards more properly his and suffered less for their misdeeds. Ralph's clean public image had been unproductive of the pleasures he thought it would bring and his bitterness about the lie he had contrived had to be balanced in his later life.

Ralph was 45 but he was single. He told me that he had never found a woman with the qualities of purity he wanted in a wife. Busy with police work, he never found the time to seek out much female companionship. He was a man to whom life and work were interchangeable terms. He knew about sex and was an experienced but not very vigorous pursuer of such contacts. Ralph called his mother at the same time each day and engaged in the same superficial conversation each time, and he got nervous if he missed this daily ritual because, after all, "she counted on my call." But it was Ralph's description of his contact with jailed homosexuals and prostitutes that first aroused my suspicions that being attached to his mother was only one of a number of Ralph's problems.

Ralph went beyond the requirements of his duties as a desk sergeant whenever prostitutes or homosexuals were brought into his bailiwick. He would, in his words, "study them and try to understand how they could possibly be so degenerate and do such filthy and despicable things." Ralph never achieved the kind of casual disinterest that most police officers finally achieve following continued exposure to social deviants caught in the toils of the law. When he was working the night shift on the desk, Ralph would wait for quiet periods, awaken the newly arrested prisoners one by one, and remove them to the interrogation room for detailed "questioning." The excitement that surged through him at those moments was something he looked forward to all day when he was assigned to the night shift.

Ralph described his psychological "studies" of fallen human beings with great enthusiasm—the enthusiasm he usually reserved for his descriptions of Nazi atrocities. Ralph wallowed psychologically in all the unsavory details of sin, seduction, drunkenness, and amoral life. As Ralph described these moments, he would become agitated as well as fascinated and he finally reported, with great shame, that he often would go to the bathroom at the police station and masturbate following a particularly exciting account of depraved life.

The problem for Ralph, of course, was that he was unable to understand that his fantasy world had long been filled with exactly those impulses and urges that criminals, prostitutes, pimps, and homosexuals were acting out for him in real life. Ralph wanted to do all the things these people did but could not tolerate the hideous thought that he was such a disgusting person.

I began to believe, although I never mentioned it to Ralph, that he was also the unsuspecting victim of his own quite transparent fantasies. An experienced prostitute taken to the interrogation room following arrest would see, from her extended acquaintance with the psychology of the adult male, that this desk officer was a little "kinky" himself. I am certain that these women, sensing what would most please him and gratify his needs, would invent for him whatever sexual detail might most vibrate his fantasy. If this speculation were true, it was likely that Ralph R. was holding a mirror to his face each time he probed the psychology of his arrested "patients."

The deep depression Ralph was suffering had to stem from some break in his defenses. Most of the time Ralph managed fairly effectively to keep his impulse life walled off from consciousness and to disguise an occasional escape in his pretentions about "psychological studies of evil persons." The study of others was a poor choice of a defense for Ralph since his basic impulses were easily recognizable beneath it and because it tricked him into spending most of his time in territory quite dangerous for him.

In a practical sense, it was a little late to say that Ralph should not have been a policeman. Ralph's disordered life had begun to assume its pattern early in childhood, and there was little he could do to alter it without help. The therapist's task, at this point in Ralph's life, was an almost hopeless one. Ralph had made the best adjustment he could, given the resources available to him and his faulty psychological structure.

Ralph could decrease his temptation by changing jobs and finding less stimulating surroundings in which to spend his time, but at this juncture in his life he would have to seek some substitute for the official contact he had found so useful. Ralph would be forced to pursue his psychological studies without portfolio if that was what it took to satisfy him.

Another approach to the case might have been to modify the stringent morality that had made him view himself as a totally clean and pure person, to temper his rejection of the impulse side of his nature until some compromise between his inner and outer life could be achieved. A number of other strategic moves were possible, but each seemed to offer less hope than the preceding one. It was apparent that meaningful contact with Ralph was necessary as a precondition to any therapeutic plan. But, Ralph had begun to sink deeper and deeper into a massive depression and was now unable to think clearly or communicate coherently with me. He was delusional about his worthlessness and sinfulness and was convinced that the whole world knew him for what he was—an abomination in the sight of God. He was certain that he was undergoing God's personal punishment for his many misdeeds and began to hallucinate the voice of Jesus and the Virgin Mary. He heard the voices asking him to kill himself and join them in the other world. This invitation was too appealing to resist.

Within a week Ralph had made two attempts on his life—wrist-slashing with fragments from a broken window and suffocation with a plastic bag. Neither attempt was successful, but the seriousness of his psychological condition dictated the prescription of a course of electroconvulsive shock treatments. This failed to achieve what we hoped it might. Ralph plunged even deeper into depression and became a vegetable. When spoken to, he seemed to pay no attention since his energies were devoted to excluding extraneous noise in order to hear more clearly the voices that now spoke to him incessantly. His regression to childish behavior, including wetting and soiling himself, boded ill for his recovery.

It has been nearly eight months since Ralph has spoken coherently to anyone. Even when suffering discomfort or unhappiness, he will not complain. He seems to feel that he deserves anything that happens to him since he is such a failure as a human being. My earlier concern about choosing from alternative strategies of therapy has been shelved since there is little prospect of putting any of them into action.

Over the past five years Ralph had always managed to marshal his waning resources and reassemble enough of his shattered defenses to return to work. It became clear that Ralph would never return to the night desk and would never re-enter the intricate path of his previous life. Ralph has progressed in that he has been moved, out of the intensive treatment ward and is now cared for as a custodial case in the maximum security ward where he is still attempting to end his life.

When does the fact that a depression has psychotic roots become apparent? As we can see in the case of Ralph R., the diagnosis of psychosis would have been in error for five of the last six times Ralph was hospitalized. While the attending professional might easily have predicted that this yearly phenomenon was bound to become permanent one day, the why and when is a little harder to forecast. Cases superficially resembling Ralph's have been returned to life outside the hospital and have found a new form of adjustment that has produced strength rather than increased weakness. Such, unfortunately, was not the case for Ralph.

If Ralph does not succeed in killing himself, he still has nothing to look forward to in the way of a satisfying life. He will probably stay in the hospital leading a meaningless life in which days are an endless repetition one of another. Ralph will hardly notice the passing of time nor will he mark the changing seasons. The probability of spontaneous remission is slight. Chemical energizers have been tried, but they have produced only a screaming agitation in Ralph in which it was necessary to control him physically and sedate him to prevent further destruction. Ralph responded unnecessarily from a deep but restless sleep. Perhaps the best we can do for Ralph is to disturb his sleep no longer.

You Can't Trust Anybody Nowadays

–Bob H.

PROLOGUE   *The paranoid state* is developed early in life and only
agitated by the normal perils of living. Most of us develop a
fundamental trust in others and view the world as a fairly stable,
dependable, helpful, and friendly place. We think we understand
ourselves and those with whom we come in contact and
anticipate being able to build satisfactory
interpersonal relations.

The person destined to become paranoid never really learns
to communicate effectively with his fellow human beings.
Anxious and frightened by events he can neither manage nor
comprehend and unable to understand the thoughts of others, the
growing child is forced to retreat to his own inner resources.
Before long, his interpretation of reality is a distorted one
based on anxiety, misunderstanding, and misinterpretation.

A paranoid view of the world often begins insidiously
and undergoes a period of incubation. Then, a sudden "insight"
or illumination reveals that the fragmented suspicions one has
always harbored are really part of an elaborate plot. Once the plot
is discovered, a host of previous experiences and current
suspicions begin to make sense and there is almost a sense of
relief that life finally has a pattern to it. He is now alert to the
existence of confirming evidence that what he has always
believed is really true. The more closely he watches others the

more confirmation he finds for what he must believe. In part, this perception is selective—he dwells only on that which confirms his beliefs—and, in part, it is an overinterpretation of events that others would treat in a casual fashion.

If the paranoiac is convinced that the "signals" he is receiving are evidence of a serious threat against his life or personal well-being, he may take several courses of action. He may naturally conclude that he must be someone pretty special and unusually important. Yet, being mistreated and hounded is also anxiety provoking and stressful, so, the victim may decide to strike back and defend himself against the imagined threat. Since gross personality disorganization is not evident in the early stages of this disturbance, the paranoid goes undetected in our society for a considerable period of time.

The paranoiac distorts reality and denies his own impulse system by attributing his negative feeling to others rather than himself. Delusions, in such circumstances, are the victim's attempt at a spontaneous cure for his emotional difficulties. Delusional beliefs crystallize his way of life and offer a pattern of action that verifies past suspicions. One's difficulties are "out there" rather than internal and can be dealt with in a way that internal problems cannot.

The possibility of cure for long-standing cases of paranoia marked by highly systematized delusions is slim indeed. Paranoia reflects a total way of life not easily undone. The very motive of the illness armors it against healing penetration from those outside the delusional system of the patient. In any form of therapy, trust, confidence, and optimism are essential forces in producing relief of one's symptoms. Paranoia effectively shuts off help from the therapist just as it has made help from others impossible. The therapist must always ask himself the same question as he begins therapy, "Can I reorganize the total way of life of another human being who from the beginning of therapy will attribute all of my words and actions to an urge to destroy him?" Mistrustful and suspicious patients can be moved, psychologically, at least to a position of watchful neutrality with regard to the therapist's motives. But, the systematized, organized delusional beliefs of paranoiacs are constructed with built-in defensive systems that protect them and maintain their invulnerability.

Asking the paranoid person to abandon his delusional system is similar to asking someone to change his way of thinking so as to contradict everything he knows to be true. We must ask the paranoid person to learn that black is white and right is wrong. There is, thus, little wonder that we fail as often as we do in treating paranoid conditions.

The case of Bob H. is best described as that of a paranoid personality undergoing decompensation or losing his ability to compensate for increasing stress. About midstream ir my casual contact with Bob H., it became apparent to me that his mistrust of others was the only visible part of a full-blown paranoid schizophrenia.

WHAT DO YOU DREAM ABOUT at night and think about during the day? For most of us the answer would be an amazingly variegated clutter of rapidly shifting thoughts, impressions, observations, feelings, and reactions impossible to catalogue. Suppose for a moment that your mental processes—waking or sleeping—were always concerned with the same set of issues and problems and that you could be distracted only by environmental stimulation of high intensity. For brief periods, everyone worries, but this obsession with problems is a brief encounter and is not typical in life's total pattern.

Recall, if you can, a moment in your life when you were very worried about the course of your personal affairs and felt trapped in an impossible situation for which you could see no satisfactory solution. Recall the resentment you may have felt at the blows life was delivering to you and your feelings that people did not appreciate your real abilities and capacities. Such emotions, brooded over for a lifetime, produce a paranoid state. It is a rough description of the state of Bob H. when he first came to see me.

Bob was another informal patient. He was unaware that his view of life and people was in any way inaccurate or distorted. He dropped in frequently to see me because he had acquired the notion that I was sympathetic to his beliefs. I was not impatient with the world as he saw it because I enjoyed talking to him. My enjoyment stemmed from his unusual brightness and personal creativity—he overflowed with original ideas and views of man that were almost but not quite workable. I worked to see if amelioration of his state was possible through nontherapeutic informal contact with him.

Bob would enter my office casually and open the conversation with a ritual gambit, "I had a funny idea the other day." Within this framework our conversations continued for two-and-one-half years until he had to be hospitalized one day when he called the police at 4 a.m. and insisted that his house was surrounded by people who were "out to get him." He was brandishing a revolver when the police arrived and had fired several warning shots into the air to frighten off his suspected assassins. I visited Bob once a week for the next eight months, but he became incoherent, grossly deteriorated in all aspects, and was finally transferred to a "back ward." By this time he had included me in his delusional system and suspected me of masterminding his hospitalization.

Paranoia is always a puzzling state to the observer who views it only in its advanced stages. It is puzzling because it is a marriage of intellect and interpersonal distortion that fits no one's idea of a rational being. Bob H. had a wife and four children, and in my contact with his wife I probed to understand how a nonparanoid person managed to live with the suspicions of a hostile, anxious husband. I discovered that several elements were needed.

Bob H.'s wife did several things to adjust to this unanticipated facet of her marriage. Unaware of the deliberate way in which she managed it, she shielded the children from very much direct contact with Bob. When he decided, on a weekend, that he ought to spend more time with his children, every child in the family was suddenly occupied with programs at the YM-YWCA. Bob never resented this for long because he was always preoccupied with responding to some new provocation. Lee, his wife, knew that Bob did not fit the ordinary mold but she never seriously thought that he was sick and needed help. She had been bothered by his sexual disinterest in her and had a hard time understanding his complex theories about how sexual intercourse drained the vital fluids from a man's body and reduced his alertness.

Lee H. seldom objected strenuously to Bob's behavior or philosophic view of life because he was so much better educated than she. She always felt at a loss for words and could never explain properly or effectively what she had in mind. She equated training with intelligence and intelligence with correctness in life. As a child she had led a somewhat barren existence, and in the following years she always felt distinctly uncomfortable in the presence of women with more than a high school education. When she sensed others knew more than she did, she became quiet and unobtrusive. In this respect she treated Bob as an educated guest in the house. She never argued, she never disagreed, she listened quietly, and she swallowed the doubts that lurked in her mind.

At one time Bob had as many as four legal suits pending in the municipal and circuit courts of the county. He sued anyone who crossed him, and at the least suggestion of indignity or inequity, he flew into a rage. He had, for example, been overpaid by his payroll department. He cashed the check and refused to refund the overpayment since he viewed it as negligence and error on their part—negligence and error for which they should be punished. He was also fighting a city order to clip his hedges to the legally prescribed 30-inch height. He insisted, with some real justification, that this ancient ordinance was being enforced capriciously, as a personal matter, by the local police and that clipping the hedge would not increase the visibility of drivers turning the corner by his house.

Then, the electric company had the poor judgment to string a power line across his property without first consulting him. He knew his property rights and insisted that the power company had exceeded its authority in his airspace. He was offered a reasonable out of court settlement, but instead he was going to fight the case to the bitter end. Finally, he waged an unceasing vendetta against his fellow office workers. He was certain they were gossiping about him and plotting behind his back to get him discharged. The intricacies of the plots and counterplots he suspected were taking place are too lengthy to recount in detail. Each plot he reported to me was, in addition, confirmed and verified by a strange brand of specious logic. A look, a strange question, an unusual greeting, a whispered conversation that ceased as he approached, or receipts that were slow reaching his office all became bits of evidence that something was going on.

Bob H. had an incredible memory for events that confirmed his suspicions. With the slightest encouragement, he would return to long dead issues, examining them microscopically and agonizingly, only to reach the same conclusion again and again. I would try to keep focus in our conversations by telling Bob that he was going over previously plowed ground. Bob would then turn his attention to more recent events, but I was aware that he was only shelving the issue for now. His fellow employees felt that Bob was out of line with his complaints about the way things were going, but they were trapped by a modern dilemma. Bob was a light-skinned Negro and his wife was white. Whenever Bob's views were called into question, he would raise the issue of racial prejudice.

In psychotherapy conducted over the years, I have often confronted issues important socially but confusing to the course of therapy. Racism and prejudice have been particularly difficult problems. Had Bob H. been white, he would have been subject to resentment by the whites who surrounded him in his work setting. He was not white, so he was self-consciously "tolerated."

Given this social and psychological climate, Bob's fellow workers felt some sense of relief that he was coming to see me regularly. I tried to explain that ours was a casual relationship, not a fully therapeutic one, but they refused to listen. They simply and blindly hoped I would somehow solve the problem for them.

Bob was not only suspicious of the motives of others, but basically, hostile toward everyone before he had evidence that they deserved such treatment. Bob never seemed to relax his vigilant awareness of everything in his environment. Fear of attack or bodily assault was a very real continuous experience for Bob, and in a rare session of self revelation he told me,

> I don't like to go into public toilets because I never know who will be in there and I worry that they will bother me in some way. If I'm standing at the urinal and somebody comes in, I just push the flush handle and walk out like I'm all finished. If it happens there is someone there already, I'll sometimes just wash my hands hoping he'll finish and leave so I won't have to stand next to him. Now and then, I get trapped with someone standing next to me and I always feel miserable and wonder if he is leaning over and looking at my privates. Usually I don't take any chances and walk right into a toilet stall even if I only have to urinate. Even then I get to thinking the guy on the next stool is listening to me or watching me in some way. Its always been like that with me ever since I was in grade school. It seems like every day you read about more and more of that kind of stuff happening so I don't go there unless I have to.

Bob's reference to homosexuality was not unusual for him. Conversations originating at any point seemed always to drift around to jokes or sly comments about homosexuals. Bob was quite moralistic about them and felt they were everywhere about him. It had shaken Bob considerably when long-haired men made their appearance on the fashion scene, because it immediately inflated the proportion of effeminate looking men.

Bob's conscious suspicions made it impossible for him to trust anyone except his wife whom he thought he could dominate completely. Toward the end of our association he avowed openly that his co-workers disliked him because they were jealous of his superior talents and abilities and suffered by comparison with him. This was a startling bit of egotism and I could not be certain if he had only recently come to this awareness or if he was just making the feeling public for the first time.

The distrust of his co-workers and his fear of homosexuals began to overlap before long. Bob began to report that he was convinced that some of the men in his office watched till he had to go to the toilet and then followed him. I was convinced that Bob was overreacting to an odd mixture of coincidence and reality. As Bob's emotional stability deteriorated, the office staff began to tease him with annoying little tricks—removing articles from his desk when he left the room and then denying they had done so when he returned.

What Bob saw in others seemed to be very much like a projection of his own inner urges and impulses. To Bob, the world was beginning to look increasingly evil and he had to take action against the plot he felt was rapidly thickening. At first Bob reacted in a strange fashion. He responded as if I knew all about the plot to get him and could in some way end it. He began to leave notes for me, such as: "I give up. They can't all be dealt with at once. Why so many?" "Why am I blocked? If you don't know, someone knows. If I can find him." "Thanks for the help. It must have cost you a lot of your valuable time." None of the notes was signed. In addition, parts of articles from newspapers and magazines began to appear on my desk with certain important thoughts or phrases underlined in red pencil: "Retarded Found Able to Think," "Some Few Have Extrasensory Powers," "Can Some Read the Minds of Others?"

Bob applied little scientific logic to the sequence of cause and effect he had constructed in his mind. For him it was simple to put together what he took to be two and two. Each bit and fragment of evidence was disputable in and by itself and could easily be explained away on rational grounds. He was regularly willing to admit the plausibility of alternative explanations when the stakes were small and the loss not great. As far as Bob was concerned, the removal of no single thread appreciably altered the broad design he was certain he detected.

"Suppose for just a minute that I am right about what is going on," he suggested one day. "You know how the CIA operates. They gather a tiny bit here and a tiny bit there—most of it from easily available public sources—and they put it together like a giant anagram till, suddenly, it spells something meaningful. If what I know is going on is true, then it makes sense that everyone denies the truth of what I am saying. Sure, it looks like there is some other good explanation for everything that happens. That's the way they would arrange it if they are smart and they are. They have tricks most of us never heard of and there are more of them than you can imagine. You watch them for a while and you learn how to catch their secret signals of recognition. They know who's what but nobody else knows it. I'm onto them and they don't know it yet. Everything looks innocent, sure. But that's the way they operate. You can't tell me that all the things that have happened are nothing but accidents. I know better."

Bob was unable to comprehend two seemingly simple sets of circumstances. First, the more suspicious he became, the more strange became his actions. Second, as the circle became complete the reactions of others to his behavior indeed became strange and mysterious since the secret they shared was the somewhat frightening observation that he was growing more than a little weird day by day. Bob's behavior was a form of self-fulfilling prophecy in which what he did made others act the way they did and their actions, in turn, confirmed the authenticity of his original suspicions. There clearly was no means to break this ring of mutually distorted perceptions. Escalation could be the only outcome of this spiraling semicircularity of decaying interpersonal relations.

Bob had on his side the weight of a mass of circumstantial evidence—evidence convincing by its mass rather than its believable substance. Too many unexplainable things happened too often to be dismissed in an unconcerned fashion. Once Bob H. had fashioned his delusions into a recognizable shape, it was no more than a matter of the simple elapse of time till the full break with reality was bound to occur. Knowing what to suspect focused Bob's attention on the most salient features of his environment and this increased attention to it only formed the burning fear that flamed within him.

It was very much like having the walls of a room close in on you inch by inch. As the suspected plot thickened, Bob became increasingly frantic, for time seemed to be running out. They were closing in for the kill and he was standing sheeplike and bleating to unhearing ears. But the revenge of the sheep is terrible to view. This aphorism crossed my mind too often for comfort.

In our conversations less and less content passed between us, and he began to act out a cloak-and-dagger sort of relationship between us. Every glance was loaded with meaning for him. I suspected that he was going through a crystallization process in which the many loose ends of suspicion, fear, and insecurity which had plagued his life were being gathered together into a single organized plot.

He also began to miss days at work and give vague excuses for his absence. Later I learned that he had spent this time watching his own house in a rented car parked inconspicuously down the street and shadowing his fellow employees home from work to see where they went and what they did. He began to keep a little black book in which he scribbled cryptic notes during the day. Whenever he did this, he would look around the room knowingly as if to say "I've got the goods on you now. You'd better stop what you are doing and be quick about it." He would then lock it in a box, place the box in a locked desk drawer, and head for the water cooler where he would pretend to drink while surveying the group to see if anyone looked guilty or frightened.

Bob's work began to suffer as he became obsessed with the idea that the enemy was closing in on him. He was sure there was a hidden message in routine requests whenever the slightest departure in procedure occurred. He was sure he was being checked so he could be proved incompetent and fired. At one point he brought me routine vouchers to ask if the signature on them "didn't look a little funny."

During this period of psychological decline, Bob was totally humorless. The elasticity of life had gone out of him. Everything worried him, the smallest things had great significance, and he began to lose weight rather markedly. He was eating only one meal a day, and he chose the meal he would eat by a system designed to outwit anyone studying his personal habits. He had even made an attempt to hire a private detective to help him discover who was after him, but the detective agency told him it was all in his imagination and to go home and forget it. He at once was convinced that they were in on it too.

The world had indeed closed in on Bob H. After an explosive scene in the office one day, he became quite agitated and could not be reassured or calmed down. His superior told him to take several days off and get some rest. The fear that prompted this action communicated itself to Bob, so he left that day and never returned. His wife told us he came home in a rage, went to his room, locked the door, and wrote a detailed account of the day's events. Bob did not sleep that night. He wandered the house mumbling incoherently and woke his wife and children early to help him do what was needed. He kept the children home from school that day, locked all the windows and doors, and pulled the shades down at every window. Bob's vigil was kept all that day and night and he allowed no one to turn on the radio or television set since it was necessary for him to hear everything going on outside the house. He armed himself and by 4 a.m. was so agitated that he roared out of the house firing shots in the air and daring his enemies to come and get him.

As I noted earlier he has become incoherent, and what psychological strength he had has waned and disappeared almost completely. It is unfortunate that there was no opportunity to unravel his early life and to discover how directly his childhood experience destined him for an early psychological collapse. Many paranoid personalities reach a kind of equilibrium in which they can survive. Bob H. had developed internal and external patterns that would not fit together comfortably, and so his internal life destroyed the outside world.

Schizophrenic Reaction:
Chronic, Undifferentiated Type

Everybody Has Nightmares. Don't They?

–SAM P.

PROLOGUE   *The problem* in classifying psychoses is that they
tend to be disorderly. The clearest evidence that our classificatory
system is crude and can only approximately describe serious
emotional disturbance is the existence of the catchall called
schizophrenic reaction—chronic and undifferentiated—
cause unknown.

Schizophrenics constitute 25 per cent of those admitted to
mental hospitals and their average stay is approximately 13 years.
Remaining hospitalized as long as they do, they along with other
psychotics, begin to accumulate in our hospitals until they
occupy every other bed. For some, the schizophrenic reaction
is a reactive syndrome that appears suddenly in a person
otherwise and ostensibly normal. For others it is a process
syndrome with a gradual onset that overtakes someone with
an essentially unstable prepsychotic personality and destroys
what feeble remnants of organization remain to him.
Victims are primarily single, urban males.

The undifferentiated schizophrenic is subject to a series
of symptoms by which the disorder is characterized. For example,
he suffers a loss of contact with reality, is unable to adjust
socially, and becomes distant and withdrawn. Reality, for him,
is something to satisfy his inner needs—a world organized to be

what he would like it to be. The fine line between fantasy
and reality is obscured. Depersonalization occurs and the
individual begins to feel unreal and disconnected
from the world as others see it.

The urges and emotions normally subject to the moderation
of ego control, get loose and may take any number of forms.
The quiet, self-contained person may suddenly become
aggressive, noisy, overactive, and euphoric and at the same time
deprived of reason by hallucinations and delusions. The thought
processes of the schizophrenic are disrupted next and wish
fulfillment displaces logic and reality. This distorted, subjective
thinking—called autistic—reflects an intrusion of primitive,
illogical thinking. The ego can no longer
distinguish real from unreal.

The defenses each of us has erected to manage our primitive
impulses break down and become highly permeable for the
schizophrenic. Repressions previously successful in hiding
unacceptable and socially revolting urges, desires, and impulses
now fail and release into the consciousness feelings that disrupt
normal adjustment. The ability to organize life and to be
creative is destroyed as the world begins to fragment and break
into small unrelated pieces. Experience can no longer be
synthesized and even casual cause and effect relationships become
disconnected and chaotic. The patient may progress from bizarre
communication with others, to incoherent mumbling to himself,
to stuporous noncommunication with anyone.

Delusions and hallucinations accompany this disorder.
Hallucinations are usually auditory although any one of the
senses can deceive if it is necessary for survival. In severe
circumstances the body is willing to comply with any demands of
the psyche. With this unusual level of disruption of the self,
dazed or confusional states may occur.

Therapy with undifferentiated schizophrenics is no more
rewarding than with any other serious psychological breakdown.
The task of undoing the damage of early life is herculean, for
once free of symptoms, the personality of the victim must still
be retrained to give it substance in the form of skills, abilities, and
the confidence it never had. The person who becomes
schizophrenic is experiencing a crisis in which his psychological
energies are devoted almost totally to managing his inner
impulse system and to making it congruent with outer reality.

The onset of this disorder has been described as similar to the
experience of driving a car when a bee is buzzing about one's
head. At first the bee is only an annoyance and modest distraction
to the driver. As the bee persists and threatens the driver with
greater harm, more of the driver's energies must be devoted to
self-defense and less is left over to cope with the problems of
safe driving. When the bee finally stings the driver, he may lose
control of his vehicle. This is a useful analogy despite its descriptive limitations. The schizophrenic is, in one sense, being attacked
by an invisible psychological bee that disorganizes his control
over the course of his life.

ALONG THE CANADIAN-AMERICAN BORDER the ease of emigration from one
country to another is phenomenal. That's how Sam P. came to America.
He turned left in Windsor, Canada, drove over the Ambassador Bridge,
rented a furnished room in a suburb of Detroit, and listened intently for
the knock of opportunity. The first few things he tried made good sense,
but something always went wrong. Without any previous business experience, Sam involved himself in money-making schemes that had an air of
optimism and grandeur that was unwarranted by knowledge of the real
world.

   For example, Sam began a cheez-chip business. From a wholesaler he
purchased a number of cartons of cheez-chip palettes—compressed, cheese
flavored potato discs that expanded into a cheese flavored chip when immersed in hot oil. For a while he spent nights frying, bagging, and labeling
the product and days selling them wherever he could get permission to set
up a little stand. He soon learned that the big money he envisioned earn-
ing was all tied up with dealerships, franchises, commissions, space rental,
and fixed profit guarantees. He had neither the capital nor the business
savvy to manage such complicated affairs, and he left the enterprise with
an enormous number of unfried cheez-chips.

   A tour of Sam's basement told the story of his business career. One saw
the unassembled parts of "revolutionary" fishing reels and poles, a bulky
machine that made cement blocks for chimneys, a collection of now illegal punchboards offering prizes for the puncher of the lucky number,
and, finally, the parts and wiring apparatus needed to install complete
home fire-alarm systems. Sam himself pointed out that his judgment
looked faulty now but that could have been said for the judgment of men
who were now rich and famous for their inventive accomplishments.

   As a person, Sam P. was at first not much more odd than many other
people one might meet. He was somewhat intense in his speech and would
now and again stare fixedly into space for a moment. Once in a while, he

would grimace, stretch his neck muscles, and run his finger inside his collar as if his tie were too tight. After a while this grimace became un-noticeable and was ignored by onlookers. His gestural patterns always interested me because they differed in some puzzling way from the aver-age. Then I discovered that whenever Sam gestured, he did so in what looked like slow motion. Some of his gestures seemed to become frozen in mid-air or to take an interminable time to be completed. I dismissed this as no more than a personal idiosyncrasy. Later I discovered it had deeper meaning.

Sam managed to maintain quite intricate interpersonal relations with a varied set of business associates in his many ventures. The sense of shock they reported at the time of his hospitalization was contributed in part by its unexpectedness and in part by the nagging suggestion that it might as easily have happened to them. Sam's exit from the stable world of normality was only one of a steady series. With each loss, those who re-mained felt just that much less secure about what tomorrow might bring.

Afterward, everyone played the game of "In Retrospect," in which they sorted through their past contacts with Sam, searching for the clue that should have been a dead giveaway to his imminent collapse. These recollections and probings were more than idle curiosity. They had a nervous and fearful quality about them, for the signs they might have detected in Sam could be the same signs useful in measuring those not in-frequent moments when secret doubts of their own surfaced in conscious-ness.

Pathology of such a severe sort was threatening to everyone. It seemed to violate every rule of common sense and made a mockery of attempts to organize life into meaningful, trustworthy patterns. What was the point of leaping out of bed every morning and pushing and shoving all day if these efforts were nothing but symptoms of sickness? Why wasn't there some easy way to tell who was sick and who was well? How much could a man reasonably take before he cracked under the strain? Why did it happen to a civilized people?

It was even more fascinating to consider how Sam's symptoms had es-caped the notice of so many persons who considered themselves excellent judges of their fellow man. In retrospect they told Doris that they were bothered, at times, by his frozen gestures and by the tension revealed in his tight collar tic. From her reports of their comments it became evident that no one of them had been able to form more than the most superficial and casual bond with Sam. Some few had a hearty hand-pumping, back-slapping, I-want-you-to-meet-a-friend-of-mine acquaintance with him and they misjudged this to be more personal than it really was. The more perceptive among them were nagged slightly by the lack of warmth and cold emotion Sam seemed to convey to them when at certain moments they exchanged confidences. It was as if they could not quite make con-

tact with the real Sam and, for a flickering moment, it was annoying because they interpreted this missing element to be something deliberately
hidden from view and revealed only to the select, intimate few.

This uniform misreading of signs was understandable, given the fashion
in which Western society is organized. Having both a public and private
life, each person accorded to the other the same privilege. Since these two
aspects of the self now and then crossed boundaries and overlapped one
another, the mixture was always unexpected, puzzling, and anxiety-laden.
So, each observer did what he had to do to restore his peace of mind. He
discussed these observations as a natural response to the strain of a com-
petitive life and treated them as transient expressions of the stress each
one of them felt from time to time. Or, he deliberately failed to decipher
the code and tucked these passing apparitions safely into an unknowable
unconscious. With this last course it became necessary to stretch one's
toleration of strangeness near to the breaking point. Most often the motive
for such an act was a mixed one—part tolerance and part a silent prayer
for sympathy if the roles in life ever happened to be reversed.

Doris, Sam's wife, told me that she was bothered by his behavior at
times but she attributed it to the pressure of business and the continuous
disasters he underwent. As Doris said,

> What hurt me most was the feeling I began to get more and
> more of the time that I was losing contact with him. It was as if
> he were drifting away from me and I didn't know what to do
> about it. I would talk to him for a while, but when I looked at
> him, I would realize he wasn't listening. He was off somewhere
> lost in thought and never heard a word I said. Then he began
> to do scary things and creepy things. I would wake up in the
> middle of the night and he would be gone. Once I found him
> sitting on the grass in the middle of the backyard at 4 a.m. and
> he didn't seem to know where he was or what was going on.
> He was confused, but he was all right the next day and never
> mentioned what had happened the night before.
>
> Once I was scared to death when the police called me in the
> middle of the night and told me they had found Sam standing
> in front of the bank knocking on the door. Sam told them it
> must be a holiday cause the bank was closed. After the police
> brought him home, he went to sleep and snored like he always
> does when he is exhausted. Then, an hour after he went to bed,
> I woke up to find him perched on the foot of the bed crowing
> like a rooster. He didn't recognize me when I tried to shake
> him awake. He didn't even wake up; he just rolled into bed
> with his eyes open.

At this juncture, Sam B. began to talk about the devil, sin, death, and
reincarnation. He stopped working and just sat around the house all day

thinking. Doris reported that she would hear him speaking but she discovered he was always talking to himself and never answered her when she spoke. He wore his pajamas all day and began to ask her strange questions—"Would God care if I didn't eat breakfast?" About three weeks after Doris spoke to me about her husband, he was arrested at 3 a.m. in a small town about 40 miles from where they lived. The police report said he was driving through town at nearly 85 miles an hour when stopped and that he told the arresting officers that he was trying to "get up escape velocity for a trip to Mars."

When Sam left the county jail he was escorted directly to the state hospital. By the time I could visit him, he was openly hallucinating and in an agitated state. He was wild, unshaven, disheveled, and incoherent. Two weeks later he was displaying all the classic symptoms of the catatonic. Some of the ideas Sam spoke about freely to doctors and fellow patients were extremely bizarre. At one time he was convinced he was Robin Hood, for example. He had not notified anyone of this sudden shift in his identity and it was discovered only when he leaped from a perch atop a door and landed on the back of an unsuspecting attendant who had just entered the room. After a brief scramble, Sam informed the hospital authorities that Robin Hood always jumped out of trees whenever the king's men approached and that the attendant looked very much like the Sheriff of Nottingham. Sam was watched closely from that time on. When I visited Sam, he was in moderately good psychological condition even though he was convinced I was there to secure his release from the hospital. He cried a little and complained about his treatment in the hospital. After a 45 minute visit with him, I contacted the psychology department of the hospital and had a frank and revealing talk with its members.

Sam's stay in the hospital had been the usual mixture of pleasant and unpleasant. At the time of admission he had been severely catatonic. He was mute, staring, and displayed the waxy flexibility of the classic catatonic, that is, his limbs could be placed in awkward positions and he would retain this pose for several hours. He was negativistic and refused to eat, drink, dress, undress, or respond to requests. When commanded firmly, raised from his chair, and escorted to the dining room, Sam would follow the lead of another but would sit staring vacantly at the food placed before him and had to be urged to eat. He remained in this state for several months and made no attempt to communicate with others. He would sit stiffly erect with his eyes focused on unknown objects in the distance. Sam's withdrawal from the real world was almost total, and attempts to make psychological or interpersonal contact with him were greeted with suspicion and violent distrust. It was, for Sam, a kind of conflict in which he could not bear to make a positive move for fear that it would in some fashion contribute to his emotional downfall and result in his destruction.

Sam emerged cautiously and slowly from his catatonic condition. One attendant had been particularly warm and gentle with him and Sam seemed to feel that at least he understood the terror Sam was experiencing. The psychiatrist assigned to Sam's case was tolerant but so busy that he had little time for anything beyond a quick reassuring arm-squeeze and a cheerily superficial greeting each day as he swept rapidly through the ward. The ward psychiatrist was blameless. In those pretranquilizer days, he was assigned responsibility for 400 ward patients.

When Sam abandoned catatonia for a related but less primitive adjustment to reality, he was briefly violent and unmanageable. Negativism was replaced by overt assault on his surroundings. When this proved to be both painful and unproductive, Sam calmed down and became a model inmate—submissive, compliant, and uncomplaining. He would stand in line quietly and he carefully adhered to all the hospital routines as if they were biblical injunctions. Sam became supernormal in his behavior, but this course of action availed him little since the attendants were aware that Sam's attention was focussed almost exclusively on the chorus of voices that he heard all day, every day.

The voices spoke to Sam about Truth, Wisdom, Justice, and the Meaning of Life. The voices told tales of a place and a way of life in which man's troubles and woes lived only as dim shades in a faulty memory. The voices invited him to relinquish pain and seek solace with them. Once convinced, Sam attempted to become one with them by committing suicide. All his attempts failed and Sam finally abandoned them. He still listens intently when they speak to him and sometimes he replies incoherently. But, the voices have become a commonplace part of his existence and, as such, are not responded to in behavior.

Sam actively hallucinates scenes in which sin, the devil, and hell-fire occupy his body and torment him immeasurably. To Sam the devil is a living personage who visits him in the night and is a constant companion during the waking hours. The devil is real, and he sometimes assumes the guise of the ward psychiatrist or looks out from the faces of the nurses and attendants. What is startling is the lack of concern Sam shows about these manifestations. He accepts them as commonplace and shows no emotional reaction. Sam has learned to live with his auditory hallucinations and probably believes everyone else is receiving such messages. What Sam hears is his own inner voice, of course, and the messages he receives are always the same and always the inner part of himself that has been unavailable to his consciousness.

Sam is quiet, does what he is told, and causes no trouble. His reaction times are slow, as are his movements, and he seems numb to the world about him. He is, psychologically, a walking dead man whose inner experience is a secret since he is unable to relate it to us meaningfully.

I made an attempt to unearth some explanation for Sam's progressive psychological breakdown by asking his wife to relate, in as much detail as she could recall, all he had told her of his early life. This means of studying another human being is only one approach, of course, because it rules out the possibility that Sam's problem was really an organically based difficulty produced by faulty metabolism, improper diet, or brain tumor. It was my belief that his early childhood experience would help us to understand him, so I looked to his early years to comprehend his ignominious end as an adult.

Although we can never be certain that the events of Sam's early life had a direct bearing on his pitiable adult status, it was apparent that Sam's childhood was a period of fear, anxiety, and trouble. His wife recalled that when Sam discussed his family and early life, it was always with bitterness, resentment, and rancor.

Sam's mother and father had conducted a running battle of 20 years duration. They fought continuously and with whatever weapon was closest at hand. Sam, it turned out, was an only child and became, thus, the instrument of convenience in marital free-for-alls. Sam, for example, was regularly employed as a message-bearer when his parents were not speaking. When the parental argument reached a fever pitch and could not be resolved, each contestant would retreat within himself and brood. Sam was then used as a communication system between them. The scene was a classic one. In earshot of his mother, Sam's father would tell Sam to inform her that he would not be home for supper tomorrow. This message dutifully repeated to the mother would be acknowledged and a reply phrased such as, "tell him who cares?" His anguish in being asked to play the role of a youthful intermediary was appreciated by both parents, but each took Sam's suffering as evidence of what the other was doing to their son. He was too young to survive. In part, the desperation of his illegal immigration to the United States expressed a need to escape he had experienced for most of his growing life.

When Sam was hospitalized, it was soon discovered that his residence in America was illegal. Having been declared mentally incompetent by the State of Michigan, he was at once subject to deportation. The process of transfer to a Canadian mental hospital took nearly a year to accomplish, and I visited Sam twice during the intervening time. His emotional and psychological status remained constant during these months, and it was apparent that unless a spontaneous remission of symptoms occurred, Sam would be hospitalized for the rest of his life.

Sam was schizophrenic and, at least in retrospect, the signs had been in early adolescence. Sam had always been a person disconnected from other people and from the usual responses to life. Yet, Sam retained the visage of the normal long enough to survive into his late 20's. Had Sam been more seriously disordered early in life, the likelihood of his survival to such a relatively late age would have been greatly diminished. In this respect Sam was an atypical schizophrenic.

Sam had experienced a stressful and perturbing childhood from which he probably emerged scarred and less than a whole person. He had fought his way into adult life trying desperately to be successful, but had failed. With each failure, a greater and greater part of his self had been whittled away. As he attempted to adjust psychologically, increasing stress pushed him to even more desperate psychological defenses. Finally, even these failed, and Sam was rendered helpless in the face of assaults too severe and too unremitting. A state mental hospital became the only kind of safe and protective environment in which he could survive and his existence within it is a minimal kind of life.

Sam's future, then, is a grim and unappetizing one. His psychological disorder was sufficient to remove him from the company of his fellow-citizens and to isolate him almost totally from normal contact with his home community. The problem is that in an environment populated only by other seriously disturbed persons, the probability of his eventual recovery is greatly diminished. In an odd fashion the penalty for disorder is immersion in an even more disordered society.

It is unlikely that Sam will ever rejoin society in any productive role. He has twice been given the full course of electric shock treatments and once underwent insulin therapy. The gains from these therapies were minimal and short-lived. In the eyes of the therapeutic staff members of the hospital, Sam is a hopeless case. He will get cursory contact in the next decade with therapy as we know it today. If he is ever to rejoin society, it will be a consequence of his own efforts or nothing at all.

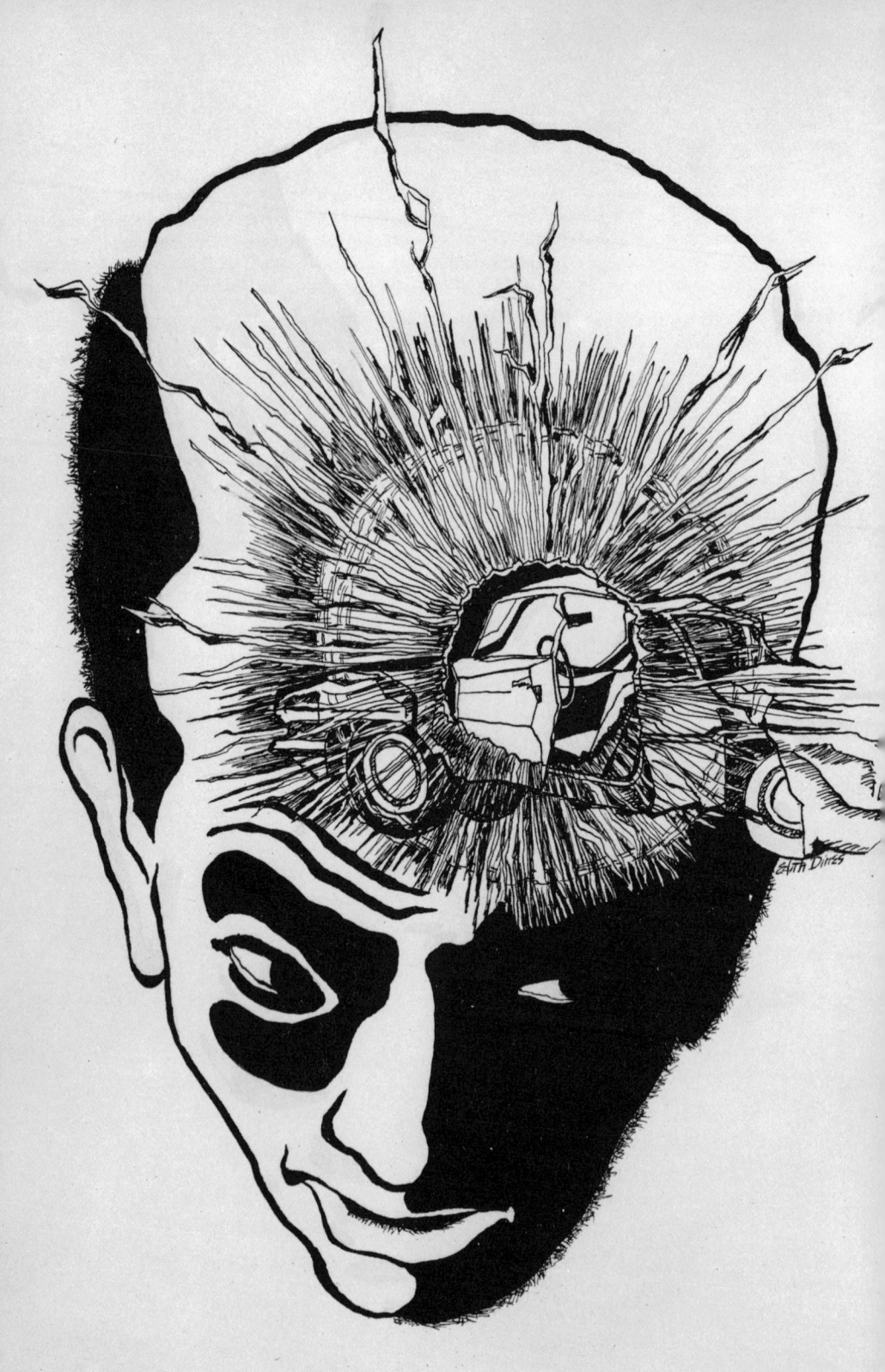

Gasoline and Alcohol—In Equal Parts
–Norm R.

PROLOGUE   *When it is calculated* that each year there are nearly
one-and-one-half million head injuries in automobile accidents
alone, the wonder is that acute or chronic brain disorder is not
more prevalent. Everyone has suffered innumerable bumps on the
head, the majority of them during childhood, but comparatively
few suffer from extensive or severe brain damage. This is true
primarily because the skull is wonderfully designed to protect
the brain. The extraordinary development of his brain freed man,
but it also made him particularly vulnerable. Man can lose an arm
or a leg or large segments of other organ systems and still remain
human, but damage to his brain is dehumanizing.

The effects of severe brain damage are not precisely
predictable since they are so much a function of the location
and form of the physical insult to the cerebral tissue. At the same
time, one's life situation and degree of personality integration
prior to the injury will effect the pattern of symptoms that will
appear. There are, however, broad classes of behavior
and general forms that symptoms may take.

As the patient becomes dimly aware that his previous ability
to deal with the world has been destroyed or badly scrambled,
he may make an attempt to restore order by compensatory
behavior. This can be an impossible task if the damage to the

brain is sufficiently severe. The victim may suffer memory
defects, he may easily become irritable, fatigued, distracted,
or excited, suffer headaches, and find himself incapable of
managing the flood of stimuli that everyday life presents to him.
He cannot concentrate for long on any problem or abstract
thought without becoming confused and bewildered
by its complexity.

Faced with such an overwhelming collapse of his world,
the damaged human begins to shrink his world to fit the reach
of his newly limited capacities. The doubts and anxieties
that always plagued him but were held back before may now
attack him as he finds himself threatened but defenseless. His
attitude may be an odd mixture of violent resentment and
apathetic acceptance of his fate. He may become terribly upset
when new details and routines are introduced into his life.

Brain injury of any sort, if sufficiently diffuse, may produce
what have been labelled "release symptoms." The controlled,
well modulated, studied management of one's impulses is a
learned affair that takes a long time to achieve. The ability to
perform properly socially is in many respects no more than a
thin veneer of civilized propriety that can be erased along with
the brain tissue. When this occurs, the patient may express openly
urges, thoughts, and feelings that he had previously suppressed.
This is shocking and repugnant to those who are accustomed to
seeing a quite different face and less frightening human. Part
of the problem of rehabilitation lies in overcoming aggression,
resentment, and repulsion on the part of relatives, wife, and
children who find themselves living with a raucous and
obscene stranger.

For the victim of the injury, brain damage may mean a
variable convalescence complicated by secondary gain. The adult
male rendered helpless by a malfunctioning brain may regress
to a level of interpersonal relations that is essentially infantile;
he may become as totally and whiningly dependent on others
as he was when a young child. Freedom from competition
can be a positive pleasure to those who were not anxious
for it in the first place.

To appreciate what happens to the severely brain damaged
person, you must visualize what it would be like to awaken
tomorrow morning to find yourself unable to tie your shoe laces,
incapable of thinking through your schedule for the day,

confused by decisions you must make regarding clothing to be
worn and the proper order for morning hygiene. Then imagine
that you have left the house and seated yourself in your
automobile. You might not only be unable to manage the
procedures for starting the car properly but would find yourself
overwhelmed by the rules of the road that were once so familiar
to you. With brain damage the simple becomes complex and the
complex becomes a serious threat. Severe brain damage may
produce quite fundamental alterations in personality. Even
moderate but diffuse cerebral damage requires that other persons
learn new ways of responding to the victim. They must learn to
become acquainted with the brain damaged person all over again.

NORM R. WOULD GET A LITTLE HIGH at parties and live it up too much but
this was harmless and most often went no further than boisterousness,
talking too loud, telling dirty jokes, and slopping his drink on other people. When he did get totally drunk, it was usually the aftermath of being
nagged by his wife who felt he always acted like a fool when he got a
little liquor in him.

The superego or conscience is one part of the human psyche that can
be dissolved by alcohol. This is what happened to Norm R. His usually
temperate, reserved, polite, cautious self faded away, and the "other"
Norm would leap vigorously onto the scene. When Norm was drunk, he
could never judge accurately if he was being hilariously funny or just
plain repulsive. If his judgment about people could be described as substantially diminished when he drank, then his judgment about his perceptual skills under the influence of alcohol could only be called disastrous.
From friends' reports, he really believed he could drive as well drunk as
he could sober. It is more probable that he was convinced he could drive
drunk better than most other drunks. He had once gotten home by driving the car with the wheels on its right side rubbing against the curb.
When he came to an intersection, the car would lurch to the right and
prod him to alertness again for another block. He made progress in this
fashion for about two miles till his car stalled and he fell asleep on the
front seat. He was more than a little startled when he was awakened
rudely by the homeowner whose driveway he blocked when he fell
asleep.

Tonight it was happening again. He was trying to hug somebody's
wife when a shoving match began with the aggrieved husband. That tore
it as far as Norm's wife was concerned and she made the mistake of chew-
ing him out in front of the others. Norm slammed out of the party filled
with righteous indignation and a gnawing sense of guilt. He took the

wheel of his station wagon, fumbled with the keys for a minute, and roared out of the driveway.

It had gotten much colder, but Norm's thinking was disconnected and focussed mostly on the indignities he had just suffered. He was talking out loud to himself as he drove and swearing fruitlessly at everything that was wrong with his wife and the world in general. The damn windshields were filthy, he thought. He missed his first pass at the windshield-washer button and when the wipers finally started to sweep the windshield it took him a few seconds to realize that the water on the windshield had frozen cutting off his forward vision completely. Norm glanced out his left hand window at the curb to keep from driving out of his lane and began, slowly, to apply the brakes. The street was icy so he eased off the brake pedal for a second when the car started to skid. This was the last Norm could remember. Norm's wife told me the rest of what happened.

> I was in a blind rage when he left the party and tried lamely to explain to everybody that Norm had been sick lately and shouldn't have had so much to drink. Boy, was I going to get him when I got home. I finally arranged to ride home with a girlfriend and he still wasn't there when I got there. That didn't bother me too much because I was mad and knew he usually went someplace to drink and sulk for a while and then would sneak home and sleep it off on the couch. He's really a good man if he doesn't drink and he doesn't act like a fool very often. Well, I was tired so I went to sleep. Then about seven o'clock in the morning the police called and said he had had an accident and was in Receiving Hospital. They wouldn't tell me how badly he was hurt so I got the kids off to school and got a taxi to take me to the hospital. The police were there and they told me he hit the steering wheel with his face and then hit the windshield with his head. He never would wear his seat belt unless I yelled at him about it and this was exactly what I thought might happen some time. His windshield was all iced over and there's a pedestrian island right there on Jefferson Avenue and a lamppost so people can see it. The police said he hit the lamppost head on and never knew what happened when he flew into the windshield. I don't know what we are going to do now. He can't work and we've got bills piling up.

Mrs. R. seemed concerned about the accident, not so much because her husband had been severely injured, but because he had irresponsibly ceased to be the family breadwinner. There was an air of revenge and poetic justice in her manner. Her emotional reaction was just the slightest bit inappropriate to the situation.

Norm R. survived the crash but he ceased to exist just as surely as if he had died in the wreckage. He was alive—if you could call it living.

When Norm's head hit the windshield, a part of his skull was depressed by the impact. A large blood vessel in the brain was ruptured by small fragments of the skull, and there was widespread cerebral laceration. Following remedial surgery, Norm was comatose for two days and survival in any form remained an unanswered question. Once past this first crisis, he was watched closely for behavioral signs that would indicate the rate at which the body was repairing itself. Progress was slow and painful, and Norm posed an unusually vexatious home care problem when he finally was well enough to leave the hospital.

Norm was bedridden for two full months at home, and when he was capable of being up and about he proved to be even more disruptive to the household. The slightest change in routine, for example, upset him and he would whine and complain at length and repetitively about it until his wife reported that she often felt "like screaming and hitting him with something." During the early period of her adjustment to caring for him, he more than once suffered neglect at her hands.

It was partly Norm's psychological condition that was worrisome. He was restless and anxious most of the time and these feelings were translated into a general fussiness about his surrounding environment. Norm's need for sameness in his world was most irritating. If breakfast were late, if furniture were moved, if the children were home from school during the day, if friends dropped in to visit his wife, or if the phone rang too often, Norm at once demanded to know what was happening. Patient attempts to give him detailed answers only confused him.

The worst part for Norm and those caring for him, especially the children, was the impairment of his memory. So many details of Norm's past life were gone that he had to invent new ones to fill in the vacant space. Where parts were missing, new and plausible substitutes were invented to take their place. Whenever Norm made an effort to reconstruct the world as it had once been, he became acutely aware of his inability to concentrate for even a brief period of time, and he would get a headache and become totally fatigued by the vain effort.

Norm easily misinterpreted the stimuli life presented to him. At night he would awaken with a start at the sound of a truck roaring along a nearby expressway and would awaken his wife to ask her if she heard it and what she thought it was. His wife found this regular and sudden awakening infuriating so she moved into the spare bedroom after two weeks of such harassment. His wife was usually exhausted by nighttime anyway, but Norm would be wide awake, having napped off and on most of the day.

It was inevitable that Norm would sooner or later confront a situation too complex and too demanding for him to manage. After he had been up and around for several months, Norm decided that he ought to go back to his old firm and resume work on a limited scale. Not nearly enough re-education or rehabilitation had been accomplished with Norm to prepare him for this. He took an inordinate amount of time to dress that morning, and he became quite irritable when a number of little things went wrong in the process. He couldn't manage the involved procedure required to drive a car—he also had suffered some loss of hearing and needed heavily corrective glasses—so he took a bus into town. The bus and the busy city were too much for him.

Norm had to transfer from one bus line to another and the exchange took place at the busiest intersection in the city. There were busses on all four corners each going in a different direction on a different route. With the traffic noise and bustle of street lights, taxis, trucks, and people, the degree of confusion Norm felt was overwhelming. Time was running short and he would be late for his appointment but he was riveted to the spot in panic and confusion. He tried to approach a traffic policeman and explain his plight, but the outcome was only a jumble of halting and incomplete sentences punctuated by intense bewilderment. Norm wandered aimlessly about the city and had little recollection of where he went and what he did until the police picked him up after a missing persons call by his wife.

It was some time before Norm ventured out into the world again. He abandoned plans to return to work and trimmed his active world to a manageable size by going no more than a block from home. Norm doesn't drink anymore since even small amounts of alcohol not only add to his confusion but make him foul mouthed and lecherous. Norm is nothing like the active, energetic person he once was. When friends come to visit he seems preoccupied by his private thoughts and pays little attention to the conversation. Social conversation does not interest Norm because he has a hard time following it. He misses the point of jokes and feels left out of most of what is going on. Since there is little in the world that Norm can understand he has retreated to an inert inner world that makes few demands on him.

Norm has been a steady visitor to the hospital in the last few months. A vigorous schedule of physiotherapy and rehabilitation has been begun with him, and at least the management of his body has shown remarkable improvement. Norm has increased confidence in himself now and has acquired again an optimism about what tomorrow may bring.

People who knew Norm R. both before and after the accident are acutely aware of how great the loss has been and what a great distance Norm has yet to travel before he comes even close to his previous self. Norm's therapy is helping his thick-tongued speech, and the retraining he is undergoing is helping intact parts of his brain take over functions other parts have lost through damage.

Norm's improvement is remarkable considering the severity of the brain damage produced by his accident, and he is becoming enthusiastic about returning to the good old days that he remembers in a fragmentary way. It is unfortunate that Norm's daydreams will never become real. Estimates, at the moment, suggest that he will recover little more than 70 per cent of his previous faculties, skills, and abilities. Norm will never be the man he once was.

The problems Norm faces are severe, but the burden borne by his wife is a weighty one. The children have almost adjusted to the new Norm during the past year, but they treat him somewhat as though he had been invalided. They still say "daddy's sick" whenever he loses his temper or becomes upset. The family's rapidly declining economic status complicates matters, and Norm's wife is now working as an executive secretary in quite a responsible position. Probably the greatest future difficulty will be lodged in the subtle change that Norm's wife is showing. At first she resented being forced to go to work, but now her spirits have lifted more than I at first anticipated they would. She finds contact with the outside world exciting and spends less and less time with Norm R. She views Norm as a hopeless cripple and has little expectation that he will ever recover. She feels he is a has-been and she plans to care for him as long as he needs it, but she has no more than a custodial interest in his welfare.

My guess is that his wife is now a prime candidate for a love affair with someone at her office—someone more capable of responding to her emotional needs and desires. She has not been fully candid with me about her feelings toward Norm R. She has begun to miss appointments and has suggested several times that she has found an answer to her problems of the past year. I think she will ask Norm for a divorce as soon as she has the courage to do so and as soon as she feels sufficiently free of guilt. Every day she cares for Norm satisfies her guilt a little more. The longer she suffers, the easier it is for her to justify the course of action she is secretly contemplating. I am certain the divorce will set Norm's recovery back and it is likely that Norm will spend a great many of the years to come trying and failing to comprehend what has happened to him.

The marriage vows say "for better or for worse, in sickness and in health," but this is easier said than done. Norm's wife had good intentions, but they had begun to waver even before the accident. The party scene that began this calamitous chain of events was typical of many in recent years. There was no serious thought of divorce between them but their marriage was a routine, stale, habitual existence. Norm's wife reported that she had more than once found herself daydreaming about the kind of life she might have led if she had not married so young and had kids right away. As she said, "When I was 18 years old the most important thing in the world was to show everybody I was marriageable and wanted and needed by someone. Just being called Mrs. made me feel better than the rest of the girls in my crowd."

Running early to marriage and motherhood kept her tied to home and hearth for 15 years. As the children grew and became less dependent on her, she longed more and more for the challenge of something new, different, and more exciting. These secret thoughts were seldom shared with the other mothers in her circle of friends since they all believed working mothers were a prime cause of delinquency and psychological damage to their children. A "good" mother ought to be satisfied with helping her husband and raising her children. Thus, when Norm was incapacitated and she had to go to work it was an honorable way out of a situation growing more unpleasant day by day.

As Norm's wife blossomed in her new life, she found a growing number of good reasons for working late at the office and spending evenings bowling with the office gang. Norm was irritated at her frequent absence, but his complaints must have been dismissed easily by reference to his wife's new role as breadwinner. Norm has begun to have periods of euphoria bordering on silliness or childishness. It is almost as if treating him as a helpless child has reinforced a regressive pattern of behavior. He is living up to the view others have of him.

A distressing accompaniment to this euphoric behavior is an element of grandiosity that was not present before. Norm has been talking of going places and accomplishing things that are clearly beyond his present capacity and would be unrealistic even in the dimly forseeable future. It appears that these plans are not particularly bizarre in themselves. It is rather that there is a childlike denial that any real obstacles stand in the way of their accomplishment. He is clear about the ends he has in mind but confused about the means to achieve them, and, after a while, brushes aside all such issues saying he will work those details out later. As he struggles to think plans through to their reasonable conclusion, the extent of his inability to manage abstract and conceptual thought becomes painfully visible. His wife reports that when anyone tries to correct him he explodes and goes off into the bedroom to sulk.

I don't know what will happen to Norm R. if his wife asks for a divorce. If his rehabilitation progresses no further than it has to date Norm will continue to need semicustodial care for the rest of his life. Perhaps, in time, he can be retrained to a set of simple work skills by which he can support himself, but at the moment he is only partly capable of managing even the daily routine of living in a city.

Norm R. is a prime candidate for a nursing home or institution if he is cut adrift from home and family by a wife bored and wearied by working and caring for what must seem like an additional and unwanted child in the family. The disorder in the lives of this husband, wife, and children started in the fraction of a second it took for Norm's head to hit the windshield. Norm's injudicious intake of alcohol, his capricious pass at

someone else's wife, his wife's intemperate criticism, and Norm's characteristic resentment over it all combined to precipitate this tragedy. The
lives of five people careened off the main road and took a devious path
leading in unknown directions. For Norm R., it is beginning to look like
a dead end road.

Chronic Brain Syndrome
(Syphilis)

The Swinger—Twenty Years Later

–JACK O.

PROLOGUE   *"In fourteen hundred ninety-two,* Columbus sailed
the ocean blue" and, perhaps, he and his sailors rewarded Queen
Isabella by bringing to Europe the scourge of syphilis contracted
in the West Indies. It is reported that on his last voyage in 1504
Columbus was so ill that he had to be carried ashore. He was
suffering what seems now to have been the unmistakable
symptoms of the terminal stage of syphilis. Whatever its source,
the great pox ravaged Europe in the late fifteenth century with a
degree of virulence that probably does not exist today. The
adventurers who sailed after Columbus may even have reinfected
the populace of the new world with a newly cultured
strain of the spirochete.

   As the disease spread, it was blamed on whatever nation was
the current national enemy of the afflicted population, until, in
1530, an Italian physician described its symptoms in a poem
about a shepherd named Syphilis who was struck with the disease
as a consequence of an insult he had rendered to the god Apollo.
It took several hundred years for the affliction to be isolated
and treated successfully.

   Syphilis is caused by a microscopic organism called a
spirochete which can enter through any small break in the skin
surface or can be absorbed through a mucous membrane such as

lines the human mouth. The course of the disease can be divided
into roughly four stages:

1. Within 10 to 40 days of the initial infection the
spirochete multiplies within the system of the host and produces
a hard chancre at the point of infection. This disappears within
four to six weeks and may be unnoticed by the victim.

2. Three to six weeks later a body rash that resembles
measles may break out—the disease was labelled the great pox to
distinguish it from smallpox. This may be accompanied by
nausea, fever, indigestion, loss of appetite, and headaches.

3. While the spirochete may be busy attacking the patient's
bone marrow, nerve cells, spleen, blood vessels, or other organs,
it becomes latent in that all clinically apparent
symptoms disappear.

4. In ten to thirty years this accumulated damage to the
brain and central nervous system makes its appearance in the
form of heart attacks, loss in motor coordination, or failure of
vision. Syphilis presents symptom patterns that may resemble
a variety of diseases.

Physiologically, the victim suffers from a chronic brain
syndrome with progressive dementia caused by widespread
destruction of the brain and its lining. As the scar cells multiply,
there is a narrowing of the brain convolutions and a widening of
the spaces between them. These spaces fill with fluid and the cells
deteriorate. Only 3 per cent of untreated syphilitics suffer brain
tissue damage, but the consequences for this group are fatal in a
short period of time, probably two to three years after the
appearance of the initial symptoms. Several clinical types of
general paresis have been described—expansive, depressive,
demented—but all types resemble one another when the damage
to the brain has been sufficiently extensive.

In general, the behavioral and psychological manifestations
of neurosyphilis involve disturbance to the speech and writing
patterns, the onset of tremors, and the loss or alteration of
pupillary and musculative reflexes. The patient begins to make
mistakes in his work, becomes sloppy, tactless, unconcerned or
imperceptive regarding his impact on others, and suffers memory
loss and defects of judgment. His emotional response may also be
blunted so that joys and sorrows responded to by most people
are either not recognized or are responded to inappropriately.

In cases in which the syphilis infestation produces euphoria,
bizarre behavior is likely to occur as a reflection of the delusions of

power, wealth, ability, and grandeur from which he is suffering.
The victim begins to overesteem himself, makes unrealistic
plans, and soon loses contact with the nature of the real world
as his euphoria and sense of excitement overwhelm him.

Despite the chemical and medical advances of science, the
incidence of syphilis is rising frighteningly. This increase is
attributable, primarily, to adolescents who participate in sexual
activity with the lack of judgment typical of youth. Massive
doses of penicillin can cure syphilis and proper prophylactic
measures can prevent infection in the first place. But, both
prevention and cure are possible only when the possible hazards
of promiscuous intercourse with a variety of partners is known.
A great number are unaware of the menace of syphilis, many
more do not understand how it is contracted in the first place,
and too few recognize the symptoms of the disease
or seek treatment for it.

As a very young man, Jack O. acquired a reputation for being a combination of Don Juan, Casanova, and Beau Brummel. He had also mastered
the difficult feat of being a man among men as well as among women. He
was a con-man, a liar, an operator, and much more.

From his first not so fumbling approach to women, he progressed
steadily to the level of master craftsman. He was the swinger in his crowd
who could always be depended upon to regale the less experienced with
his tales of conquest. His graphic and colorfully exaggerated portrayal of
the exquisite and intimate details of sexual encounter commanded a breath-
less audience of novices. It was the same tale told a thousand times but, on
first hearing, it enthralled an eager audience caught up in a fantasy of
future successes.

Jack's view of sex seemed fixed at a level that may be characterized as
all sensation and no relationship. He practiced sex as an exercise that somehow made him more attractive in the eyes of others.

In 1943 he was drafted, and he was not in the least unhappy about it.
Every eligible male was in uniform and to be a civilian was to be really
out of it. In the service he was transformed into a uniformed prowler with
the war effort running a bad second to his extramilitary affairs.

His single state, his charm, his good looks, his fastidiously tailored uniform, his glib but convincing approach to women, and his practiced
devil-may-care attitude proved to be highly successful. He especially
loved the challenge of the difficult female who seemed unattainable and,
like a chameleon, he assumed whatever colors were necessary to gain his
objective.

For a bright and worldly person Jack had a surprising number of blank spaces in his comprehension of what life was all about. As he polished his performance in the role of soldier-seducer he contracted gonorrhea several times but treated each instance as no more than the cost of admission to the theater of life. He treated gonorrhea as an annoying evidence of how little trust could be invested in the apparently "nice" girls of the world. His manner was casual and flavored slightly with bragaddocio as he recounted the circumstances of the infection and the discomfort of its treatment. It was, to Jack O., no more than an inescapable occupational hazard. No worse than a bad cold, as he described it.

Jack spoke unashamedly of his conquests and, among men, swapped stories with the best of them, managing always to relate an escapade slightly more erotic and flamboyant than the tale last told. When the group included both male and female avid listeners, Jack tempered his stories hardly at all and seemed to fashion the details, calculatedly, to create an excessively reckless image projected squarely at the female. As he insisted, this gambit more often advanced his seductive cause and less often interfered with it. Jack maintained it paid to advertise.

Jack seemed to know the feminine mind as few males do. His capacity to empathize with their feelings, urges, impulses, and inhibitions was so acute that he knew how to be whatever kind of person he had to be in order to reach his end. His collection of reported conquests included all social classes, ethnic groups, races, religions, and ages.

If it could be said that Jack O. had a specialty, it would have to be educated women. As Jack noted, "If you tell them they are all talk and no action, they have to prove you a liar, because they know deep down in their hearts that it is true. They will try anything to prove they are sophisticated." His approach had about it a fixed and patterned quality that succeeded more often than not. When he did fail, Jack accepted it with such grace that it acted only to rekindle the desire of the female and increase her conflict regarding the wisdom of her decision. Such women then became a potential for future exploitation when the time and circumstances were right. He maintained that they always responded after a delay of several weeks. After a complicated campaign and final success, Jack seemed to lose interest and began to cool off his newly found and passionate partner.

Jack had no idea which of his many paramours had given him the original syphilitic infection. It was irrelevant, of course, since he was never aware that he had contracted syphilis in the first place, and by the time it became apparent, it was too late to care one way or another. Jack had always been a gay and socially active person, so the euphoria he finally suffered was, at first, hardly distinguishable from his behavior when he was a little high at a cocktail party. Jack worked hard, partied hard, and regularly slept too little. Suffering from insufficient rest and hangovers, he did not notice that his hand tremor had reached unusual proportions or the subtle increase in difficulty he had in speaking and writing.

Jack was always sensitive to the female and accommodating when it served his ends. He never pressed the issue when he judged the move to be inappropriate and he designed an assignation as a masterpiece of blended danger and safety each in the proper proportion. And, Jack was a man among men as well as among women. His sensitivity to the needs of the female had its counterpart in his capacity to "read" the male insurance prospect and to judge which form of approach offered the best odds for monetary success. Jack sold insurance where others had failed and he sold an excessive amount of insurance where others would certainly have settled for less. Jack was, unconsciously, the perfect chameleon. He knew instinctively how to disarm others and to warm them to the issue at hand. He viewed insuperable barriers as challenges and regarded each sale as a demonstration of his personal worth. Jack was one hell of a salesman and he relished the three times he managed to join the inner circle of members of the million dollar round table of insurance sellers.

Jack had always made some mistakes in the paperwork required of an insurance agent because he had a rather cavalier attitude toward this part of his job. These mistakes began to increase in frequency and seriousness and brought him several reprimands from his boss as well as causing him to lose clients. The real financial loss to Jack came with his steadily growing insensitivity to the attitudes and feelings of potential insurance buyers. Where Jack once was tuned carefully to the frequency of his target and always managed to home in for the kill, he was now beginning to receive false signals that would send him in the wrong direction. If the prospective client told a moderately off-color joke, Jack would top it with one quite filthy, pointless, and inappropriate to the mood and the setting. He began to get the brush-off but failed to recognize it for what it was.

Jack had devoted a great deal of his time to being a fastidious dresser who was always close to the newest fashion trends. He knew style, had excellent taste, and would fuss over some tiny detail of his attire until it was just right and suited him exactly. But, Jack started to get sloppy. He did only an approximate job of shaving and sometimes he forgot to do it at all. His shirts were worn more than once, his shoes lost their unfailing luster, his tie knot became lumpy, and he went too long between haircuts. His eating habits became gross and his apparel was stained with a variety of foods. This was so out of character for Jack that it evoked comment by all who knew him.

Jack began increasingly to respond inappropriately to events around him. He laughed loudly and too long at things others thought grisly and unfortunate. Jack got sad and melancholy at odd moments when everyone else was having a good time. A certain amount of this off-center response was attributed, by those who knew him, to the usual mood swings all of us experience now and again. With Jack, however, things went from bad to worse. His responses became stranger, and little remained of his old, smooth self.

Jack had always taken an extroverted approach to life, but now it appeared unmistakably for all to see. He was wildly optimistic about almost everything, but the twin focus of his euphoria came to rest on sex and job success.

He began to proclaim his sexual prowess loudly and long for all to hear. That his audience was bored by the tedious recital was not apparent to him, and before long he began to repeat himself telling the same story two or more times with a complete disregard for minor details which differed from telling to telling. His stories were told at the wrong times, in the wrong places, and to the wrong people. It was not long before he found himself talking to the wall as his audience beat a hasty retreat to less colorful narrators.

On the job Jack matched every real failure with fanciful plans about what he was going to do tomorrow. He began dictating memos to the district supervisor suggesting sales schemes that could never work in a sane world. As the memos piled up and wandered farther from reality, a new man was assigned to his territory, and Jack was eased out of his job. Since Jack did not seem to get the hint from the home office, he was told bluntly by mail that his services were no longer needed. Jack ignored the letter and went to Washington, D.C., for the annual sales conference and award ceremonies.

His appearance at the convention was uncomfortable for all who knew his true relationship to the company but it was decided not to make a fuss about it. At the award banquet Jack got drunk and made a grossly vulgar and uninvited sexual advance to the startled and staid wife of the district manager. Jack was escorted uncomprehendingly from the banquet room, put on a plane, and greeted unceremoniously at the district office two days later.

My contact with Jack was on a referral basis from the company physician who wanted psychological tests done on him. Jack was quite willing to be tested but he was a difficult subject since he ran off at the mouth at great length about past accomplishments and future grandiose plans. The degree of intellectual and cognitive deterioration revealed by the tests was severe. The loss in his capacity to reason, to solve problems, and to perform visual-motor tasks was astonishing in such a young man, and much of the content of the projective tests was distorted, bizarre, and disconnected. Tests designed to reveal organic impairment suggested diffuse damage to the central nervous system and these findings fit closely the results obtained by a complete neurological examination.

Jack was hospitalized the next day and continued to decay at an accelerating rate. He began to have sensory distortions in his sense of taste, smell, and touch, and although he remained euphoric, he became more and more bewildered and confused. Jack's ability to communicate in a coherent way with others began to disappear as his speech became slurred and tremor in his extremities became more pronounced. The content of his thinking became quite bizarre and unrelated to reality.

Medical treatment has kept Jack alive but, there is little in his behavior or appearance that resembles the man he once was. Jack's case is unusual in this day and age, but cases like it appear with a distressing frequency despite medical advances. The means Jack chose to convince himself and others that he was a complete and admirable man were unfortunate. As his life was reconstructed through interviews with those who knew him best, it became increasingly apparent that his ceaseless pursuit of females was not just the uninhibited, vigorous expression of extreme masculinity. Jack chased because he felt less than a person when he was not chasing. The experience of sexual contact convinced him he was a man and he never became aware that the entire process was emotionless and unreal to him.

The feminine traits Jack was known for—fastidious dress, interest in style and appearance, careful grooming—made him beautiful to behold, but it was not masculine beauty as it is usually defined. Jack was delicately rather than ruggedly handsome. He was fussy as few males are and he was single when almost all other males his age had committed themselves to marriage. My suspicion was that Jack really was quite frightened of women but had decided to conquer his fear by conquering women. With every victorious encounter he dispelled one more microscopic fragment of anxiety, but he was doomed never to reach the end point of his quest. Jack had probably never felt secure enough to take females or to leave them alone. Jack had become a sexual miser who accumulated tokens of the good life but never comprehended why he was collecting them in the first place.

I have speculated a number of times about what might have happened had Jack not gotten syphilis or if the spirochete had not invaded his central nervous system and destroyed him physically. I think that Jack's fate was an unhappy one under any circumstances. There was little in the way of a firm foundation in his life to stabilize him in those years ahead when sexuality was no longer a reliable measure of the man. Middle age would have been a catastrophe for Jack and he probably would have destroyed himself by becoming a ludicrous social misfit.

Old Folks at Home

–JOHN AND NANCY B.

PROLOGUE *We have witnessed* the terrible effects of damage to
the human brain from head injury and syphilis infestation of the
central nervous system. The kind of brain damage the reader is
most likely to encounter as an integral part of daily life is that
suffered by those who live long enough to experience the
ravages of senility. Senility is an expression of brain damage in
older persons characterized by an insidious, gradual onset of
cerebral incompetence beginning at ages 60, 70, or 80.

   Senility is not just a straightforward process of cerebral
decay. It is, in addition, a reaction to the consequences of decay
and, as such, involves some understanding of the entire
personality and its previous history of adjustment. Interestingly—
as with a number of other diseases—it is primarily a male rather
than a female affliction. With normal aging, the benefits of
experience outweigh losses in brain capacity. With extreme old
age, the degree of deterioration tips the balance and decay begins.
The senile older person suffers a diffuse atrophy of tissues of the
central nervous system and these cerebral-vascular changes—
arteriosclerotic alteration of the blood vessels—reduce the
individual's capacity to adapt to new challenges in life.

   The pattern of symptoms that the patient will display are
heavily dependent on the individual's premorbid personality.

The senile person may withdraw from interpersonal relations with others and narrow his social interests to a select few. He reduces the world to a size he can manage with his reduced mental alertness, lower tolerance for newness and change, and damaged capacity to comprehend life. As his thoughts become self-centered he begins to putter his way through life, to sleep less well, and to be suspicious of others. He now becomes a problem to the younger persons who surround him. He may become personally sloppy, cry easily, suffer deteriorated judgment, become anxious or agitated, live in the past, and indulge impulses long denied and well controlled in his past life.

The senile patient may continue the repetition of a simple performance long past its usefulness. He may recall and relate every insignificant detail of past events even though he is unable to recall that he has repeated this story endlessly. He may also construct out of fantasy the details that his memory has mislaid. He makes a new whole out of a fragmented collection of intact bits left over from the past.

One way to comprehend the actions of the senile person is to understand that those social sophistications most recently learned are the patterns of behavior to be discarded first. The social façade of circumspection and propriety will drop away revealing the impulsive and least acceptable part of the self. When the destruction of cortical cells reaches its apex, the primitive person that lies close behind the mask of civilization reappears.

Senility is simple brain damage that comes with age. It produces changes in behavior that may not be socially acceptable or popular, but these changes are closer to the truth of humankind than most of us are willing to accept. Each of us builds an image of the kind of person our parents are, and we are not easily or comfortably disposed to alter that picture to include facets of the self that have long been hidden. If our conception of our fellow men could encompass a truly developmental orientation including continuous change throughout life, we would be less shocked to discover that our parents or grandparents change with age.

There is a fixed period in life in which the brain remains intact and continues to function as it always has. As the brain cells die and fail to be reproduced by the growth of new cells, personality alterations are inevitable. The management of these

changes in the aged, damaged self are of crucial importance in
our consideration of senility. How we treat the aged constitutes
a meaningful commentary on the way our society has evolved.

John and Nancy B. were the kind of aging couple that regularly had
pictures taken as they celebrated anniversary after anniversary. He was
76 and she was 77 years old. In most such marriages, he would have died
at least ten to twenty years earlier. Local reporters often interviewed them
and asked the same wearisome questions about the secret of living to a ripe
old age.

Their early years had been a model of morality, circumspection, and
clean living. They met at an assembly of the Young People's Christian
Association and they courted during the evening meetings and socials of
the First Presbyterian Church in their town. Their evenings were spent in
the family parlor singing around the piano and viewing the stereopticon.

Neither one smoked, drank alcoholic beverages, danced, played cards
on Sunday, or visited unrefined places. They gossiped in shocked tones
about "the sinful goings on" in the world but had, ostensibly, little if any
firsthand contact with it. As John now and then noted, it was true that
there was some pretty rough talk down at the barbershop on Saturday
night, but he appeared unscathed by this encounter. John and Nancy never
travelled very far from their small, midwestern, farm community. But,
as they pointed out, "there wasn't any reason to." They did recall a trip to
the fair in St. Louis, or maybe it was Chicago, but this was the greatest
distance they ever cared to travel.

In the last several years John and Nancy's daughter and son-in-law had
begun to find it increasingly burdensome to have them as continual house
guests. These survivors of what seemed to be an ancient past slowly began
to change and seem less and less charming. Their physical deterioration
had been much more noticeable in the last year—they were both confined
to wheel chairs—and the necessary nursing care increased drastically. Their
hours of wakefulness and sleeping no longer coincided with those of the
rest of the family. They were up at strange hours of the night calling for
help or attention and drifted off into brief naps all during the day. Sometimes they even slipped into a light sleep while you were talking to them.

In the middle of a conversation, either or both of them might suddenly
burst into tears over the least trifle. Sometimes John would get weepy
and insist he was being mistreated and Nancy would join in the unhappy
demonstration without the slightest justification. As rapidly as they cried,
they could also express bitterness and recrimination. Often it was about
the behavior of people at the moment, but just as often the resentment
was directed at persons long dead and involved incidents that had taken
place as long as 50 years ago.

Most recently, the fuss usually made over the grandparents when dinner guests came to call was eliminated from the social ritual. Guests, in the past, had anticipated this polite and meaningless exchange with the old folks and unconsciously rehearsed new approaches to admiring recognition of how long they had survived.

This regular holding of court for the aged ceased, but not because it was burdensome and wearying. In fact, the children seemed to use their aged relatives as a kind of conversation piece. In addition, they prided themselves on their devoted self-sacrifice in a world little accustomed to such nurture of aged parents. John and Nancy began to appear less and less frequently because John had fallen into the habit of goosing female guests whenever they came within his reach or that of his extended cane.

John, in particular, began to be so foul-mouthed and vulgar that even the children of whom he seemed so fond were no longer safe around him. He talked like a drunken sailor at the most inappropriate times, and this was particularly shocking in light of the form and quality of his past life. As his daughter once commented, "It certainly must have been educational at that barbershop on Saturday night."

John's memory began to fade rapidly, but he persisted in a tiresome and detailed repetition of events recalled from his youth. As these stories droned on and on they were punctuated by Nancy's critical commentary. She seemed to delight in correcting every detail of every story. From her interruptions, it appeared that John had every name, date, and sequence totally incorrect. When John had accumulated sufficient frustration, he would wheel his chair about, raise his cane in a threatening gesture and shout, "You damned old fool, what do you know about the price of tea in China?"

Nancy seemed better preserved than John, but she was beginning to talk loosely of plots to get her money, and she became coarse if not vulgar. Her food seemed poisoned to her and her eyes would flash with suspicion at every meal. She would taste the food tentatively, watch to see if anyone looked guilty or was watching her, and in a loud, stagey voice announce, "I'm not very hungry today. I think I won't eat." With a look of ultimate triumph, she would push her plate aside and resist all appeals to eat. Then, within an hour of each meal, she would carp unendingly to all within earshot that, "My stomach is so empty it thinks my throat is cut. Why don't we ever get fed around here?" Attempts to remind her that she had refused to eat less than an hour ago met with little success. It only convinced her of the serious mistreatment she was undergoing. Poisoned or not, she always ate a hearty supper.

When John and Nancy's children came to see me, they were at their wits' end. Their carefully nurtured admiration for old people was fading as reality intruded on their fantasy of how it should be. These middle-aged "children" were tortured by guilt over secret wishes that their parents would die and spare them further embarrassment. But, at the same time, they feared these deaths because they felt the longer the old folks lived, the greater seemed to be their own chances of extended survival. Torn by mixed emotions, they were frantic and helpless. They did not understand what was happening, had no notion of how to cope with it, and felt guilt which they had never admitted to one another. Instead, they were trying to maintain the status quo in the face of an obviously deteriorating situation.

My first therapeutic efforts were devoted to a detailed explanation of the cause and effect relationship that becomes apparent when people live long enough to suffer the ravages of the brain deterioration called senility.

It was necessary to help the children understand that their romantic notions about the beauty of life's twilight years were not always true of everyone reaching extreme old age. The children were victims of an illusion carefully nurtured by parents who had throughout life hidden the normal human impulses that are everyone's heritage. They were convinced that their parents had never had an evil thought or engaged in any behavior subject to social criticism. As a consequence of this not unusual deception, the children idealized their parents and felt guilty whenever their own behavior was less than perfect.

John and Nancy were regressing to earlier and less complex patterns of behavior. The impulses they had so carefully kept in check were slipping through holes in their ego structure—holes that appeared as the flow of oxygen and other brain cell nutrients failed to penetrate the far reaches of the brain. John and Nancy were responding through a filter of brain damage, the penalty of surviving beyond the age at which the body can function efficiently. In addition, this release of long-repressed impulses came at a time when it was natural for John and Nancy to wonder why some of their former values and standards had seemed quite so important to them. Most of their friends had died, and there was little opportunity for contact with the few who had survived. There was a quality of "don't give a damn anymore" in some of the behavior of these old folks which was particularly irritating to the children.

The children were faced with a limited number of possible alternatives. One possible path involved learning to live with John and Nancy in terms completely different from those to which the children had been accustomed in previous years. It would be much like dealing with very young children and learning to accept the provocation and unpredictability that is characteristic of young ones. It meant ignoring behavior that was offensive, finding ways to live their own lives free of the domination of their parents, and seeing after their physical well-being while curbing their behavior. Parents would have to become children and children would have to become parents. This role reversal is not easy to learn, and, psychologically, it can be quite painful. The children would have to acquire the capacity to give loving custodial care to strangers who resembled people they once knew.

If John and Nancy were to be cared for at home, the children would have to prepare for the day when one or both would die. The guilt children feel about things they failed to do for their parents, and the frequent, occasionally conscious wish for their early death were not easy feelings to deal with but they were part of such an arrangement.

On the other hand, the children could turn over the nursing chores to professionals in a retirement home. There were calculated risks in such a course of action since this frequently seems to hasten the rate of senile deterioration and bring on sudden and unexpected death. Guilt over sending one's parents away to be cared for by strangers becomes a gnawing feeling that one is without character or strong moral fiber. A child's unspoken fear of being abandoned comes aliive with a special urgency when he does to his parents the very thing he most dreaded they might do to him. Even in our modern society—antiseptic, sterile, and medically oriented—it is not a move free of subtle social criticism.

The children discussed each of the alternatives at great length and even tried to invent some additional ones. In a family council, an elaborate scheme was constructed in which each of the children would care for the parents for a fixed number of months each year. Another plan involved hiring a nurse to come in and tend to John and Nancy's needs, but this proved to be prohibitively expensive even if such care were available. During the months of discussion, John and Nancy deteriorated rapidly, and John had to be hospitalized when he fell and broke a hip. Nancy seemed only dimly aware that he had gone to the hospital. It was pathetic, but very little remained of the old bond of affection between John and Nancy.

Three weeks later Nancy died quietly in her sleep. The immediate cause was cardiac arrest but the real cause was old age. John was never told of Nancy's death. He remained in the hospital for several months, and his hip fracture healed very slowly. The doctors felt he would be bedridden for an indeterminate period and suggested that he be placed in a medical nursing home nearby. This solution to the problem was immediately accepted by the children who then spent a great deal of time reassuring one another that "it really is the best thing for him" and that "the doctor certainly knows best."

Freed socially and personally of guilt for finding their parents burdensome, and provided with an excellent excuse for their action, the family is much gayer now. Visits to see John in the nursing home have decreased in frequency since a great number of things seem to come up that make it inconvenient. I sense that a subtle death watch has begun for John and just recently heard the children discussing openly the need to make prearrangements for John's funeral and burial. That minister who did such a beautiful service for mother has been elected to preside again.

The treatment accorded John and Nancy is far from atypical in

America. The children who went through this trying period will themselves grow old. There is a real possibility that their treatment of John and Nancy will return to haunt their own twilight years. If senile deterioration occurs, they may express the conviction that their own children do not treat them properly and are trying to get rid of them. Without a reliable social tradition in our care of the aged, we may be perpetrating an unbroken cycle of action and reaction.

DATE DUE